CONSTRUCTIVIST
ASSESSMENT

THE COUNSELING PSYCHOLOGIST
CASEBOOK SERIES

SERIES EDITOR: BRUCE R. FRETZ
University of Maryland

Sponsored by the Division of Counseling Psychology of the American Psychological Association, this series focuses on four major topics: counseling, career psychology, normal development/student development, and training and supervision. Each casebook includes four to six cases and delineates key topics. They also provide background and assessment information with actual dialogue from counseling sessions (all cases are edited and disguised with participants' consent). Authors also provide commentary alerting the reader to new concepts, where appropriate.

1. **Organizational Consultation**
   by **Robert K. Conyne & James M. O'Neil**

2. **Constructivist Assessment**
   by **Greg J. Neimeyer**

CONSTRUCTIVIST
ASSESSMENT
A Casebook

edited by
GREG J. NEIMEYER

THE COUNSELING PSYCHOLOGIST CASEBOOK SERIES

SAGE Publications
International Educational and Professional Publisher
Newbury Park   London   New Delhi

For information address:

SAGE Publications, Inc.
2455 Teller Road
Newbury Park, California 91320

SAGE Publications Ltd.
6 Bonhill Street
London EC2A 4PU
United Kingdom

SAGE Publications India Pvt. Ltd.
M-32 Market
Greater Kailash I
New Delhi 110 048 India

Printed in the United States of America

Library of Congress Cataloging-in-Publication Data

Constructivist assessment : a casebook / Greg J. Neimeyer.
        p.   cm.   —(The counseling psychologist casebook series; 2)
     Includes bibliographical references and index.
     ISBN 0-8039-4830-1.   —ISBN 0-8039-4831-X (pb.)
     1. Counseling.   2. Personality assessment.   3. Constructivism
(Psychology)   I. Neimeyer, Greg J.   II. Series.
BF637.C6C563   1993
158'.3—dc20   92-33021

93   94   95   96   10 9 8 7 6 5 4 3 2 1

Sage Production Editor: Tara S. Mead

Contents

1

Defining the Boundaries
of Constructivist Assessment

GREG J. NEIMEYER

ROBERT A. NEIMEYER

PSYCHOLOGICAL and human sciences have been undergoing a period of critical reappraisal regarding their commitments to what constitutes science. Derived largely from the positivistic worldview, this account of science has imposed significant restrictions on the conduct of inquiry within the clinical and counseling professions (Howard, 1985; Mahoney, 1991; Polkinghorne, 1984, 1991). Awareness of these restrictions has prompted recent efforts to harvest meaningful modes of inquiry from disciplines less wedded to objectivist stances. As a result, prominent scholarship has been directed toward issues of self-agency, hermeneutics, and theories of intentional action and narrative knowing (Hoshmand, 1989; Howard, 1989; Polkinghorne, 1988), approaches that are broadly consistent with the rapidly emerging field of constructivist counseling and psychotherapy (Carlsen, 1988; Efran, Lukens, M., & Lukens, R., 1990; Mahoney, 1991; Mahoney & Lyddon, 1988; Neimeyer, R. & Neimeyer, G., 1987).

Despite their diversity, members of this interdisciplinary family of constructivist orientations all share a common premise: We do not have direct access to a singular, stable, and fully knowable external reality. All of our understandings instead are contextually embedded, interpersonally forged, and necessarily limited. Founded on the idea that "humans actively create and construe their personal realities" (Mahoney & Lyddon, 1988, p. 200), constructivist theories have spawned a distinctive array of innovative methods designed to "fit the study of humans as active, interpreting agents" (Borgen, 1984, p. 458).

Following from their distinctive beliefs, constructivist approaches orient toward fundamentally different types of assessment strategies. Emphasis is placed, for example, on the primacy of personal meaning, the active role of the person as a co-creator of meaning, and the self-organized and developmentally progressive nature of our knowledge structures (see Lyddon & Alford, Chapter 2, this volume). Constructivist traditions emphasize processes of knowing and orient toward assessing the viability (utility) as opposed to the validity (truth) of an individual's unique worldview.

This chapter discusses each of these features and develops the ways in which they articulate with broader changes occurring within our allied mental health professions. Divided into two sections, the chapter first reviews some common assumptions of constructivist traditions and then illustrates several of their distinctive contributions to assessment by comparing constructivist with more traditional forms of cognitive-behavioral assessment.

This comparison sets the stage for subsequent chapters by describing and distinguishing features of constructivist assessment and by laying the conceptual groundwork for the assimilation of these methods into informed professional practice. In Chapter 2, for example, Lyddon and Alford call attention to the critical developmental processes that undergird constructivist orientations and illustrate the convergence of multiple strategies in framing a relationship-sensitive approach to assessment. R. Neimeyer (Chapter 3) extends this discussion by illustrating a variety of vehicles for the measurement of personal meaning, assessment strategies that attend to structural and process-oriented aspects of personal construction. A complementary focus on the qualitative assessment of content constitutes Chapter 4, where Viney richly illustrates diverse content analytic schemes. Broader patterns of interpersonal construction are the focus of Feixas, Procter, and G. Neimeyer's Chapter 5, where they illustrate the convergence of family systems and constructivist orientations in a variety of innovative assessment techniques. And finally, extending these themes more broadly still, Hoshmand (Chapter 6) attends to the role of personal narratives as they are forged within the communal process of social construction. The volume concludes (Chapter 7) with a review of the central, common features of constructivist assessment.

Taken collectively, the chapters that comprise this volume illustrate diverse applications of assessment and intervention strategies, strategies that nonetheless converge on the central assumptions of a constructivist position. As Polkinghorne (1984) noted, "It takes a great effort for a discipline to move from the recognition of the need to use alternative systems of inquiry to the production of clear descriptions of what these systems will look like" (p. 427), and this volume represents a tentative effort toward accomplishing that goal.

Constructive Assumptions

We are seeing in our lifetimes the collapse of the objectivist worldview that dominated the modern era, the worldview that gave people faith in the absolute and permanent rightness of certain beliefs and values. The worldview emerging in its place is constructivist. If we operate from this worldview we see all information and all stories as human creations that fit, more or less well, with our experience and within a universe that remains always beyond us and always mysterious. We honor the search for truth and knowledge and values but regard what we find as the truth and knowledge and values of people—of people in our time. (Anderson, 1990, p. 268)

Constructivism refers to a family of interrelated theories that challenge realist and objectivist versions of science. Although contemporary versions of constructivism reflect diverse historical influences (see Mahoney, 1988a, 1991; Mahoney & Lyddon, 1988), they share a common assumptive framework that emphasizes the necessarily limited and fallible nature of all our quests to know. Foremost among these assumptions are beliefs that human beings (a) are oriented actively toward a meaningful understanding of the world in which they live, (b) are denied direct access to any external reality, and (c) are continuously in the process of development and change. According to this perspective, being human necessarily entails a partial, situated "effort after meaning" (Bartlett, 1932), a position that restores to prominence processes of self-agency in human action (Howard, 1985). These efforts are marked by attempts to represent and comprehend a reality symbolically, however, that can never be fully comprehended. Instead we can have little more than indirect, mediated, and partial access to a series of transformed and forever shifting "realities," flickering images given shape and substance by the very processes that yield them. Attention to each of these human features, the fundamental orientation toward meaning, the denial of direct access to reality, and the continuous processes of change distinguish the substance and style of constructivist assessment.

Making Meaning

Man has, as it were, discovered a new method of adapting himself to his environment. Between the receptor system and the effector system, which are to be found in all animal species, we find in man a third link which we may describe as the symbolic system. This new acquisition transforms the whole of human life. As compared to other animals man lives not merely in a broader reality; he lives, so to speak, in a new dimension of reality. . . . Man lives in a symbolic universe. (Cassirer, 1972)

Constructivism is founded on the premise of meaning making; being human entails active efforts to interpret experience, seeking purpose and significance in the events that surround us. "We seem to be neurologically 'wired' to classify our experiences," reflected Mahoney (1982, p. 92), "and to transform the 'buzzing booming confusion' of sensation into some codified and dynamic representation of the world." It is this drive toward meaning, this effort to forge significance and purpose from elements of experience, that typifies the human enterprise and that serves as the cornerstone of constructivist thinking.

Efforts to understand processes of meaning making are the common cause of constructivist thinkers who have combed diverse forms of human activity for evidence of symbolic representation. Within psychology, many of these efforts have converged on processes of *languaging,* attempts to signify experience in semantic space. "For better or worse, we live in a world of language," observed Efran et al. (1990, pp. 31-32), noting that "it is in languaging that meanings are created" (see also Korzybski, 1933).

Languaging can be defined broadly, extending beyond the pale of spoken representation, across verbal and nonverbal, behavioral and cognitive, conscious and unconscious terrains (Maturana, 1980). Even within its narrower confines, however, meaning making takes rich and diverse forms. Vehicles for introducing structure and organization into the flow of experience include such processes as metaphorical representation and narrative transactions.

Sarbin (1986), for example, proposed a narratory principle that holds that human beings think, perceive, imagine, and act according to narrative structures, a position strongly supported by studies of narrative knowing (Polkinghorne, 1988). We routinely develop stories or accounts of significant life events, changes, and loss, for example, in an effort to infuse these occurrences with some coherence and meaning (Harvey, 1989; Harvey, Orbuch, Weber, Merback, & Alt, 1992). "We live in and through stories," Mair (1988, p. 127) noted. "They conjure worlds. We do not know the world other than as story world. Stories inform life" (see also Hoshmand, Chapter 6, this volume; Mair, 1989a, 1989b).

Like stories, metaphors provide potent vehicles for symbolic representation. Metaphorical knowing permeates therapeutic interventions (Bryant, Katz, Bevcar, R., & Bevcar, D., 1988) and has served as the basis for the development of *cognitive linguistics,* a constructivist discipline dedicated to the study of metaphorical understanding (Lakoff, 1987; Lakoff & Johnson, 1980). Like other constructivist theories, the essential argument of cognitive linguistics is that our constructions of the world emerge from our interactions with it. These interactions are constrained by our corporality, by the size and shape of our bodies, the nature and limitation of our movements, and the physical concomitants of being human. Gradually this physical embodiment is extended to other domains as we develop our capacities for abstractions and cognition. At first, when a novel experience is encountered for which no existing class or category of understanding is available, the event remains unclassified and unassimilated. It acquires meaning as a "structural coupling" (Maturana, 1980) occurs between aspects of that experience and aspects of preexisting constructions. "The recognition of partial similarity on some construct provides the basis for analogy, and if linguistic translation is necessary, the partial similarity is expressed in metaphor" (Sarbin, 1986, p. 4). So, for example, in helping a divorcing client anticipate his impending experience, we might speak of the "emotional roller coaster" that he can expect in the coming months, importing a physical referent to help structure and organize his anticipations of events in the emotional realm.

"In all aspects of life," observed Lakoff and Johnson (1980, p. 158), "we define our reality in terms of metaphors and then proceed to act on the basis of the metaphors. We draw inferences, set goals, make commitments, and execute plans, all on the basis of how we in part structure our experience, consciously or unconsciously, by means of metaphor."

One of the clearest descriptions of the process of *meaning making* was detailed by Kelly (1955) in his *Psychology of Personal Constructs.* Kelly stipulated that individuals attend to recurring aspects of their experience and abstract salient perceived similarities and differences from among these events, fashioning categories or forging distinctions that he called *personal constructs.* Personal constructs are bipolar distinctions (e.g. tall vs. short; shy vs. outgoing; religious vs. not religious) that, once formed, serve to channelize subsequent anticipations, perceptions, and actions (see Kelly's [1955] fundamental postulate). The very process of forging such distinctions brings events into phenomenal existence, enabling them to stand out against an otherwise seamless blur of events. Constructivist accounts therefore regard *perceived distinctions* as elemental to the process of meaning making; by noting differences, we literally call events into existence for ourselves. Consistent with its Latin origin (*existere,* meaning to "stand out against"), existence presupposes distinction. "To say that something exists," noted Efran et al. (1990, p. 36), "simply means that it has been discriminated from a background. A 'this' has been separated from a 'that'."

Such distinctions enable us to navigate our way through an ocean of experience in vessels of our own making. They allow us to impose structure and impute significance to the events of our world. In all its varied forms, the processes of meaning making constitute the very heart of being human. "We are language-related, symbol-borne, and story-sustained creatures," noted Fowler (1984, p. 50). "We do not live long or well without meaning."

Making Reality

Meaning making is central to constructivist conceptualizations of the person (Carlsen, 1988; Kegan, 1982). Like Kelly (1955), Bateson (1972) regarded meaning making as an active process of construction that owes no direct allegiance to the contours of the external world. "The division of the perceived universe into parts and wholes is convenient and may be necessary, but no necessity determines how it shall be done" (Bateson, 1979, p. 38). The distinctions that we forge are not prefabricated givens delivered directly to our senses by an external world; "man creates his own ways of seeing the world in which he lives," proffered Kelly (1955, p. 12), "the world does not create them for him."

Even in the realm of sensation, long regarded as the domain best suited to a realist understanding of the individual as a passive recipient of external events, active processes of construction are increasingly evident. In contrast to the direct and immediate access to the world that our visual system may appear to give us, for instance, active organismic processes are clear participants in the construction of what we see. Light, for example, may bathe the retinal surface of our eyes, but it does not directly penetrate beneath it, so its properties alone cannot determine what we take as perceptual givens. Nor does it directly trigger neurochemical activity that fully determines vision in any immediate line of efficient causation. Rather it joins the ongoing pattern of activity that is continuously occurring within our visual system, the vast majority of which is self-referential. As Mahoney (1991, p. 101) noted, "Numerically speaking, there are 10 motor (efferent) neurons for every sensory (afferent) receptor; and for every motor neuron, there are 10,000 interneurons (neurons that connect only with other neurons). If we accept the traditional notion that one's sensory receptors constitute one's contact with the outside world, we are forced to conclude that one is much more extensively connected with oneself than with the external environment (at a ratio of 100,000 to 1)." These quick calculations lend palpable support to Hayek's (1952, pp. 6-7) earlier observation that "much that we believe to know about the external world is, in fact, knowledge about ourselves" (see also Weimer, 1977).

Evidence such as this challenges the classical subject-object dualism, blurring the boundaries between what is viewed as "internal" and "external" to the person and underscoring the essential theory-ladeness of all our observations. Gone is the high-contrast distinction between theory and fact, and with it the assurance of any eventual one-to-one correspondence between our interpretations and features of a fixed and stable external world (Lauden, 1990; Polkinghorne, 1984, 1988). Preference instead shifts to the mediated, contextualized, and transactional nature of the relationship between the individual and the world.

Importantly, however, the utility of our perceptions is not necessarily limited by their correspondence to some presumed "objective" reality. In distinguishing properties of a gas (a concept meaningful as distinct from solids or liquids), for example, we frequently study the relationship between two other invented concepts: temperature and pressure. The covariation of these can provide a reliable (consistent) index of gaseous properties, but this fact in no way verifies the "reality" of any of these concepts. "That pressure and temperature are real properties of real entities or that their measurements provide us an unmediated view of the natural world as it is does not follow from their covariation" (Longrino, 1990).

Because neither our perceptions nor their utility is tied directly to features of the external world, any event is subject to a wide variety of alternative constructions. It is this capacity that offers equal promise to personal and scientific pursuits. As Kelly (1970, p. 1) remarked, "Howsoever the quest for truth will turn out in the end, the events we face today are subject to as great a variety of constructions as our wits will enable us to contrive. This is not to say that one construction is as good as any other. . . . But it does remind us that all our present perceptions are open to question and reconsideration and it does broadly suggest that even the most obvious occurrences of everyday life might appear utterly transformed if we were inventive enough to construe them differently." This position, dubbed *constructive alternativism* (Kelly, 1955), is a cornerstone of constructivist thinking, and it highlights the contingency of observation on human construction. Albert Einstein noted that the theory decides what we can observe (Heisenberg, 1972), and our current convictions do indeed form the basis for our future anticipations (Bateson, 1972; Kelly, 1955). Each construct or representation "actively creates and constrains new experience and thus determines what the individual will perceive as 'reality'" (Mahoney & Lyddon, 1988, p. 200; see also Bateson, 1972; Efran et al., 1990).

The Challenge of Change

The subject of experience, the individual, is a nexus of interpretation coming into existence at the boundary of nature and culture. What we contribute to the structure of experience can change over time, as the cultures in which our sensory capacities develop and are educated change. These capacities seem to be transparent transmitters of information from the external world until juxtaposition with another version of the same state of affairs reveals their opacity—their role in the formation of experience. (Longrino, 1990, p. 221)

Change is endemic to being human. Most constructivists assume that the world exists along a dimension of time and that time brings changes. Changes call for continued reconstruction of events, and for that reason Kelly (1955) defined *psychopathology* in terms of a system of constructions that was impervious to change. Psychological health is characterized by an ongoing process of revision and fluctuation. "Each day's experience," argued Kelly (1955, p. 14), "calls for the consolidation of some aspects of our outlook, revision of some, and outright abandonment of others."

Within scientific circles, too, change is the rule. Constructivists challenge the conception of science as a series of systematic approximations to an objective reality, but they embrace a conception of science as consisting of dynamic and humanly constituted worldviews periodically punctuated and transformed by radical reconceptualizations (Kuhn, 1970). Even once-cherished and seemingly unassailable worldviews gradually accede to change and reconstruction.

Because each construction carries implications for future anticipation and action (see Kelly's [1955] fundamental postulate), it follows that shifts in those constructions necessarily enable new courses of action. "Each set of distinctions creates new action possibilities," noted Efran et al. (1990, pp. 35-36); "for example, in education the invention of such notions as adult education, community college, work study, cooperative education, and correspondence courses all generated options that were not previously available." Because our constructions simultaneously enable and disable particular courses of action, constructivist assessment is directed in part at assessing these processes of personal construction, and therapy is directed in part at dislodging the person from a trenchant adherence to the "reality" of current constructions.

"Unfortunately," noted Efran et al. (1990, p. 32), "we become so accustomed to the parts we have created that we act as if these divisions were intrinsic aspects of nature and that they predate our arrival on the scene. We reify our distinctions and become so attached to them that we can hardly imagine other ways of doing it." We forget, in short, that we are the authors of these constructions and attribute them instead to intrinsic properties of an extrinsic world, a process that Kelly (1955) is reported to have irreverently dubbed "hardening of the categories."

In summarizing constructivist assumptions, their restricted knowledge claims merit emphasis. The world is never fully knowable, and for that reason the pursuit of ultimate meaning or ultimate truth is, for the constructivist, illusory. "As human beings," noted Polanyi (1958, p. 3), "we must inevitably see the universe from a centre lying within ourselves and speak about it in terms of a human language shaped by the exigencies of human intercourse. Any attempt to rigorously eliminate our human perspective from our picture of the world must lead to absurdity." Objectivists, in contrast, believe that our constructions in some sense correspond ever more accurately to a real and external reality, gradually converging at the point of truth. Constructivists temper this optimism with the realization that all knowledge is contextualized and constrained by the organizational features of our biological, psychological, and cultural embeddedness (see Lyddon & Alford, Chapter 2, this volume). "What we think we know about the world is always determined by the exigencies of our own situation," noted Efran et al. (1990, p. 32), reminding us that "neither science nor any of our other human pursuits yields privileged access to the sort of information of which a diehard realist dreams."

Constructive Comparisons

So far, we have reviewed a few of the central tenets of constructivism and in so doing have set the stage for better understanding what distinguishes constructivist assessment. One way to further this goal along pragmatic lines is to build a bridge to constructivist assessment techniques by comparing and contrasting them with more traditional methods that target roughly the same domain of experience—namely, cognitive-behavioral techniques for the assessment of beliefs, thoughts, and "self-statements" (Kendall & Hollon, 1979; Merluzzi, Glass, & Genest, 1981; Segal & Shaw, 1988). Similar comparisons could be made in relation to other schools of thought (existential, psychodynamic). Readers interested in the relationship between constructivist therapies and existential therapies may be interested in Soffer's (1990) comparison of these approaches. Likewise Soldz (1988) traced constructivist developments within recent psychodynamic therapies and noted several points of contact between these two therapeutic traditions. Here we will limit our comparisons to cognitive-behavioral orientations because these are broadly familiar to practitioners across disciplines and frequently are viewed as most closely related to constructivist developments. This comparison of constructivist

TABLE 1.1 Features of Cognitive-Behavioral and Constructivist Approaches to Cognitive Assessment

Feature	Cognitive-Behavioral Approach	Constructivist Approach
Intended effect of assessment	neutral, non-"reactive"	change generating
Target	isolated thought unit, self-statements, beliefs	construct *systems*, personal narratives
Characteristic focus	frequency of thought, degree of belief	implicative relations between constructs
Temporal focus	present	present, but more developmental emphasis
Form of cognition studied	proposition, e.g., "I am worthless."	fundamental distinction or bipolar construct
Assumed relations between cognitions	associationist, (para) logical	hierarchical; emphasis on core ordering processes
Level of analysis	individualistic	individualistic to systemic
Diagnostic emphasis	disorder-specific	comprehensive, general
Mode of administration	self-administered questionnaire	interactive interview or program, personal "diary"
Format of instrument	highly structured and standardized	less structured, idiographic
Scoring	quantitative	both quantitative and qualitative
Criteria for adequacy	psychometric	both psychometric and hermeneutic

and cognitive-behavioral assessment techniques yields several clear bases of distinction. Twelve of these are depicted in Table 1.1.

Intended Effect of Assessment

In the ideal case, most cognitive-behavioral assessment strategies are designed to be neutral in their effect on the subject, and "reactivity" to the assessment procedure is regarded as a troublesome side effect to be strictly controlled; that is, in keeping with the "objectivist" tradition to which they subscribe (Neimeyer, R. & Feixas, 1990), most cognitive methodologists tacitly assume that their procedures merely reflect rather than change the thinking process of the subject. It follows that assessment strategies that demonstrably influence the very processes they measure (e.g., as when a think-aloud protocol alters the form of a subject's thoughts) should be regarded with suspicion, leading to the conclusion that any "reactive" technique "may be limited in its utility" (Genest & Turk, 1981, p. 247).

Although this criticism may carry force in the context of traditional methods, it is less pertinent in the context of clinical assessment that is linked to treatment. Constructivists in particular reject the notion that our methods allow us wholly unobtrusive access to the activity of our subjects, and in this way they ally themselves with contemporary shifts in the physical sciences (Keutzer, 1984). Instead constructivists argue that any *assessment* should be seen as an *intervention* that prompts subjects to reconstrue the concerns being evaluated (cf. Neimeyer, R., 1988). When a therapist employs a circular question (Selvini-Palazzoli, Boscolo, Cecchin, & Prata, 1980), for example, he or she is assessing simultaneously the assumptions that family members bring to bear on a presenting problem and is staging an intervention. "What would happen in this family if this identified problem were to disappear?" for instance, might serve the therapist in two ways: It might reveal the multiple meanings attached to the presenting concern, while at the same time possibly suggesting alternative actions, promoting the rehearsal of new solutions, and challenging earlier notions concerning the intransigence of the problem. According to this framework, the development and articulation of personal constructions are themselves processes of construction and for that reason necessarily introduce some degree of change or development. Indeed recent research by Feixas, Moliner, Montes, Mari, and R. Neimeyer (1992) supports this view insofar as the serial administration of repertory grids prompted subjects to "tighten" or clarify the implicit predictions in their construct systems, resulting in more organized or coherent thinking about the domain of elements being considered. From this perspective, *assessment* is inherently a change-generating process that can be harnessed and directed toward promoting personal reconstruction, the ultimate goal of counseling and psychotherapy.

Target of Assessment

In keeping with popular models of psychological distress that view emotional disturbance as a consequence of dysfunctional or irrational thinking (e.g., Beck, Rush, Shaw, & Emery, 1979; Ellis, 1962), cognitive assessment techniques tend to target specific, relatively isolated self-statements or "self-indoctrinating" beliefs assumed to have a negative impact on mood and behavior. For example, Hollon and Kendall's (1980) Automatic Thoughts Questionnaire (ATQ) lists 30 "thoughts that pop into people's heads," such as "I've let people down" and "No one understands me." Subjects then rate the frequency with which each thought occurred to them over the last week (from *not at all* [1] to *all the time* [5]). Alternatively Sichel and Ellis's (1984) RET Self-Help Form prompts respondents to consider the irrational belief triggered by an activating event, which in turn leads to an emotional consequence. Thirteen typical dysfunctional beliefs are provided (e.g., "It is awful or horrible when major things don't go my way") as options, although the respondent may identify others if he or she desires.

Despite the differences in item format, most forms of cognitive-behavioral assessment focus on single cognitions without considering their connections with the subject's more comprehensive framework of personal knowledge. Ironically this tends to be the case even when more flexible "think-aloud" approaches are employed, insofar as the flow of the subject's verbal report is typically "chunked" or "unitized" prior to analysis (Genest & Turk, 1981). This tendency to assess cognitions as tidy, isolable units rather than as more complex networks of meaning was criticized by Sarason (1979), who contended that this ignores the dynamic interaction among cognitions that is vitally important to the clinician and cognitive scientist alike. The tendency of constructivists to assess interconnected systems of personal constructs through a variety of repertory grid techniques (Bell, 1990; Kelly, 1955; Neimeyer, G. & Neimeyer, R., 1981; Neimeyer, R., Chapter 3, this volume) and metaphorical constructions, or to observe the sequence and transition in clients' therapeutic narratives (Kelly, 1955; cf. White & Epston, 1990), reflects their attempts to redress this concern.

The essential point is that constructivist orientations typically place greater emphasis on the concept of *semantic holism,* the belief that any given construction can be best understood within the context of the broader system of meaning that supports it. A client who claims that she is "passive to a fault," for example, may in fact be enacting a hidden rationality if her image of passivity is understood within the broader framework that gives it meaning. *Passivity,* for example, may be contrasted with *aggressiveness,* and she may view aggressive people as "stubborn, angry, and unlikable people who go through life getting what they want at the expense of others." Tracing the specific implications of otherwise isolated thoughts or beliefs can yield valuable information regarding a client's resistance to change, and several formalized assessment techniques have been designed precisely for this purpose (see Fransella & Bannister, 1977).

Characteristic Focus

Perhaps as a carryover from the behavioral tradition from which they emerged, many forms of cognitive-behavioral assessment measure the frequency with which certain thoughts occur for the subject, echoing Skinner's (1953) contention that the frequencies of various responses are the basic data for a science of behavior. Like the ATQ described above, the Crandell Cognitions Inventory (CCI; Crandell & Chambless, 1986) requires the respondent to rate on 5-point scales how often he or she thinks certain "self-statements," such as "There's no way out of this mess" or "I'm just a nobody." Glass and Arnkoff (1982) and Segal and Shaw (1988), however, criticized the ambiguity of such ratings, which actually may represent the impact of such thoughts rather than their frequency per se. Some other measures require ratings of *degree of belief* or *typicality* as their basic data. An example of the former is the Hopelessness Scale (HS; Beck, Weissman, Lester, & Trexler, 1974), which asks for simple true or false ratings of 20 items reflecting pessimism (e.g., "My future seems dark to me"). The latter approach is reflected in Lefebvre's (1981) Cognitive Error Questionnaire (CEQ), which directs the respondent to read a series of vignettes outlining a situation (e.g., spouse's failure to comment on work you have done), followed by a hypothetical interpretation (e.g., "She must think I did a poor job"). The subject then is asked to rate how typical or characteristic such a response is of him or her.

In contrast to these approaches, constructivist assessment methods tend to focus not on the frequency or degree of belief/typicality of a thought but on the implications of a particular construction of oneself or others for other aspects of one's construing. A good example of this is the *implications grid* (Caputi, Breiger, & Pattison, 1990; Fransella & Bannister, 1977), which invites individuals to consider the ramifications of certain fundamental changes in their identity constructs. Other measures of implicative linkages within a client's system of constructs are exemplified by the repertory grid and laddering techniques described elsewhere in this volume (see Neimeyer, R., Chapter 3, this volume). In each of these methods, it is clear that the importance and personal significance of a client's construction derive less from the frequency of occurrence than from the centrality within the broader network of constructions that gives it meaning, and these methods are directed at assessing that centrality.

Temporal Focus

The instructional sets for many cognitive methods direct the respondent to focus on thoughts experienced either in the present or in the immediate past (e.g., the "past week," in the case of the ATQ). As such, these questionnaires can be faulted for failing to take into consideration subjects' "cognitive histories" (Sarason, 1979), the often complex developmental process that gives an individual's current belief system its form and power. Some constructivist approaches to assessment are also present oriented. For example, standard repertory grid methods essentially depict a "slice of psychological life" rather than the process of construing across time (Neimeyer, G. & Neimeyer, R., 1981). Other constructivist methods, however, are avowedly developmental in emphasis, such as Mahoney's (1991) autobiographical *life review project,* or a specially adapted *biographical repertory grid* or Biorep, which elicits the dimensions of continuity and change that the respondent uses to compare and contrast him- or herself at different ages or periods (Berzonsky, Rice, & Neimeyer, G., 1990; Neimeyer, R., 1985a). As Mahoney (1988b, p. 302) noted, "The emphasis placed on historical dimensions by some constructivist therapists is exceeded only by that in psychoanalysis." Importantly, however, he went on to note that such a "developmental history [or assessment] is not an objective recounting of temporal facts but a necessarily subjective reconstruction of the etiology of an experienced order."

Constructivist approaches to assessment therefore are generally respectful of developmental features, acknowledging the critical role of earlier constructions in shaping and framing subsequent interpretations. The primacy of early constructions is highlighted in the work of developmental constructivists who are advancing the interface between object relations and constructivist orientations to therapy (see Lyddon & Alford, Chapter 2, this volume).

Form of Cognition Assessed

In practice, many cognitive-behavioral assessment techniques seem to assume that the most molecular form of thought is *propositional,* as expressed in items like "I'm worthless" (ATQ) or "It all seems so useless" (CCI). In contrast, personal construct theorists would agree with Bateson's (1976, p. xiv) suggestion that "the primary data of experience are differences. . . . A report of a difference is the most elementary idea—the indivisible atom of thought." For this reason, methods such as the reptest and laddering technique (see Neimeyer, R., Chapter 3, this volume) are designed to elicit the fundamental distinctions or *bipolar constructs* that clients use to order their experiences and to chart their behavior. A wide range of variants on these basic methods likewise ask clients to sort, group, or systematically compare aspects of their experience (Heinemann & Shontz, 1985; Neimeyer, R., Chapter 3, this volume) in similar efforts to elicit bipolar distinctions of personal significance to the individual. One provocative implication of this assessment strategy is that the client who consistently construes others as either aggressive or passive implicitly is declaring this as an *avenue of movement* for herself; if dislodged from her current placement on that dimension, she simply may exercise its contrast (Neimeyer, G., 1987). Thus the constructivist therapist might exercise caution in prompting a client to be less "passive" in a given relationship, insofar as behaving "aggressively," as the client sees it, may be the clearest available alternative (Winter, 1987).

Assumed Relations Between Cognitions

In keeping with the tendency to conceptualize problematic cognitions as relatively isolated self-statements, typical cognitive assessment measures ignore the relationships among beliefs, internal dialogues, and so on. It is tacitly assumed that various negative cognitions are related in an incidental, associationist way, as are the sequences of automatic thoughts captured by the Dysfunctional Thought Record, devised by Beck and his associates (1979) and popularized by Burns (1980). Increasingly, however, cognitive-behaviorists have recognized the limits of this implicit model of cognitive organization and have begun to advocate assessment of cognitions at multiple levels. This trend is represented by the work of Persons (1989), who argued for the use of a "two level model" of case formulation. The distinctive aspect of this model is its assumption of an "underlying mechanism" that "produces" or "manifests itself in" overt difficulties in the sphere of mood, behavior, or cognition. For example, the underlying belief that "No one cares about me" could be expressed overtly as loneliness, withdrawal, and "surface level" ruminations about the difficulty of making friends and so on. In this case, the overt difficulties follow "logically" from an underlying belief, much as a conclusion might be compelled by a major premise. Persons (1989, p. 6), however, noted that "direct, objective measures of underlying psychological mechanisms are not yet available," and so the therapist is required to infer them from the client's self-report and observed behavior.

Constructivist assessment strategies, by comparison, are typically explicit in assuming that an individual's cognitive structure is *hierarchically organized,* with some constructions occupying a more central, and other constructions a more peripheral, role in the person's construct system (Kelly, 1955; Neimeyer, R., 1987). Thus constructivists have concentrated to a relatively greater extent on procedures for tapping into the "core ordering processes" that provide the individual with a deeply felt sense of reality, identity, and control (Mahoney, 1991). Significantly, the more tacit and elusive character of an individual's core structure requires an approach to assessment that is sometimes "looser," more evocative, and more symbolic than conventional cognitive-behavioral procedures for both assessment and psychological change, which tend to require relatively "tight," articulate, and verbal self-reports (cf. Neimeyer, R., 1988). For this reason, constructivist counselors are likely to work with the client to elaborate idiosyncratic imagery or metaphors (Mair, 1989a) used by the client, in addition to conducting "vertical exploration" of the more concrete or abstract implications of a client's straightforward verbalized constructions (e.g., Landfield, 1971; Neimeyer, R., 1986). It is interesting that as the cognitive-behavioral tradition has matured, it has come to recognize the vital significance of assessing such core cognitive processes and has begun to establish explicit bridges to the efforts of personal construct theorists concerned with similar issues (Safran, Vallis, Segal, & Shaw, 1986).

Level of Analysis

Both cognitive-behavioral and constructivist assessment strategies tend to focus on individuals rather than on families or groups, although the latter are more prone to elicit the idiosyncratic personal constructions used by the person to anticipate events (Bannister & Mair, 1968; Neimeyer, G. & Neimeyer, R., 1981). Over the past decade, however, constructivism has revolutionized the field of family therapy, as represented in the work of von Glasersfeld (1984), Hoffman (1988), Boscolo and Cecchin (Boscolo, Cecchin, Hoffman, & Penn, 1987), Efran et al. (1990), and many others. As a consequence, a growing number of constructivists have begun exploring systemic methods for mapping the interdependent "family construct systems" that in some senses constrain the individual constructions of family members (Procter, 1987). Examples of the practical therapeutic tools resulting from these efforts include the Family Characterization Sketch, which elicits a narrative account of dimensions that regulate family interaction (Alexander & Neimeyer, G., 1989; Feixas, Procter, & Neimeyer, G., Chapter 5, this volume), and the "bowtie diagram," which portrays the way in which the behaviors of various family members (unintentionally) validate the constructions of others (see Neimeyer, R., Chapter 3, this volume).

Diagnostic Emphasis

To a significant extent, cognitive methodologists have followed the lead of the psychiatric community in devising measures that purport or attempt to be "diagnosis specific." For example, both the ATQ (Hollon & Kendall, 1980) and the CCI (Crandell & Chambless, 1986) were designed to assess cognitions associated with depression, whereas the Distressing Thought Questionnaire-Anxiety (Clark, 1986) targets self-statements characteristic of anxiety disorders. These attempts at diagnostic specificity notwithstanding, reviewers of this literature have concluded that most such inventories fail to display discriminant validity (Clark, 1988; Segal & Shaw, 1988), although some measures, such as the Cognitions Checklists devised by Beck and his colleagues (Beck, Brown, Steer, Eidelson, & Riskind, 1987), do differentiate between individuals suffering from anxiety and from depression.

Constructivists, on the other hand, tend to eschew traditional diagnostic schemes based on affective symptomatology, just as they have radically questioned contemporary theories of emotion (Bannister, 1977; Mascolo & Mancuso, 1990). As a result, it is not surprising that constructivist assessment techniques rarely are designed to target specific diagnoses or affective states but instead attempt to provide a broader glimpse into the respondent's constructions of self or others. A prototypical example is

Kelly's (1955) self-characterization, which requests that the client simply describe him- or herself sympathetically in the third person, without imposing any structure or outline that would prompt the subject to focus on any particular content or set of concerns. As Kelly (1955, p. 324) noted, "The result of imposing such an outline upon the client is a considerable loss of spontaneity and, more important, a failure to discover what his own outline of conceptualization about himself happens to be." Thus cognitive-behavioral and constructivist assessment strategies often serve two distinct goals: the former situating clients within an externally validated set of diagnostic constructs, the latter eliciting from clients that unique set of personal constructs with which they structure their own identities (Berzonsky & Neimeyer, G., 1988; Berzonsky, Rice, & Neimeyer, G., 1990).

Mode of Administration

In addition to these broad theoretical and methodological differences, cognitive and constructivist measures tend to differ in a number of important procedural respects as well. In general, cognitive assessments rely on *questionnaires* (Clark, 1988), which require respondents to choose among a limited number of response options (e.g., true/false ratings in the case of the Hopelessness Scale, Likert-type ratings in the case of the ATQ, CCI, etc.). A few instruments require more elaborate responses in addition to these standard ratings. For example, the Attributional Style Questionnaire (Peterson et al., 1982) prompts the respondent to write a brief description of the probable "cause" of several hypothetical positive and negative events, followed by ratings of the internality, stability, globality, and importance of these factors in affecting similar future outcomes. Only the numerical ratings, however, usually are subjected to further analysis. Importantly the items to which the subject responds in virtually all of these measures are determined in advance by the evaluator or test designer; they are invariant across subjects and administrations. Exceptions to this general rule do exist, however, as illustrated by the Dysfunctional Thought Record (Beck et al., 1979), thought listing (Cacioppo & Petty, 1981), or think-aloud techniques (Genest & Turk, 1981), which permit the elicitation of more open-ended or subject-directed reports of cognitions.

Constructivist assessment strategies, on the other hand, typically represent some form of *interactive interview* rather than prefabricated questionnaire. Some of the assessment procedures described in this chapter and elsewhere in this volume literally are conducted in interview fashion with the respondent (such as laddering or the downward arrow, illustrated in Chapter 3, this volume), while others may rely on elaborate "interactive" computer programs for sequentially eliciting repertory grids from subjects, scoring them, and feeding back the results (Bringmann, 1992; Mancuso & Shaw, 1988; Sewell, Adams-Webber, Mitterer, & Cromwell, 1992). Finally some assessment techniques (broadly construed) preferred by constructivists foster primarily an interaction of the subject with him- or herself, with the counselor only indirectly involved in the process, if at all. The use of personal journals to capture and reflect on one's stream of spontaneous thoughts and feelings represents one illustration of this latter approach, as does the use of "mirror time" exercises to promote greater awareness of self-evaluative reactions (cf. Mahoney, 1991).

Format of Instrument

As implied in the above paragraphs, cognitive-behavioral assessments tend to be highly structured and standardized, permitting careful assessment of their reliability and validity in traditional psychometric terms (Segal & Shaw, 1988). In contrast, constructivist assessment strategies are often intentionally less clearly defined at the outset, instead permitting the client essentially to construct his or her own "test" and then to respond to it. Although this free-form style of assessment may reach its limit in something like an unstructured journal, it is present in subtler ways even in the more structured forms of constructivist assessments. For example, repertory grids conventionally prompt a respondent to compare and contrast important individuals in his or her life, including the self, and to describe these distinctions in terms of idiosyncratic personal constructs that may have deep personal significance (e.g., good Christian vs. no real spiritual feeling) but that are unlikely to appear on a standardized questionnaire. The grid procedure then requires the respondent to rate or rank each figure on each construct, yielding a matrix of numbers amenable to a variety of quantitative analyses (Bell, 1990; Fransella & Bannister, 1977). Despite the idiographic nature of these structural scores, they often have demonstrated impressive reliability in controlled studies (Feixas et al., 1992). The essential point is that constructivist approaches are less likely than traditional orientations to sacrifice an introspective, idiographic approach to assessment for an extrospective, nomothetic one, even though they may be interested similarly in issues of psychometric control.

Scoring

Scoring of most cognitive assessment instruments is primarily a computational exercise: A tally of responses provides an index of the frequency of negative self-statements, the strength of internal attributions for failure, and so on. In exceptional circumstances, as in the case of the procedures used by Anderson (1981) to assess imaginal processes, coding of transcripts of narrative reports permits the researcher to measure a broader range of dimensions, such as the level of detail present in the subject's imagery or changes in detail with practice in visualization. Even here, however, the approach is primarily quantitative, requiring the "unitizing" of narrative responses prior to numerical scoring of different content categories.

Some research tools popular with constructivists also follow this content analysis procedure, as is the case with scoring "cognitive anxiety" and other emotional dimensions studied by Viney and her colleagues (Gottschalk, Lolas, & Viney, 1986; Viney, 1990; Chapter 4, this volume). Moreover some forms of repertory grid yield highly abstract yet precise and reliable measures of construing, such as the percentage of positive/negative like and unlike-self judgments of others, which have been derived by Adams-Webber (1990) to test an "algebraic model of ethical cognition." Many ways of analyzing the results of constructivist assessments are more qualitative than quantitative, however, making them well suited for use in therapeutic situations. For example, even in the case of repertory grids, Taylor (1990) advocated a "hermeneutic" approach to interpretation, and Landfield and Epting (1987) provided a number of useful heuristics for generating clinical hypotheses based on the content of the constructs that the grid elicits. Constructivist assessment frequently incorporates both quantitative and qualitative features into its design in an effort to provide methodological triangulation (Neimeyer, G. & Resnikoff, 1982). The practical utility of these more qualitative measures in the context of counseling and psychotherapy is emphasized in each of the chapters in this volume.

Criteria for Adequacy

In light of the quantitative orientation of conventional cognitive assessment questionnaires, it is not surprising that their originators and reviewers have shown consistent concern for their *psychometric adequacy,* defined in fairly traditional terms of internal consistency, test-retest reliability, and convergent and discriminant validity (Clark, 1988; Segal & Shaw, 1988). Tests that meet these criteria are deemed acceptable for research and clinical use; those that do not are considered candidates for improvement or replacement.

The reactions of constructivists to these traditional psychometric canons are more variable. On the one hand, a number of constructivists share the values of the broader community of researchers concerned with test design and development, advocating that repertory grids and other measures be considered "mental tests" that are subject to all of the usual requirements for statistical and conceptual adequacy (e.g., Bell, 1990). From this perspective, some constructivist researchers have devoted years to the construction and validation of measures that meet or exceed the psychometric criteria displayed by conventional instruments (e.g., Moore & Neimeyer, R., 1991; Neimeyer, R. & Moore, 1988).

On the other hand, constructivists also have taken the lead in questioning the assumptions implicit in traditional test theory. Yorke (1989) for one has been an outspoken critic of the mathematical reductionism entailed in many uses of the repertory grid, the most statistically sophisticated technique in the armamentarium of constructivists. Among his principal objections to the method is his concern that the psychologist and subject necessarily operate on the basis of different "symbolic idiolects" or personal construct systems, which effectively block the communication of the "connotative meaning" of the subject in the usual quantitative summaries provided by grid-scoring programs. As a corrective to such a barren quantitative approach, he advocates

a radical change in analytical methodology. Gone would be the clean-cut elegance of mathematics. This would be replaced by something similar to textual or legal analysis in which an understanding of the respondent would be built up hermeneutically by testing part against part, and part against emerging whole. . . . [The] researcher would probe the deeper significance of what the respondent has made manifest, while at the same time putting the manifest under suspicion in order to demystify it. It is unlikely that this approach would yield a neat and tidy picture of the respondent, but an impressionist blur might prove more meaningful than a few superficial crisscross scratches. (Yorke, 1989, p. 75)

From this perspective, the criteria for adequacy of any constructivist assessment strategy would be primarily interpretive and phenomenological rather than normative and statistical (Hoshmand, 1989; Longrino, 1990; Madison, 1988). In recent years, a number of constructivists have attempted to elaborate or revolutionize existing approaches to assessment and research along these lines, advocating dialogical (Taylor, 1990), conversational (Mair, 1989a), and mutual orientation (Viney, 1988) models of psychological inquiry. As has been suggested elsewhere, our indebtedness to a restricted range of quantitative approaches may have set the stage for a "crisis of methodology," which may be resolved only through recourse to methods originating outside psychology altogether, in fields such as linguistics, ethnomethodology, symbolic interactionism, and cognitive anthropology (Hoshmand, 1989; Neimeyer, G. & Resnikoff, 1982; Neimeyer, R., 1985b). This volume attempts to push back the boundaries of traditional psychological assessment and provide an introduction to practically useful methods that have a generally hermeneutic orientation.

Constructive Diversity

Every cobbler thinks leather is the only thing. Most social scientists . . . have their favorite methods with which they are familiar and have some skill in using. And I suspect we mostly choose to investigate problems that seem vulnerable to attack through these methods. But we should at least try to be less parochial than cobblers. Let us . . . get on with the business of attacking our problems with the widest array of conceptual and methodological tools that we possess and they demand. This does not preclude discussion and debate regarding the relative usefulness of different methods of the study of specific problems or types of problems. But that is very different from the assertion of the general and inherent superiority of one method over another on the basis of some intrinsic qualities it presumably possesses. (Trow, 1957, p. 35)

As our discipline has renewed its critical appraisal of its commitments to a traditional view of science, calls for methodological reform in psychology have become increasingly frequent (Gelso, 1991; Goldman, 1989; Hoshmand, 1989; Patton & Jackson, 1991; Polkinghorne, 1991; Strong, 1991). And gradually the field has begun to respond by developing and borrowing methods better attuned to the detection and analysis of symbolic structures. Representative case research (Gordon & Shontz, 1990), Q-sort methodology (Heinemann & Shontz, 1985), and repertory grid technique (Neimeyer, G., 1989) all have been advanced as methods of demonstrated utility in the clinical context that nonetheless retain their fidelity to the ideographic and phenomenological nature of experience. They join other methods of "thick description" and "high context" borrowed from qualitative sociology, cultural anthropology, hermeneutics, and cybernetics (see Hoshmand, 1989) as complements to an existing battery of tools focused on the articulation and interrogation of personal meanings.

Constructivist theory offers the advantage of providing a conceptual template framework within which these and other assessment tools can be orchestrated and integrated without falling prey to "epistemological eclecticism" (Borgen, 1989). Consistent with recent radical changes in the philosophy of science (Rorty, 1979), constructivism supports the idea that no single or certain foundation exists for valid and justified knowledge claims. Only within the current century has justificationism, "the stubborn quest for 'authorized' knowledge and the dream of ultimate, absolute certainty" (Mahoney, 1991, p. 46), begun to erode, and constructivism has flourished in the possibilities that this has exposed.

Because no single system yields privileged access to knowledge of the world, constructivism places a special premium on variety, seeking to cultivate a diversity of meaningful modes of inquiry. It endorses and embraces all our ways of knowing, acknowledging the essential interplay between process and outcome and recognizing the many viable windows onto the same event or experience. Each of these windows provides access to, but also imposes limitations on, the panorama of perceived experience. The chapters that follow have been written to complement more traditional modes of quantitative assessment. As such, they can assist in a triangulation of methods that collectively will yield more rich and varied insights into the personal experiences we seek to understand (Neimeyer, G. & Resnikoff, 1982). Our hope is that these assessment tools will help supplement, not eclipse, existing methods of assessment because, as Polkinghorne (1991, p. 103) noted in his discussion of constructivist theory, "only the call for diversity is consistent with contemporary philosophy of science."

References

Adams-Webber, J. R. (1990). Some fundamental asymmetries in the structure of personal constructs. In G. J. Neimeyer & R. A. Neimeyer (Eds.), *Advances in personal construct psychology* (Vol. 1, pp. 49-85). Greenwich, CT: JAI.

Alexander, P., & Neimeyer, G. J. (1989). Constructivism and family therapy. *International Journal of Personal Construct Psychology, 2,* 111-121.

Anderson, M. P. (1981). Assessment of imaginal processes. In T. Merluzzi, C. Glass, & M. Genest (Eds.), *Cognitive assessment* (pp. 149-187). New York: Guilford.

Anderson, W. T. (1990). *Reality isn't what it used to be.* New York: Harper & Row.

Bannister, D. (1977). The logic of passion. In D. Bannister (Ed.), *New perspectives in personal construct theory* (pp. 21-37). London: Academic Press.

Bannister, D., & Mair, J. M. M. (1968). *The evaluation of personal constructs.* London: Academic Press.

Bartlett, F. C. (1932). *Remembering: A study in experimental and social psychology.* Cambridge, UK: Cambridge University Press.

Bateson, G. (1972). *Steps to an ecology of mind.* New York: Ballantine.

Bateson, G. (1976). Foreword. In C. E. Sluzki & D. C. Ranson (Eds.), *Double bind* (pp. i-xi). New York: Grune & Stratton.

Bateson, G. (1979). *Mind and nature: A necessary unity.* New York: E. P. Dutton.

Beck, A. T., Brown, G., Steer, R., Eidelson, J., & Riskind, J. (1987). Differentiating anxiety and depression utilizing the Cognition Checklist. *Journal of Abnormal Psychology, 96,* 179-183.

Beck, A. T., Rush, J., Shaw, B., & Emery, G. (1979). *Cognitive therapy of depression.* New York: Guilford.

Beck, A. T., Weissman, A., Lester, D., & Trexler, L. (1974). The measurement of pessimism: The Hopelessness Scale. *Journal of Consulting and Clinical Psychology, 42,* 861-865.

Bell, R. C. (1990). Analytic issues in the use of repertory grid technique. In G. J. Neimeyer & R. A. Neimeyer (Eds.), *Advances in personal construct psychology* (Vol. 1, pp. 25-48). Greenwich, CT: JAI.

Berzonsky, M. D., & Neimeyer, G. J. (1988). Identity status and personal construct systems. *Journal of Adolescence, 11,* 195-204.

Berzonsky, M. D., Rice, K. G., & Neimeyer, G. J. (1990). Identity status and self-construct systems: Process X structure interactions. *Journal of Adolescence, 13,* 251-263.

Borgen, F. H. (1984). Are there necessary linkages between research practices and the philosophy of science? *Journal of Counseling Psychology, 31,* 457-460.

Borgen, F. H. (1989). Evolution of eclectic epistemology. *Counseling Psychologist, 17,* 90-97.

Boscolo, L., Cecchin, G., Hoffman, L., & Penn, P. (1987). *Milan systemic family therapy.* New York: Basic Books.

Bringmann, M. W. (1992). Computer based methods for the analysis and interpretation of personal construct systems. In R. A. Neimeyer & G. J. Neimeyer (Eds.), *Advances in personal construct psychology* (Vol. 2, pp. 57-90). Greenwich, CT: JAI.

Bryant, L., Katz, B., Bevcar, R. J., & Bevcar, D. S. (1988). The use of therapeutic metaphor among members of AAMFT. *American Journal of Family Therapy, 16,* 112-120.

Burns, D. (1980). *Feeling good.* New York: Signet.

Cacioppo, J. T., & Petty, R. E. (1981). Social psychological procedures for cognitive response assessment. In T. Merluzzi, C. Glass, & M. Genest (Eds.), *Cognitive assessment* (pp. 309-342). New York: Guilford.

Caputi, P., Breiger, R., & Pattison, P. (1990). Analyzing implications grids using hierarchical models. *International Journal of Personal Construct Psychology, 3,* 77-90.

Carlsen, M. B. (1988). *Meaning-making: Therapeutic processes in adult development.* New York: Norton.

Cassirer, E. (1972). *Language et mythe: A propos des norms de dieux* [Language and myth: Regarding the norms of God]. Paris: Les Editions de minuit.

Clark, D. A. (1986). Factors influencing the retrieval and control of negative cognitions. *Behaviour Research and Therapy, 24,* 151-159.

Clark, D. A. (1988). The validity of measures of cognition: A review of the literature. *Cognitive Therapy and Research, 12,* 1-20.

Crandell, C. J., & Chambless, D. L. (1986). The validation of an inventory for measuring depressive thoughts: The Crandell Cognitions Inventory. *Behaviour Research and Therapy, 24,* 403-411.

Efran, J., Lukens, M. D., & Lukens, R. J. (1990). *Language, structure, and change.* New York: Norton.

Ellis, A. (1962). *Reason and emotion in psychotherapy.* Secaucus, NJ: Lyle Stuart.

Feixas, G., Moliner, J., Montes, J., Mari, M., & Neimeyer, R. A. (1992). The stability of structural measures derived from repertory grids. *International Journal of Personal Construct Psychology, 2,* 217-257.

Fowler, J. W. (1984). *Becoming adult, becoming Christian.* San Francisco: Harper & Row.

Fransella, F., & Bannister, D. (1977). *A manual for repertory grid technique.* London: Academic Press.

Gelso, C. J. (1991). Caliko, Aristotle, and science in counseling psychology: To theorize or not to theorize. *Journal of Counseling Psychology, 38,* 211-213.

Genest, M., & Turk, D. C. (1981). Think aloud approaches to cognitive assessment. In T. Merluzzi, C. Glass, & M. Genest (Eds.), *Cognitive assessment* (pp. 233-269). New York: Guilford.

Glass, C. R., & Arnkoff, D. B. (1982). Think cognitively: Selected issues in cognitive assessment and therapy. In P. C. Kendall (Ed.), *Advances in cognitive-behavioral research and therapy* (Vol. 1, pp. 36-71). New York: Academic Press.

Goldman, L. (1989). Moving counseling research into the 21st century. *Counseling Psychologist, 17,* 81-95.

Gordon, J., & Shontz, F. (1990). Representative case research: A way of knowing. *Journal of Counseling and Development, 69,* 62-66.

Gottschalk, L. A., Lolas, F., & Viney, L. L. (1986). *Content analysis of verbal behavior.* Berlin: Springer Verlag.

Harvey, J. H. (1989). People's naive understandings of their close relationships. *International Journal of Personal Construct Psychology, 2,* 37-48.

Harvey, J. H., Orbuch, T. L., Weber, A. L., Merback, N., & Alt, R. (1992). House of pain and hope: Accounts of loss. *Death Studies, 16,* 99-124.

Hayek, F. A. (1952). *The sensory order.* Chicago: University of Chicago Press.

Heinemann, A. W., & Shontz, F. C. (1985). Methods of studying persons. *Counseling Psychologist, 13,* 111-125.

Heisenberg, W. (1972). *Physics and beyond.* New York: Harper Torchbooks.

Hoffman, L. (1988). A constructivist position for family therapy. *Irish Journal of Psychology, 9,* 110-129.

Hollon, S. D., & Kendall, P. C. (1980). Cognitive self-statements in depression: Development of an Automatic Thoughts Questionnaire. *Cognitive Therapy and Research, 4,* 383-396.

Hoshmand, L. L. S. (1989). Alternative research paradigms: A review and teaching proposal. *Counseling Psychologist, 17,* 3-80.

Howard, G. (1985). Can research in the human sciences become more relevant to practice? *Journal of Counseling and Development, 63,* 539-544.

Howard, G. S. (1989). *A tale of two stories: Excursions into a narrative approach to psychology.* Notre Dame, IN: Academic Publications.

Kegan, R. (1982). *The evolving self: Problem and process in human development.* Cambridge, MA: Harvard University Press.

Kelly, G. A. (1955). *The psychology of personal constructs* (Vols. 1 & 2). New York: Norton.

Kelly, G. A. (1970). A brief introduction to personal construct theory. In D. Bannister (Ed.), *Perspectives in personal construct theory* (pp. 1-29). New York: Academic Press.

Kendall, P. C., & Hollon, S. D. (1979). *Cognitive-behavioral interventions.* New York: Academic Press.

Keutzer, C. S. (1984). The power of meaning: From quantum mechanics to synchronicity. *Journal of Humanistic Psychology, 24,* 80-94.

Korzybski, A. (1933). *Science and sanity.* Lakeville, CT: International Non-Aristotelian Library.

Kuhn, T. (1970). *The structure of scientific revolutions* (2nd ed.). Chicago: University of Chicago Press.

Lakoff, G. (1987). *Women, fire, and dangerous things: What categories reveal about the mind.* Chicago: University of Chicago Press.

Lakoff, G., & Johnson, M. (1980). *Metaphors we live by.* Chicago: University of Chicago Press.

Landfield, A. W. (1971). *Personal construct systems in psychotherapy.* Chicago: Rand McNally.

Landfield, A. W., & Epting, F. R. (1987). *Personal construct psychology.* New York: Human Sciences.

Lauden, L. (1990). *Science and relativism.* Chicago: University of Chicago Press.

Lefebvre, M. F. (1981). Cognitive distortion and cognitive errors in depressed psychiatric and low back pain patients. *Journal of Consulting and Clinical Psychology, 49,* 517-525.

Longrino, H. E. (1990). *Science as social knowledge.* Princeton, NJ: Princeton University Press.

Madison, G. B. (1988). *The hermeneutics of postmodernity.* Bloomington: Indiana University Press.

Mahoney, M. J. (1982). Psychotherapy and human change processes. In J. H. Harvey & M. M. Parks (Eds.), *The master lecture series* (Vol. 1, pp. 73-122). Washington, DC: American Psychological Association.

Mahoney, M. J. (1988a). Constructive metatheory I: Basic features and historical foundations. *International Journal of Personal Construct Psychology, 1,* 1-36.

Mahoney, M. J. (1988b). Constructive metatheory II: Implications for psychotherapy. *International Journal of Personal Construct Psychology, 1,* 299-315.

Mahoney, M. J. (1991). *Human change processes.* New York: Basic Books.

Mahoney, M. J., & Lyddon, W. J. (1988). Recent developments in cognitive approaches to counseling and psychotherapy. *Counseling Psychologist, 16,* 190-234.

Mair, M. (1988). Psychology of story telling. *International Journal of Personal Construct Psychology, 1,* 125-138.

Mair, M. (1989a). Kelly, Bannister, and story-telling psychology. *International Journal of Personal Construct Psychology, 2,* 1-14.

Mair, M. (1989b). *Between psychology and psychotherapy: A poetics of experience.* London: Routledge.

Mancuso, J. C., & Shaw, M. L. (1988). *Cognition and personal structure.* New York: Praeger.

Mascolo, M., & Mancuso, J. C. (1990). Functioning of epigenetically evolved emotion systems: A constructive analysis. *International Journal of Personal Construct Psychology, 3,* 205-222.

Maturana, H. R. (1980). Biology of cognition. In H. R. Maturana & F. J. Varela (Eds.), *Autopoeisis and cognition: The realization of the living* (pp. 2-62). Boston: Reidel.

Merluzzi, T., Glass, C., & Genest, M. (Eds.). (1981). *Cognitive assessment.* New York: Guilford.

Moore, M. K., & Neimeyer, R. A. (1991). A confirmatory factor analysis of the Threat Index. *Journal of Personality and Social Psychology, 60,* 122-129.

Neimeyer, G. J. (1987). Personal construct assessment, strategy, and technique. In R. A. Neimeyer & G. J. Neimeyer (Eds.), *Personal construct therapy casebook* (pp. 127-152). New York: Springer.

Neimeyer, G. J. (1989). Applications of repertory grid technique to vocational assessment. *Journal of Counseling and Development, 67,* 585-589.

Neimeyer, G. J., & Neimeyer, R. A. (1981). Personal construct perspectives on cognitive assessment. In T. V. Merluzzi, C. R. Glass, & M. Genest (Eds.), *Cognitive assessment* (pp. 188-232). New York: Guilford.

Neimeyer, G. J., & Resnikoff, A. (1982). Qualitative strategies in counseling research. *Counseling Psychologist, 10,* 75-85.

Neimeyer, R. A. (1985a). Personal constructs in clinical practice. In P. C. Kendall (Ed.), *Advances in cognitive-behavioral research and therapy* (Vol. 4, pp. 275-329). New York: Academic Press.

Neimeyer, R. A. (1985b). *The development of personal construct psychology.* Lincoln: University of Nebraska Press.

Neimeyer, R. A. (1986). Personal construct therapy. In W. Dryden & W. Golden (Eds.), *Cognitive-behavioural approaches to psychotherapy* (pp. 225-260). London: Harper & Row.

Neimeyer, R. A. (1987). An orientation to personal construct therapy. In R. A. Neimeyer & G. J. Neimeyer (Eds.), *Personal construct therapy casebook* (pp. 3-19). New York: Springer.

Neimeyer, R. A. (1988). Integrative directions in personal construct therapy. *International Journal of Personal Construct Psychology, 1,* 283-297.

Neimeyer, R. A., & Feixas, G. (1990). Constructivist contributions to psychotherapy integration. *Journal of Integrative and Eclectic Psychotherapy, 9,* 4-20.

Neimeyer, R. A., & Moore, M. K. (1988). Assessing personal meanings of death. *Death Studies, 13,* 227-245.

Neimeyer, R. A., & Neimeyer, G. J. (Eds.). (1987). *Personal construct therapy casebook.* New York: Springer.

Patton, J., & Jackson, A. J. (1991). Theory and meaning in counseling research: Comment on Strong (1991). *Journal of Counseling Psychology, 38,* 214-216.

Persons, J. B. (1989). *Cognitive therapy in practice.* New York: Norton.

Peterson, C., Semmel, A., Von Baeyer, C., Abramson, L., Metalsky, I., & Seligman, M. (1982). The Attributional Style Questionnaire. *Cognitive Therapy and Research, 6,* 287-300.

Polanyi, M. (1958). *Personal knowledge: Towards a post-critical philosophy.* Chicago: University of Chicago Press.

Polkinghorne, D. E. (1984). Further extensions of methodological diversity for counseling psychology. *Journal of Counseling Psychology, 31,* 416-429.

Polkinghorne, D. E. (1988). *Narrative knowing and the human sciences.* New York: State University of New York Press.

Polkinghorne, D. E. (1991). In conflicting calls for methodological reform. *Counseling Psychologist, 19,* 103-114.

Procter, H. G. (1987). Change in the family construct system. In R. A. Neimeyer & G. J. Neimeyer (Eds.), *Personal construct therapy casebook* (pp. 153-171). New York: Springer.

Rorty, R. (1979). *Philosophy and the mirror of nature.* Princeton, NJ: Princeton University Press.

Safran, J. D., Vallis, T. M., Segal, Z. V., & Shaw, B. F. (1986). Assessment of core cognitive processes in cognitive therapy. *Cognitive Therapy and Research, 10,* 509-526.

Sarason, I. G. (1979). Three lacunae of cognitive therapy. *Cognitive Therapy and Research, 3,* 223-235.

Sarbin, T. R. (1986). The narrative as a root metaphor for psychology. In T. R. Sarbin, *Narrative psychology* (pp. 3-21). New York: Praeger.

Segal, Z. V., & Shaw, B. F. (1988). Cognitive assessment: Issues and methods. In K. S. Dobson (Ed.), *Handbook of cognitive behavioral therapies* (pp. 39-84). New York: Guilford.

Selvini-Palazzoli, M., Boscolo, L., Cecchin, G., & Prata, G. (1980). Hypothesizing-circularity-neutrality. *Family Process, 19,* 3-12.

Sewell, K., Adams-Webber, J., Mitterer, J., & Cromwell, R. L. (1992). Computerized repertory grids: A review of the literature. *International Journal of Personal Construct Psychology, 5*(1), 1-24.

Sichel, J., & Ellis, A. (1984). *RET self-help form.* New York: Institute for Rational Emotive Therapy.

Skinner, B. F. (1953). *Science and human behavior.* New York: Macmillan.

Soffer, J. (1990). George Kelly versus the existentials: Theoretical and therapeutic implications. *International Journal of Personal Construct Psychology, 4,* 357-376.

Soldz, S. (1988). Constructivist tendencies in recent psychoanalysis. *International Journal of Personal Construct Psychology, 1,* 329-348.

Strong, S. R. (1991). Theory-driven science and naive empiricism in counseling psychology. *Journal of Counseling Psychology, 38,* 204-210.

Taylor, D. S. (1990). Making the most of your matrices: Hermeneutics, statistics, and the repertory grid. *International Journal of Personal Construct Psychology, 3,* 105-119.

Trow, M. (1957). Comment on participant observation and interviewing: A comparison. *Human Organization, 16,* 33-35.

Viney, L. L. (1988). Which data collection methods are appropriate for a constructivist psychology? *International Journal of Personal Construct Psychology, 1,* 191-203.

Viney, L. L. (1990). A constructivist model of psychological reactions to physical illness and injury. In G. J. Neimeyer & R. A. Neimeyer (Eds.), *Advances in personal construct psychology* (Vol. 1, pp. 117-151). Greenwich, CT: JAI.

von Glasersfeld, E. (1984). On radical constructivism. In P. Watzlawick (Ed.), *The invented reality* (pp. 17-47). New York: Norton.

Weimer, W. B. (1977). A conceptual framework for cognitive psychology: Motor theories of mind. In R. Shaw & J. Bransford (Eds.), *Perceiving, acting, and knowing* (pp. 267-311). Hillsdale, NJ: Lawrence Erlbaum.

White, M., & Epston, D. (1990). *Narrative means to therapeutic ends.* New York: Norton.

Winter, D. A. (1987). Personal construct psychotherapy as a radical alternative to social skills training. In R. A. Neimeyer & G. J. Neimeyer (Eds.), *Personal construct therapy casebook* (pp. 107-127). New York: Springer.

Yorke, M. (1989). The intolerable wrestle: Words, numbers, and meanings. *International Journal of Personal Construct Psychology, 2,* 65-76.

2

Constructivist Assessment:
A Developmental-Epistemic Perspective

WILLIAM J. LYDDON

DARLYS J. ALFORD

A developmental-epistemic approach to clinical assessment is founded on certain philosophical assumptions identified with constructivism in general and the developmental constructivist perspective in particular. It is our intent first to describe these assumptions briefly and how they influence our theoretical commitments and assessment practices. The second part of this chapter is devoted to a case study meant to exemplify the practical dimensions of developmental-epistemic assessment. It is important to emphasize that the approach described herein is not meant to supplant existing methods of clinical assessment but rather is intended to illustrate what we believe are some unique assessment considerations that may be derived from the developmental constructivist perspective.

Philosophical and Theoretical Contexts

The emergence of the constructivist perspective in the psychological and human sciences is founded on a core of philosophical assumptions that underscore the active and proactive nature of human knowing (see Neimeyer, G. & Neimeyer, R., Chapter 1, this volume). Although most constructivists tend to share these fundamental assumptions about the constitutive nature of human knowing, knowledge, and reality, what distinguishes developmental constructivists is their commitment to the causal principle of *structural differentiation* (Mahoney & Lyddon, 1988). Constructivists who endorse structural differentiation assume that knowledge is fundamentally dynamic and directional; that is, over time, knowledge systems and structures are presumed to undergo qualitative transformations in the direction of increased complexity and abstraction. According to this perspective, human experience is conceptualized as a lifelong, developmental unfolding of knowing processes whereby old forms of knowing give way to more comprehensive forms as the knower constructs more epistemologically powerful (inclusive, viable, integrated) ways of making sense of the world (cf. Basseches, 1984; Carlsen, 1988; Ford, 1987; Guidano, 1987, 1990; Mahoney, 1991).

Constructivist philosophical assumptions necessarily predicate certain theoretical conceptualizations. For example, our philosophical commitment to the notion of structural differentiation is reflected in our affinity for various developmentally based theories, constructs, and models of change. Most influential to the assessment approach that we will describe are Kegan's (1982) *constructivist developmental theory,* Bowlby's (1977, 1988) *attachment theory,* and models of change that focus on clients' *stages, levels,* and *types of change* (Lyddon, 1990; Prochaska & DiClemente, 1986). Our adherence to the general constructivist view that individuals actively create their personal realities similarly undergirds our interest in studying individual differences in the way persons order and validate their experiences. An important contribution to this line of investigation—and one most relevant to a developmental-epistemic approach to assessment—is Royce's (1964; Royce & Powell, 1983) constructivist theory of knowledge and his identification of three distinctive personal "ways of knowing," or *epistemic styles* (rational, empirical, and metaphorical). Because these theoretical frameworks most directly inform our assessment procedures and practices, the salient conceptual features and assessment implications of each of these influences will be discussed in turn.

Developmental and Attachment Theories

Recent descriptions of constructivist counseling and psychotherapy seek to understand personal and emotional adjustment within a lifespan-developmental framework (Carlsen, 1988; Guidano, 1987, 1990; Guidano & Liotti, 1983; Kegan, 1982; Liotti, 1984; Mahoney, 1991; Safran & Segal, 1990). From this perspective, the life cycle involves both a series of social contexts and time periods in which a person must cope with a sequential unfolding of central life tasks. Although this emerging developmental perspective owes much to the formative work stemming from Piaget's (1970) genetic epistemology and Erikson's (1959) theory of psychosocial development, valuable contributions to this paradigm also derive from the scholarly writings of Roger Gould, Daniel Levinson, Jane Loevinger, George Herbert Mead, William Percy, and Heinz Werner. As previously noted, Kegan's (1982) constructivist developmental theory and Bowlby's (1977, 1982, 1988) theory of attachment serve as particularly influential guides to our assessment practices.

Kegan's (1982) developmental theory is founded on the premise that human beings are essentially "constructive meaning makers" who are continually working to make sense of their experience. According to Kegan, development (or meaning making) is a "simultaneously epistemological and ontological activity; it is about knowing and being, about theory-making and investments and commitments of the self" (1982, pp. 44-45). Kegan suggested that as a person develops, he or she passes through various "balances in subject-object relations," whereby the self redefines or reconstructs its relationship to the world in a manner that is increasingly more integrated and coherent. Central to his theory is the concept of *holding environments*—the successive interpersonal contexts or "cultures of embeddedness" that ideally provide the significant developmental functions of confirmation (support and recognition), contradiction (opportunities to explore and differentiate), and continuity (personal coherence and consistency). Holding environments include those salient social spheres of influence—primary caregivers, extended family members, educational groups, peer and intimate relationships, and so on—that contribute to each person's developing self-identity and beliefs about personal trust, power, value, and intimacy. Understanding the unique way in which each person makes meaning of these interpersonal experiences is at the heart of Kegan's developmental framework and is a primary focus of constructivist counseling and assessment.

Another significant conceptual link between the domain of development and constructivist psychotherapy is *attachment theory*. Bowlby
(1977) stated:

> Attachment theory is a way of conceptualizing the propensity of human
> beings to make strong affectional bonds to particular others and of explain-
> ing the many forms of emotional distress and personality disturbance, in-
> cluding anxiety, anger, depression, and emotional detachment, to which
> unwilling separation and loss give rise. (p. 127)

On the one hand, in Bowlby's terms, a child will develop a *secure* pattern
of attachment if parents are readily available and lovingly responsive to
his or her bids for comfort and/or protection. Such parental responsiveness is presumed to undergird the development of a safe base from which
the child may leave to explore his or her surroundings and subsequently
return to receive comfort. *Insecure* attachments, on the other hand, are
identified with one or more patterns of parenting characterized by inconsistencies in responding to the child's care-eliciting behaviors, discour-
agement of the child's exploratory attempts, rejection of the child's bids for
closeness, threats of loss of love, and/or actual separation, abandonment,
and loss. Because the personal organization of attachment (or internal
"working model") is believed to be a relatively enduring component of
an individual's self-system, insecure working models are thought to give
rise to a range of personal and emotional difficulties over the course of
development (Ainsworth, 1989; Belsky & Nezworski, 1988; Koback &
Sceery, 1988; Sroufe, 1983; Weiss, 1982). In recent years, a growing body
of empirical research has corroborated the relevance of attachment theory
to counseling and various other relationship-based domains (cf. Bowlby,
1988; Collins & Read, 1990; Feeney & Noller, 1990; Guidano, 1987;
Hazan & Shaver, 1987, 1990; Heesacker & Neimeyer, G., 1990; Liotti,
1984; Lyddon, Bradford, & Nelson, in press; Mahoney, 1991; Pistole,
1989a, 1989b; Safran & Segal, 1990; West & Sheldon, 1988).

Lifespan Developmental Assessment. From a constructivist perspective,
Kegan's developmental model and Bowlby's attachment theory provide
an organizing framework for understanding the way clients' personal systems of meaning may be actively generated, maintained, and transformed
in the context of emotional attachments (and detachments) throughout the

lifespan. Within this context, the way that a client constructs or makes sense of his or her relationship and developmental history is a central theme for assessment and counseling. The assumption here is that our client's behavior has an inevitable developmental logic and that even the most extreme client behavior makes developmental sense once we understand it in the context of his or her developmental and attachment history (Ivey, 1991).

In our own clinical work, we have found West and Sheldon's (1988) classificatory scheme to be a helpful framework for assessing clients' insecure attachment patterns. West and Sheldon identify four clinical patterns based on Bowlby's (1977, 1982) descriptions of insecure attachment: compulsive self-reliance, compulsive care giving, compulsive care seeking, and angry withdrawal. Clients who exhibit a pattern of *compulsive self-reliance* relegate self-sufficiency to a place of prominence in their lives and as a result avoid turning to significant others for help, affection, or closeness. According to Bowlby (1988), this pattern derives from attachment interactions in which a child's desires for comfort and protection are met by consistent parental rebuffs and rejections. Although close relationships may be established in the *compulsive care giving* pattern, clients who exhibit this attachment style place highest priority on others' needs and regularly assume a giving role, rarely allowing themselves to receive care. Bowlby (1977) pointed out that a common childhood experience of these individuals is to have been prematurely forced into a caring role for a parent and/or sibling. The *compulsive care seeking* pattern is based on Bowlby's (1977) notion of anxious attachment and is exemplified by clients who maintain a sense of personal security through urgent and frequent care seeking behaviors. Compulsive care seekers are highly dependent on attachment figures for decision making and problem solving and tend to react intensely to anticipated or actual separations. Bowlby (1977) pointed out that this pattern derives from attachment experiences that give way to personal doubt and anxiety about the consistency of significant others' availability and responsiveness. Rather than experiencing pervasive feelings of anxiety, clients exhibiting a pattern of *angry withdrawal* react to the perceived unavailability and/or unresponsiveness of the attachment figure with strong feelings of anger. As implied by the pattern name, these persons often choose to withdraw spitefully from the significant other rather than to express their anger directly.

It is significant to note how the four patterns of insecure attachment may be organized along a continuum ranging from distant/detached patterns to close/enmeshed patterns. Compulsive self-reliance and angry withdrawal, for example, are similar to the extent that in each pattern the person tends to deny his or her own attachment needs. By way of contrast, persons exhibiting the compulsive care seeking and compulsive care giving patterns tend to possess a low threshold for manifesting attachment behavior (West & Sheldon, 1988).

Although the foregoing patterns of insecure attachment may be assessed via a 40-item self-report instrument developed by West and Sheldon (1988), we prefer to use their organizational scheme as a heuristic device to guide the clinical interview process. A sample of various attachment and developmentally relevant questions that we employ with clients appears in Table 2.1.

On the basis of the responses to these and other developmentally focused questions, we begin to formulate hypotheses concerning our clients' significant attachment themes and issues. As clients reveal the content of their personal stories, we attempt to look for recurring patterns with regard to such core developmental issues as trust, autonomy, identity, and intimacy. When attending to clients' unfolding life stories, we also find that it is important to recognize the basic elements of their narratives: the major participants, roles, sequencing of events, causal attributions, salient metaphors, and personal meanings associated with significant life events. From a developmental-epistemic perspective, our clients' stories provide us with examples of their present attempts at creating a coherent structure, a way of making sense of their lives.

Finally, because insecure attachment styles that have been established and maintained by the significant interpersonal relationships in the client's life often appear in the relationship with the counselor, we believe that it is important for the counselor to monitor his or her own emotional reactions to the client in the assessment process. Counselor sensitivity to the "interpersonal pull" of the client not only may serve to corroborate certain hypotheses about the nature of the client's attachment style but also holds significant therapeutic implications. For example, from a strategic viewpoint, we believe that it is important for the counselor to refrain from responding to the client in a complementary fashion—that is, in a way that confirms the client's characteristic insecure attachment pattern and working models. For example, the counselor who can disengage appro-

TABLE 2.1 Sample Lifespan Developmental Assessment Questions

Relationship with parents

Could you tell me about your life from the earliest age you can remember?

Could you tell me about you and your parents? Who spent the most time with you during your childhood? Were there any periods of separation? How did you feel about the separation?

How close did you feel to your parents as a child? How emotionally close are you to your parents now? What changes have taken place in your relationship with your parents?

Are there any patterns from your early childhood (childhood, adolescence, etc.) that continue in your present life?

Relationship with others

Were there other important people in your childhood? Who are other important people in your life now? Could you describe these relationships?

Could you tell me about your best childhood friend? Who is your best friend now? What does this relationship mean to you?

Could you tell me about an important relationship that ended?

How did this happen? How did you feel about it at the time?

How do you feel about it now?

When you are having difficulties, whom do you go to for assistance? When you are feeling unhappy, what other person would be most likely to notice?

Relationship with self

Tell me about some of the earliest statements others made about you that began with "You are ____ ."

If you were to make a list of true statements about yourself, what would it include?

What kind of friend (son/daughter, parent, husband/wife, lover, student, employee) are you?

What does being dependent (independent) mean to you? Do you find it easy to make decisions?

Do you find it difficult to get close to others?

How open are you to experiencing your feelings? What feelings are most difficult to express? Could you tell me about anger and frustration in your life? How do you deal with your anger?

What do you hope for? What do you fear?

priately from the compulsive care seeking client's need to have the counselor solve his or her problems disconfirms the client's view that he or she is a helpless person who must rely continually on others for decision making and problem solving.

Stages, Levels, and Types of Change

Recent trends of development in counseling theory indicate a growing interest in understanding fundamental principles and processes of change (Bandura, 1977; Frank, 1985; Goldfried, 1982; Highlen & Hill, 1984; Mahoney, 1991; Prochaska & DiClemente, 1982). An important contribution to this endeavor is reflected in the research program of James Prochaska and his colleagues that has attempted to identify how people change both as a result of their own efforts and as a response to counseling and psychotherapy (McConnaughy, Prochaska, & Velicer, 1983; Prochaska & DiClemente, 1982, 1986). Their findings suggest that people use a variety of strategies of change that can be located reliably at differing stages of the change process. In their conceptualization, a stage of change is both a duration of time and a set of tasks to be accomplished before moving into the next stage. Prochaska and DiClemente (1986) identified four basic stages of change: (a) precontemplation (people are either unaware of a problem or have no desire to change), (b) contemplation (people are aware of a problem and begin to think about making a commitment to change), (c) action (people actively have begun to alter their behavior or environment), and (d) maintenance (people have made significant progress toward the desired change and are working at continuing therapeutic gains and at preventing relapse). Similar conceptualizations have been offered by Howard, Nance, and Myers (1986), who identified various stages of client readiness for change.

In addition to the stage of change concept, Prochaska and DiClemente (1986) put forward a hierarchy of levels of change: (a) symptoms/situational, (b) maladaptive cognitions, (c) interpersonal conflicts, (d) family/systems conflicts, and (e) intrapersonal conflicts. Theoretically the *levels of change* concept represents an attempt to assess psychological problems along the dimension of complexity (from least to most complex) and, as Prochaska and DiClemente suggested, holds implications for goal setting and choice of strategic intervention.

Another related distinction that we find helpful in the assessment and goal formulation process is that between two types of change: first- and second-order change (Lyddon, 1990; Sinnott, 1989; Watzlawick, Weakland, & Fisch, 1974). Briefly *first-order change* is essentially "change without change," or any change that does not produce a change in the structure of the system. Examples of first-order change include immediate symptomatic relief and/or the reestablishment of equilibrium. Individuals for whom first-order change is indicated typically exhibit a secure attachment style, are comfortable with their core assumptions about self and world, and tend to require only peripheral adjustments in their personal system. Second-order change, on the other hand, is "change of change," a type of change that alters the fundamental structures of the system. Constructivists refer to second-order change as "deep" (Guidano, 1987) or "core" (Mahoney, 1980) and suggest that it (a) involves a restructuring of a client's personal identity and most basic assumptions about self and world and (b) is often accompanied by intense and sometimes painful emotions. Lyddon (1990) offered several potential indicators suggestive of a need for second-order change:

> (a) the presence of a perceived developmental life crisis accompanied by significant emotional disequilibrium; (b) the need for core personality change and/or fundamental changes in one's assumptions about self, world, or reality; (c) openness to exploring, experiencing, and expressing feelings; (d) unsuccessful attempts to resolve the conflict through first-order change strategies; and (e) prior experience with second-order, or transformational change. (p. 125)

With regard to developmental and attachment themes, individuals for whom second order change is indicated tend to exhibit a pattern of insecure attachment, to reveal conflicts of an intrapersonal and developmental nature (conflicts involving such basic issues as trust, autonomy, identity, or meaning), and to require a significant constructive revision in their assumptions about self and world.

Change Assessment. The consideration of client stage, level, and type of change dovetails nicely with general developmental theory by building the dynamic of client change into the conceptualization of the client and his or her presenting concerns. Assessment of client stage of change may be accomplished via the Change Assessment Scale (CAS; McConnaughy, DiClemente, Prochaska, & Velicer, 1989). The CAS is a 32-item self-report measure designed to assess "clients' readiness for involvement in change at the start of therapy" (McConnaughy et al., 1983, p. 368) by operationalizing Prochaska and DiClemente's (1986) four theoretical stages of change. Clients are asked to indicate in a Likert-scale fashion the extent to which they agree with statements about their presenting problem. Raw total scores for each subscale (Precontemplation, Contemplation, Action, and Maintenance) are transformed to T-scores and subsequently plotted in a stage of change profile form. The four subscales have reported coefficient alphas of .88 (Precontemplation), .88 (Contemplation), .89 (Action), and .88 (Maintenance). Principal components analyses have yielded a clear four-component solution, suggesting that the items measure the theoretical constructs of interest (McConnaughy et al., 1983, 1989).

Although empirical support bearing on level and type of change is not available, we find the distinctions to be heuristically valuable in that assessing these dimensions of clients' problems has direct implications for both goal setting and mode of strategic intervention. For example, students at the end of their college careers often seek counseling to cope with their anxieties about the job interview process. In these cases, the level of change tends to be less complex, involving first-order adjustments in skills, cognitions, and emotional responses to the job interview situation. Role playing, cognitive restructuring, and relaxation training have demonstrated utility with this level and type of change. Some students facing the same developmental task, however, reveal conflicts of a more intense, intrapersonal nature. At this point in their college careers, these students—some for the first time—are questioning their basic values, expressing dissatisfaction with their major field of study, and contemplating the meaning and purpose of their educational experience. In these cases, the level of change tends to be more complex, indicating a need for possible second-order revisions in personal values, choices, and identity. When second-order changes are indicated, we find a more process-oriented counseling approach—one that promotes client self-exploration of values, emotions, and personal meanings—to be most beneficial.

With regard to the distinction between first- and second-order change, it is important to remember that initial assessments and goal setting are always open to negotiation. As previously suggested, clients often enter counseling to make first-order changes in their lives, requesting skill acquisition and/or symptomatic relief. For most, this is an achievable and appropriate goal. Occasionally, however, what initially is assessed to be a first-order problem is discovered to reflect a history or pattern of difficulty with some core developmental issue. In these cases, we encourage counselors to suggest to the client what developmental issues may be at stake and describe to them the process and possibilities of second-order change. At this point, the client ultimately must decide whether to proceed with the initial commitment to first-order adjustments or to permit a shift to deeper psychological exploration. If a client chooses to continue with his or her first-order goals, we believe that having introduced the possibility of second-order change encourages (and often results in) the client's return to counseling specifically to accomplish deeper change when he or she is ready.

Epistemic Style

On the basis of a research program that spans more than three decades, Royce and his colleagues developed a conceptual framework that identifies three basic epistemic styles or approaches to knowing the world: empiricism, rationalism, and metaphorism (Diamond & Royce, 1980; Royce, 1964; Royce & Mos, 1980; Royce & Powell, 1983). These "ways of knowing," which he termed *epistemic styles,* are construed as higher order personality factors that are believed (a) to be a function of a subhierarchy of component cognitive abilities and (b) to account for individual differences in the way persons test the validity of their beliefs. The *empirical* style of knowing is an inductive, perceptually based way of knowing that involves a commitment to (a) relating to the world through one's senses and (b) evaluating the validity of one's beliefs in terms of their reliable correspondence to relevant observations. The *rational* epistemic style is a deductive, conceptually based approach to knowing that entails a commitment to (a) understanding the world via rational/analytic abilities and (b) testing the validity of one's beliefs in terms of their logical consistency. The *metaphoric* style is an analogical, symbolically based epistemology that involves a commitment to (a) relating to the world through symbolic experience and (b) evaluating the validity of one's beliefs in terms of their generalizability to various domains of experience. Although Royce's three epistemic styles are conceptualized as interdependent to the extent that all knowing involves empirical, rational, and metaphorical component processes, Royce and Powell (1983) pointed out that persons tend to exhibit a dominant epistemic style. It is this notion of epistemic dominance that we believe has implications for assessment and counseling.

Epistemic Assessment. It is our experience that clients with a dominant empirical epistemic style, on the one hand, tend to provide concrete and detailed "facts" about specific situations and events. The facts that they provide lead to theories or conclusions about self and others which are then "justified." An empirical thinker often has kept careful mental documentation of his or her own and others' misbehavior to explain emotional reactions. The process of justification by fact must not necessarily be logical in cause-effect connection; there simply must be an overwhelming balance of evidence for something to be perceived as true. Clients with a dominant rational epistemic style, on the other hand, tend to be abstract and intellectual in their descriptions of their concerns. Rational knowers typically seek to establish a high degree of logical consistency and coherence to their personal narratives and tend to talk about feelings rather than experience or to explore their personal affect. Metaphorical knowers, by way of contrast, tend to describe their experiences in what may be termed a "felt-sensed" modality. They seem to value intuitive awareness, employ symbols and metaphors, and at times, are capable of viewing life events from several perspectives. Although cognitively abstract in their thinking, metaphorical individuals tend to be more open to exploring their feelings and to utilizing novel and artistic avenues of expressing (e.g., guided imagery, dramatic enactments, journal work, etc.).

Assessing epistemic style may be done formally via the Psycho-Epistemological Profile (PEP; Royce & Mos, 1980) or more informally in the interview process. The PEP is self-administered, contains 90 items (30 items per epistemic dimension) presented in Likert fashion, requires approximately 25 minutes to complete, and yields a profile of one's epistemic hierarchy. The 1980 manual (Royce & Mos, 1980) reported strong test-retest reliability, as well as considerable data supporting the instrument's concurrent and construct validity.

When individual differences in epistemic style are assessed, this information may be applied in several ways. We believe that if counselors initially can adapt their interview/assessment style to the epistemic style of the client, the development of rapport and understanding of the client's view of the world will be enhanced. Matching therapeutic strategies with client epistemic styles also may prove beneficial. For example, highly rational clients may be more responsive to a rationalist cognitive approach (Ellis, 1962; Ellis & Dryden, 1987) that emphasizes the use of reason and logical persuasion, whereas an individual with a dominant empirical style may be more open to the behavioral "experiments" and data-gathering techniques common to Beck's (1976) cognitive therapy (see Lyddon, 1991, 1992, for further discussions of these issues).

Another possible outcome from the assessment and observation of epistemic style is that the counselor may discover that the client's dependence on a particular mode of knowing borders on the absolute; that is, it tends to be utilized to the exclusion of other modes. For example, an overly empirical client may be unaware of others' symbolic gestures of kindness and caring that are not necessarily easily quantifiable (e.g., attentive listening, calm deference in decision making). In this instance, the person may benefit from a more metaphorical exploration of the meanings and intentions of subtle interpersonal communication—that is, developing an understanding for "what is not being said." In sum, a case can be made for both matching or mismatching therapeutic styles with clients' epistemic styles, depending on what therapeutic goals are most relevant at a particular point in the counseling process.

A Case Example

Robbin is a 20-year-old single female attending a small community college in the southeastern United States. She is presently in her third semester of college and lives in the campus dormitory. She was referred for evaluation by the Dean of Students when concerns were raised about her expressed depression and threats of self-harm related to difficulties in a current romantic relationship. During her high school years, Robbin received counseling through a local community mental health center for similar depressive symptoms and suicidal gestures.[1]

Lifespan Developmental Assessment

As noted earlier, understanding the way a client orders her or his life experience is central to a developmental-epistemic approach to assessment. In initial sessions, Robbin was provided the opportunity to construct a coherent life narrative and to review life issues, such as family and peer relationships, significant life events, and problems experienced. Thus, rather than starting with the current life problem (relationship difficulties), Robbin was encouraged through a series of open-ended, developmentally related questions to review various life stages and to explore their impact on her present cognitive model of the world. A sample of some of the salient themes in Robbin's relationships with parents, others, and self is provided below.

Relationship With Parents. In attempting to recall her earliest memories of her mother, Robbin stated: "I'm sure my mother held me when I was a child, but I don't really remember." Her recollections of her father, however, were more detailed.

> I miss our fishing trips. Our time just being together. . . . I miss the excitement of hearing his truck pull up in the drive each evening. I miss just sitting and watching TV with him. I miss his coming in and giving me a kiss and hug before he went to work in the morning. That always seemed to get the day started off so great. Damn, I really miss Daddy.

Most significant to Robbin's childhood experience is the fact that when she was 10 years of age, her father left the home and her parents subsequently divorced. In the second session, Robbin described this period of her life.

Robbin   He was the one who didn't show up for 2 years! (angrily)

Dr. A   It seems that you're really angry about that. I wonder if that would be something to tell him—just how angry you are at him. Have you ever told him that? That he just left you and didn't show up for 2 years?

Robbin   No. Because he would just say that Mom wouldn't let him see us [Robbin and her younger brother]. How do we know? But, if it were my kids, I'd fight like hell to see them. There wasn't any court order saying that he couldn't see us. He had plenty of opportunities to get us—just as much as Mom did and instead he walked in and said, "I decline custody."

After her parents were divorced, Robbin continued to live with her mother. During Robbin's high school years, her mother became legally blind, and Robbin subsequently assumed major responsibility for her mother's care, as well as for the care of her younger brother. Because of the reversal of caretaking roles, Robbin eventually came to view her mother as incapable of providing love and support. When queried about her current feelings toward her mother, Robbin stated:

I wish I had a mother who was loving and caring. (sadly) One that I could talk to. . . . One who would make me feel like her special daughter. . . . Down deep I know I really love her but my immediate feelings are almost hate.

Robbin's evaluation of her current relationship with her father is revealed in the following session excerpt.

Robbin   If I were to call right now and say I needed to talk, he would say, "Not now. I have something else to do." It's always been like that. We tried to get together for a birthday. It didn't happen. He said it was because his wife was in the hospital. No card, no call, nothing. I must sound like a 2-year-old.

Dr. A   I don't think you sound like a 2-year-old.

Robbin   I send him cards at Christmas and Father's Day.

Dr. A   He doesn't call to say he got them?

Robbin   No (pause) What makes me angry is I love him so much, but then I hate him. It feels like there's an attachment there somehow, somewhere, but I don't know why. Then after thinking about all the years that have gone by that I've missed [with him] how could I ever make up for them? Even if I did kill myself tonight, what would he say? "Oh, she was just all confused about something." Would he even show up to the funeral? I've been told he won't show up to my wedding, so why would he show up to my funeral?

Dr. A   Who told you he wouldn't come to your wedding?

Robbin   Ellen [his wife]. It's not fair for me to love him and miss him so much when he doesn't give a damn. He tries to make excuses. . . . If I had one of my parents who gave a damn, it would make a difference.

The assessment of Robbin's relationship with her parents generally reveals that she perceives them to be unresponsive to her emotional needs. Her feelings for both parents appear to vacillate between love and anger. In a poem that Robbin wrote and shared with the counselor, she underscores her longings for her parents' love and support:

A Simple I Love You

I sit here as the tears begin to fall,
Wondering why our family had to fall.
No morning hugs or I love you,

Just a seldom call and Christmas card or two.
I long to hear my father say,
"Come my daughter and sit on my knee."
Or with my mother take a walk,
And have a warm heart to heart talk.
My Father in Heaven has given me a Christian family so dear,
For love and support and even a tear.
But I would trade all the riches, and even more too,
To hear my mom and dad simply say, "I love you."

Relationships With Others. Someone who did provide emotional support for Robbin during her formative years was her grandmother, whom she affectionately refers to as "Mawmaw." This close relationship ended, however, when Mawmaw died during Robbin's high school years. Robbin often writes to Mawmaw in her daily journal:

Mawmaw, if you were here things would be OK. I need you to hug me and tell me you love me and that everything's alright. I thought back alot today on times you and I spent together. God I miss them. I know there will never be any more times like those and it hurts. You're the only one I believe truly loved me and now you're gone. Your hugs and your talks and especially your stories. Why did God have to take you from me? It's not fair. I'm the one who needs you. I could never fool you. You always saw right through me and always knew what to do.

It is important to note that the significant changes in Robbin's life during her high school years—Mawmaw's death and the added responsibilities for the care of both her mother and younger brother—culminated in Robbin's initial bout with depression and her first experience with counseling.

Another important person in Robbin's life is a young man whom we will refer to as James. Robbin met James during her first year of college. Up to the time that Robbin was referred for counseling, she and James had been seeing each other for several months. During this period of time, Robbin developed strong feelings of love for James and subsequently began to imagine the possibility of marriage. In a journal entry, Robbin wrote:

I have to confront my feelings with him before it destroys me and my thoughts and feeling for him. I can't lose them [feelings] they're all I have, they're what I need. They're also what I want. I'm becoming more aware and sure of that. If he doesn't feel the same about me then I'm finished. . . . I can't picture my future without him. I more than just care, I love him. I wonder if he knows?

Before Robbin took the opportunity to express the depth of her feelings to James, he announced his intentions to enter the ministry. In session, Robbin described her response to this revelation:

Robbin Damn. Everything's over. James and I got together and talked. We ended up arguing. I can't take him going into the ministry right now. That is so damn unfair. What about us? What about how I feel? God took Mawmaw from me, and now he's taking James. Sometimes I wonder why have religion. Why believe in it? It's just getting me all screwed up. It's shooting my life straight to hell. God, it's not fair. I'm the one having to hurt and cry. Why did he have to make this decision now? Or why didn't he say something to me earlier? Wasn't it fair for me to know? I'm so hurt and angry.

Dr. A Angry at James?

Robbin More at God. It's not fair. It's no damn fair.

It is this relationship change that seemed to precipitate Robbin's most recent depression and suicidal ideation.

Relationship With Self. Part of the initial assessment process included asking Robbin to make a list of true statements about herself. Robbin wrote:

I'm not comfortable with myself
I'm confused
I'm alone
I'm empty
Unpredictable
Scared
Shakey
Suddenly helpless
Living in present and past with no future
Lost 20 lbs. and feels good

A student
A singer

When writing to herself in her journal shortly after her argument with
James, typical daily entries took the following tone:

> Good morning hell. It's time to put the mask back on. It's time to start acting
> out another day. Who am I going to fool today?
>
> Each day I feel less. When will I be completely empty?
>
> Today I just feel so horrible. I feel so lonely. Then reality hit. Why can't I
> love again?
>
> I really don't know who in the hell I am. I know how I used to be, I'm not
> sure what I want to become and I don't know who I am.

Perceptions of an impending loss of self also were expressed in a poem
that Robbin wrote entitled "The Mask."

The Mask

The mask into which I hide,
is laced with days of forgotten pride.
It hides the tears and a heart that's broke,
With sounds of laughter from a silly joke.
Others think the mask is the real me,
But it's only a glimpse of what I once wanted to be.
So as I remove the mask and let it fall without a sound,
They will lay me into the cool, peaceful ground.
The remnants of the mask will soon be rotten,
And I will eventually be quietly forgotten.
So each time you see someone with a mask to hide their gloom
Let them know you care with a hug so the mask will fall away—
allowing them to bloom.

Robbin's developmental and attachment history reveals themes of
disappointment, abandonment, anger toward parents and God, and a
personal sense of helplessness and loss of self. Robbin perceives both

parents as having been unresponsive to her emotional needs and tends to exhibit an insecure attachment pattern of angry withdrawal. In her case, she even contemplates the ultimate withdrawal (suicide) and imagines that even this step would not elicit a reaction from her father; that is, she believes that he would not even attend her funeral. Robbin also experiences a strong sense of loss for both Mawmaw and James; however, her anger and withdrawal are directed toward God in these instances. It seems that she perceives both Mawmaw and James as being capable of providing her with love and support but that they were both taken from her by God—one through death, and the other through a "higher calling."

Change Assessment

Stage of Change. Robbin's responses on the Change Assessment Scale (CAS; McConnaughy et al., 1983, 1989) revealed the following T-scores for each subscale: 35, Precontemplation; 55, Contemplation; 40, Action; 50, Maintenance. The high Contemplation score suggests that Robbin is aware that she needs to make changes in her life and is willing to expend the effort to bring about self-improvement. Strongly endorsed Contemplation subscale items included the following:

"I've been thinking that I might want to change something about myself." (Item 8)

"I have a problem and I really think I should work on it." (Item 15)

"I wish I had more ideas on how to solve my problem." (Item 19)

It is also significant to note that Robbin's second-highest stage of change score was on the Maintenance subscale, suggesting that she may view her difficulties as a recurrence of a former problem that she thought was resolved. This perception is best captured by her strong agreement with the following Maintenance subscale items:

"I thought once I had resolved the problem I would be free of it, but sometimes I find myself struggling with it." (Item 18)

"It is frustrating but I feel I might be having a recurrence of a problem I thought I had resolved." (Item 28)

Stage of change impressions gleaned from the CAS were corroborated in the initial counseling session, during which Robbin talked about her need to "do something about the mess I'm in" and her fear that her previous experience with depression and suicidal thoughts were being "played out again."

Level and Type of Change. Although Robbin's current crisis was precipitated by an interpersonal conflict (relationship with James), indications are that her difficulties go beyond this level and are fundamentally intrapersonal in nature. Her current relationship impasse seems to be symptomatic of a pattern of insecure attachments established in her formative relationships with significant others (parents and Mawmaw) and intrapersonal struggles related to such core issues as trust, personal worth and power, intimacy, and especially self-identity. The presence of these developmental life issues, coupled with Robbin's patterning of emotional disequilibrium, suggests the need for second-order structural change in her personal assumptions about self and relationships. The need and desire for basic redefinition of self are perhaps most poignantly expressed in Robbin's own words.

I just want to try and find out who I am before I give up. I'm at the end of my rope trying like hell to pull up, but I keep slipping back. When will I find a knot to help me?

Epistemic Assessment

Robbin completed the Psycho-Epistemological Profile (PEP; Royce & Mos, 1980) after her first interview. Her response to the PEP revealed an epistemic profile highest in Metaphorism, followed by Rationalism, and Empiricism (raw scale scores were 115, 102, and 97, respectively). This result suggests that Robbin's predominant way of understanding the world is through symbolic thinking and intuitive awareness. Her epistemic commitment to metaphorism is evident in her attempts to understand herself and her intrapersonal conflicts through self-initiated journal work, poetry writing, and a rich use of metaphor. Regarding the latter, one dominant metaphorical theme used by Robbin was expressed in a recurrent "self as child" metaphor. For example, when describing her relationships with her mother, father, and Mawmaw, Robbin would end with the repeated wish that she could once again become a child and be held and nurtured.

> Sometimes I wish I could feel like a little girl again. I wish she [Mother] could just hug me.

> I wish I had my daddy back. How I wish Daddy was just holding me again like I was his little girl.

> Sometimes I wish I were a kid again and Mawmaw was holding me in her lap like when we sang hymns together. But that can't be.

When asked to elaborate on the personal significance of this metaphor, Robbin stated:

> Maybe I sound like a child but I can't help it. I feel like I'm in pieces right now and a hug would hold the pieces together just for a moment.

Another striking metaphor used by Robbin as an attempt to understand her present loss of purpose and meaning for life was what could be termed a "resilient tree" metaphor.

Robbin   I was just sitting there and I started looking at one of the trees . . . and it was like I was thinking to myself how it would be good to be like that tree.

Dr. A   In what way?

Robbin   That tree stood there strong and tall through life's storms. It may lose a limb here and there and a few leaves, but it comes through the storms. Sometimes the trees do fall to the ground, but they're even useful that way. They can become furniture for comfort or beauty, a playhouse for children, or even firewood to keep people warm. See, those trees, no matter what their condition, they are always useful somehow. I think that's what I long for—a purpose.

Summary and Implications for Counseling

Understanding personal patterns of meaning—that is, the way a client organizes and makes sense of his or her experience over time—is a fundamental goal of constructivist counseling and psychotherapy. Similarly a developmental-epistemic approach to assessment seeks to understand clients' current problems in the context of their unique developmental histories, patterns of attachment, and epistemic styles. For example, Robbin's dramatic reactions to her relationship breakup with James are meaningful when situated in the context of her attachment and developmental history; that is, Robbin seems to have arrived at young adulthood with an "emptiness" and longing for the nurturing and support that in her words "left her life" following her parents' divorce and the death of Mawmaw. In her recent attempt to establish a love relationship, she once again feels emotionally abandoned—this time by a person who, in her mind, appears to put God and the ministry above her needs for love and support.

Although the foregoing discussion and description of developmental-epistemic assessment imply a clear differentiation between assessment and counseling, in reality we view these dimensions as reciprocal and to a large extent interchangeable. We find that each dimension informs the other and that both entail diagnostic and therapeutic value. For example, we view the developmental questioning process itself as a critical therapeutic intervention. Although a comprehensive overview of the counseling implications of developmental-epistemic assessment is beyond both the focus and scope of this chapter, a few salient guidelines and considerations will be offered.

First and foremost, we believe that the primary crucible for client change is the counseling relationship. From a developmental-epistemic perspective, the counseling relationship is construed as a powerful developmental milieu—what Bowlby referred to as a "secure base"—from which the client may explore (a) working models of self and attachment figure relationships, (b) how these models may have developed during childhood and adolescence, and (c) how they continue to influence his or her personal and emotional development (Bowlby, 1988). As mentioned earlier, we believe that it is important for the counselor to recognize how the client's attachment pattern may reveal itself in the interactions with the counselor. For example, in Robbin's case, her pattern of angry withdrawal tended to take the form of anger and resentment toward the counselor as various practical and professional limitations of the counseling relationship were enacted (confidentiality limitations, session length limits, limitations on phone contacts, unexpected scheduling conflicts, etc.). By both acknowledging Robbin's anger in a matter-of-fact way and encouraging her to explore these feelings in light of her past resentments and rejections, Dr. A was able eventually to help Robbin make connections between her current feelings and past experiences. In our opinion, a counselor's sensitivity to attachment patterns also better equips him or her to anticipate and appropriately respond to client emotional reactions, thereby facilitating the development of a safe base for client self-exploration, risk taking, openness to novelty, and emotional experience.

Procedurally—and as exemplified throughout this chapter—our general approach to constructivist assessment and counseling entails a developmentally focused reconstruction of the history and patterning of the client's presenting concerns. From this focus, we tend either to discover a history of relatively secure attachment or to identify one or more patterns of insecure attachment. In the former case, first-order change usually is indicated. As suggested earlier, the person with a secure attachment style tends to seek counseling in response to a situational crisis or a perceived skill deficit, and the counseling need is generally short term with an emphasis on support, direction, and technical intervention. With regard to the presence of an insecure pattern of attachment, however, the counseling agenda takes on a different quality. In these instances, we invite the person to take a second look (Novey, 1968) at his or her working models so that the impact of past attachment experiences on present relationships can be examined.

When working with a client who exhibits an insecure pattern of attachment, an initial therapeutic goal is what we term *pattern awareness*—the recognition on the part of the client of recurrent themes in the content and emotional experiences of his or her life story. In our own work with clients, it is not uncommon for insecure persons to provide a detailed history of unfavorable attachment experiences and at the same time appear unaware of the influence of these experiences on their present relationships. For example, although Robbin was able initially to describe recurrent experiences of separation and loss, it was not until the fourth session that she began to recognize this pattern and to raise questions about its possible connection to her current emotional crisis.

When a sense of pattern awareness is achieved and the client begins to see connections between the present and the past, we use this bridge to move therapy toward a level of *process awareness*. At this juncture, therapeutic goals include (a) a gradual elaboration of the client's tacit cognitive models of self and world that are no longer viable, (b) a full exploration of the feelings associated with this newly experienced self-knowledge, and (c) therapist support for the construction of new meaning structures and personal possibilities. In general, each counseling session seeks to demonstrate how working models that have led to the development of insecure attachment relations involve cognitive and affective components that were adaptive solutions to earlier attachment conflicts but that now are no longer viable. The primary therapeutic goal at this stage of the counseling process is the cognitive and affective revision of the client's working models. Often this second-order revision takes the form of significant corrective emotional experiences accompanied by a dramatic shift in the client's experiential world—that is, a change in meaning. For some clients, the experience is saliently affective, as in the grieving of a symbolic (or actual) attachment loss. For Robbin, however, this shift was primarily cognitive in nature; that is, personal change took the form of an attributional shift in which she began to perceive that her father's unresponsiveness stemmed from his own problems rather than from her basic inadequacy or personal sense of worthlessness.

When client and counselor choose to navigate through second-order change, the significance of the counseling relationship in facilitating such change cannot be underestimated. In her description of second-order change, Carlsen (1988) underscored this point when she stated:

> [The] dramatic reordering of the bases for experience can cause a kind of existential terror. Although the old ways are painful they are known ways, and the resistances of therapy can reflect the fear and confusion which comes with the breakup of a meaning system. Any resistance which occurs, therefore, can represent a protection of the old system as the client seeks to maintain its integrity and continuity. . . . In this cognitive reordering the therapist can play an important role as facilitator and supporter. (p. 9)

As client and counselor explore the process of personal change, the counseling relationship has the potential to become a working model of healthy attachment. More specifically, if effectively employed, the counseling relationship can be a powerful medium for extending the client's process and pattern awareness to the "lived-in moment." To the extent that the counselor can create a safe context for client self-exploration, the client may for the first time begin to feel the security necessary to negotiate successfully the realm of human relationships.

Note

1. The primary purpose of this case example is to demonstrate the salient aspects of a developmental-epistemic approach to assessment. Because of the potential life-threatening nature of this client's presenting concerns, it is important for the reader to understand that although the client exhibited suicidal ideation, she reported no overt means or intention of harming herself. In spite of this initial assessment, levels of depression and suicidal ideation/intent were monitored on an ongoing basis.

References

Ainsworth, M. D. (1989). Attachments beyond infancy. *American Psychologist, 34*, 932-937.
Bandura, A. (1977). Self-efficacy: Toward a unifying theory of behavioral change. *Psychological Review, 84*, 191-215.
Basseches, M. A. (1984). *Dialectical thinking and adult development.* Norwood, NJ: Ablex.
Beck, A. T. (1976). *Cognitive therapy and emotional disorders.* New York: International Universities Press.
Belsky, J., & Nezworski, T. (Eds.). (1988). *Clinical implications of attachment.* Hillsdale, NJ: Lawrence Erlbaum.
Bowlby, J. (1977). The making and breaking of affectional bonds: I. Etiology and psychopathology in the light of attachment theory. *British Journal of Psychiatry, 130*, 421-431.
Bowlby, J. (1982). *Attachment and loss: Vol. 1. Attachment* (2nd ed.). New York: Basic Books.
Bowlby, J. (1988). *Clinical applications of attachment: A secure base.* London: Routledge.
Carlsen, M. B. (1988). *Meaning-making: Therapeutic process in adult development.* New York: Norton.
Collins, N. L., & Read, S. J. (1990). Adult attachment, working models, and relationship quality in dating couples. *Journal of Personality and Social Psychology, 58*, 644-663.
Diamond, S., & Royce, J. R. (1980). Cognitive abilities as expressions of three "ways of knowing." *Multivariate Behavioral Research, 15*, 31-36.
Ellis, A. (1962). *Reason and emotion in psychotherapy.* New York: Lyle Stuart.
Ellis, A., & Dryden, W. (1987). *The practice of rational-emotive therapy.* New York: Springer.

Erikson, E. (1959). *Identity and the life cycle.* New York: International Universities Press.

Feeney, J. A., & Noller, P. (1990). Attachment style as a predictor of adult romantic relationships. *Journal of Personality and Social Psychology, 58,* 281-291.

Ford, D. H. (1987). *Humans as self-constructing living systems: A developmental perspective on behavior and personality.* Hillsdale, NJ: Lawrence Erlbaum.

Frank, J. D. (1985). Therapeutic components shared by all psychotherapies. In M. J. Mahoney & A. Freeman (Eds.), *Cognition and psychotherapy* (pp. 49-79). New York: Plenum.

Goldfried, M. R. (1982). *Converging themes in psychotherapy.* New York: Springer.

Guidano, V. F. (1987). *Complexity of the self: A developmental approach to psychopathology and therapy.* New York: Guilford.

Guidano, V. F. (1990). *The self in process: Toward a post-rationalist cognitive therapy.* New York: Guilford.

Guidano, V. F., & Liotti, G. A. (1983). *Cognitive processes and emotional disorders.* New York: Guilford.

Hazan, C., & Shaver, P. (1987). Romantic love conceptualized as an attachment process. *Journal of Personality and Social Psychology, 52,* 511-524.

Hazan, C., & Shaver, P. (1990). Love and work: An attachment-theoretical perspective. *Journal of Personality and Social Psychology, 59,* 270-280.

Heesacker, R. S., & Neimeyer, G. J. (1990). Assessing object relations and social cognitive correlates of eating disorder. *Journal of Counseling Psychology, 37,* 419-426.

Highlen, P. S., & Hill, C. E. (1984). Factors affecting change in individual counseling: Current status and theoretical speculations. In S. D. Brown & R. W. Lent (Eds.), *Handbook of counseling psychology* (pp. 334-396). New York: John Wiley.

Howard, G. A., Nance, D. W., & Meyers, P. (1986). Adaptive counseling and therapy: An integrative, eclectic model. *Counseling Psychologist, 14,* 363-442.

Ivey, A. E. (1991). *Developmental strategies for helpers: Individual, family, and network interventions.* Belmont, CA: Brooks/Cole.

Kegan, R. (1982). *The evolving self.* Cambridge, MA: Harvard University Press.

Kobak, R. R., & Sceery, A. (1988). Attachment in late adolescence: Working models, affect regulation, and representations of self and others. *Child Development, 59,* 135-146.

Liotti, G. A. (1984). Cognitive therapy, attachment theory, and psychiatric nosology: A clinical and theoretical inquiry into their interdependence. In M. A. Reda & M. J. Mahoney (Eds.), *Cognitive psychotherapies: Recent developments in theory, research, and practice* (pp. 211-232). Cambridge, MA: Ballinger.

Lyddon, W. J. (1990). First- and second-order change: Implications for rationalist and constructivist cognitive therapies. *Journal of Counseling and Development, 69,* 122-127.

Lyddon, W. J. (1991). Epistemic style: Implications for cognitive psychotherapy. *Psychotherapy, 28,* 588-597.

Lyddon, W. J. (1992). Cognitive science and psychotherapy: An epistemic framework. In D. J. Stein & J. E. Young (Eds.), *Cognitive science and clinical disorders* (pp. 171-184). New York: Academic Press.

Lyddon, W. J., Bradford, E., & Nelson, J. P. (in press). Assessing adolescent and adult attachment: A review of current self-report measures. *Journal of Counseling and Development.*

Mahoney, M. J. (1980). Psychotherapy and the structure of personal revolutions. In M. J. Mahoney (Ed.), *Psychotherapy process: Current issues and future directions* (pp. 157-180). New York: Plenum.

Mahoney, M. J. (1991). *Human change processes*. New York: Basic Books.

Mahoney, M. J., & Lyddon, W. J. (1988). Recent developments in cognitive approaches to counseling and psychotherapy. *Counseling Psychologist, 16,* 190-234.

McConnaughy, E. A., DiClemente, C. C., Prochaska, J. O., & Velicer, W. F. (1989). Stages of change in psychotherapy: A follow-up report. *Psychotherapy, 26,* 494-503.

McConnaughy, E. A., Prochaska, J. O., & Velicer, W. F. (1983). Stages of change in psychotherapy: Measurement and sample profiles. *Psychotherapy: Theory, Research, and Practice, 20,* 368-375.

Novey, S. (1968). *The second look*. Baltimore: Johns Hopkins.

Piaget, J. (1970). *Psychology and epistemology: Toward a theory of knowledge*. New York: Viking

Pistole, M. C. (1989a). Attachment in adult romantic relationships: Style of conflict resolution and relationship satisfaction. *Journal of Social and Personal Relationships, 6,* 505-510.

Pistole, M. C. (1989b). Attachment: Implications for counselors. *Journal of Counseling and Development, 68,* 190-193

Prochaska, J. O., & DiClemente, C. C. (1982). Transtheoretical therapy: Toward a more integrative model of change. *Psychotherapy: Theory, Research, and Practice, 19,* 276-288.

Prochaska, J. O., & DiClemente, C. C. (1986). The transtheoretical approach. In J. C. Norcross (Ed.), *Handbook of eclectic psychotherapy* (pp. 163-200). New York: Brunner/Mazel.

Royce, J. R. (1964). *The encapsulated man: An interdisciplinary search for meaning*. Princeton, NJ: Van Nostrand.

Royce, J. R., & Mos, L. P. (1980). *The Psycho-Epistemological Profile manual*. Edmonton, Canada: University of Alberta Press.

Royce, J. R., & Powell, A. (1983). *Theory of personality and individual differences: Factors, systems, and processes*. Englewood Cliffs, NJ: Prentice-Hall.

Safran, J. D., & Segal, Z. V. (1990). *Interpersonal process in cognitive therapy*. New York: Basic Books.

Sinnott, J. D. (1989). Changing the known; Knowing the changing: The general systems metatheory as a conceptual framework to study complex change and complex thoughts. In D. A. Kramer & M. J. Bopp (Eds.), *Transformation in clinical and developmental psychology* (pp. 51-69). New York: Springer Verlag.

Sroufe, L. A. (1983). Infant caregiver attachment and patterns of adaptation in preschool: The roots of maladaptation and competence. In M. Perlmutter (Ed.), *Minnesota Symposium on Child Psychology* (Vol. 16, pp. 41-81). Hillsdale, NJ: Lawrence Erlbaum.

Watzlawick, P., Weakland, J. H., & Fisch, R. (1974). Theories of knowledge restructuring in development. *Review of Educational Research, 57,* 51-67.

Weiss, R. S. (1982). Attachment in adult life. In C. M. Parkes & J. Stevenson-Hinds (Eds.), *The place of attachment in human behavior* (pp. 171-184). New York: Basic Books.

West, M., & Sheldon, A. (1988). Classification of pathological attachment patterns in adults. *Journal of Personality Disorders, 2,* 153-159.

3 Constructivist Approaches to the Measurement of Meaning

ROBERT A. NEIMEYER

O NE of the distinctive features of constructivist metatheory is its twin focus on both the *structure* and *process* of human knowing and the implications that both carry for the counseling context. Mahoney (1988), for example, discussed the "morphogenic nuclear structure" that characterizes personal knowledge systems, referring to the way in which more central constructions influence the form of more peripheral beliefs and actions. Moreover constructivists conceive of human experience as inherently "proactive" and "self-organizing," insofar as we co-create the "external" realities to which we respond, and evolve in directions that maintain the integrity of our "internal" organization (Mahoney, 1988).

Thus, at a practical level, it may be useful to distinguish between methods of assessment that attempt to elucidate the implicit structure or organization of a client's belief system and those that focus on the process, flow, and change of such constructions across time. This distinction is also compatible with the prototypical constructivist perspective on psychotherapy—personal construct psychology (Kelly, 1955)—whose corollaries can be grouped into those that concern (a) the structure of personal knowledge, (b) the process of construing, and (c) the social embeddedness of our personal epistemologies (Neimeyer, R., 1987). This third emphasis

TABLE 3.1 Goals of Selected Structural and Process-Oriented Approaches to Constructivist Assessment

Method	Goal
Structural	
Laddering	Identify core issues or central identity constructs
Dialectical laddering	Reconcile conflicting meanings or behaviors
Downward arrow	Trace chain of implication triggered by distressing event
Repertory grid	Elucidate implicit networks of personal meanings and interpersonal relationships
Process-oriented	
Self-characterization	Assess client's view of self and avenues for change
Stream of consciousness	Tap into client's spontaneous flow of thoughts, images, feelings
Family "bowties"	Diagram interlocking positions of members of family system

on the interpersonal context of construing is compatible with both a structural and a process-oriented approach to assessment and will be integrated into several of the examples that follow.

Constructivist Assessment: Structural Methods

To provide an orienting framework for this chapter, I have presented selected structural and process-oriented assessment techniques in Table 3.1, along with the main objectives of each. These methods range from informal interview procedures to more elaborate written assignments and target both enduring and evanescent aspects of the client's ongoing attempts at meaning making. Beginning with structural assessments, I hope to illustrate some representative constructivist methods that can assist the counselor and client in understanding the personal meaning systems of the latter and facilitate their revision or elaboration.

Laddering

Albert F. is a 41-year-old salesman who referred himself to therapy for his alcohol abuse and related marital distress. In his opening remarks, he argued that "alcoholism is a learned problem" rather than a "genetic disease" and contended that he could quit his daily, moderate intake for "periods of time." As we broadened our exploration of his background, he described himself as a "chemist by education" who, following college, pursued a highly successful career with an American pharmaceutical company in Hong Kong. Following the breakup of his first marriage to a Hong Kong citizen partly as a result of his "gentlemanly but domineering behavior," he decided that "there was more to life than titrating some solution" and sought counseling for the first time. His self-description as a "scientist" was still very much in evidence, however, leading him to want to know "*why* problems happen, especially the alcohol abuse." When I engaged him in a hypothetical inquiry into what therapy would need to provide in order for our work together to be successful (cf. Neimeyer, R., 1980), he began by describing his unsatisfactory experience with an inpatient treatment program for alcoholics that "tried to tell him how to do things" and gave him "rules to follow." In contrast, Albert described "good doctors" as those who "explain *why* and draw pictures of your problem." This implicit request to offer a contextual explanation for his problem, preferably in pictorial form, prompted me to consider eliciting a personal construct "ladder" with Albert to explore the meanings surrounding his problematic construction of his identity.

First introduced by Hinkle (a student of George Kelly) in 1965, the laddering procedure consists of a simple structured interview with the goal of examining the superordinate or higher order implications of some important personal construct that the respondent uses to construe the world (cf. Bannister & Mair, 1968). In Albert's case, I was intrigued by his repeated allusions to a "scientific" attitude in his self-presentation and decided to use laddering as one means of fleshing out the connotations that this carried for his approach to life. I therefore began by eliciting the contrast pole to this personal construct and by asking him a recursive series of questions, as summarized below:

> You've described yourself today as a *scientist,* and it might be interesting to find out more about what that implies for you. What would be the contrast or opposite to being a scientist, in your view?

Albert answered that the opposite to being a scientist, for him, was being a "product of your environment." I then asked him which he preferred to be, and he responded without hesitation "a scientist." Recording

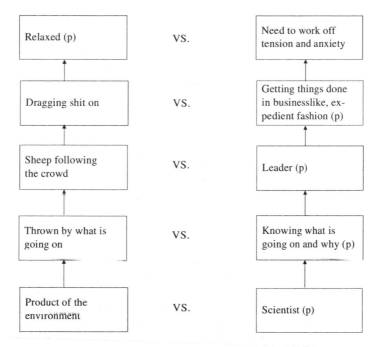

Figure 3.1. Personal Construct Laddering for Albert F.
NOTE: (p) indicates Albert's preferred self-construal.

his response, I followed this with the question, "Why? What would be the advantage of that?" He elaborated by saying that a scientist "knows what's going on," which contrasted with being "thrown by what's going on." Recording this new construct dimension, I repeated the cycle of inquiry, eliciting a new preference, advantage, and contrast, and continued with this recursive questioning until Albert could no longer articulate more abstract or superordinate implications of his choices. The resulting "ladder" of personal constructs is presented in Figure 3.1.

As I had suspected, Albert's description of himself as a scientist was far more than simply a statement about his college major; indeed it functioned as a key identity construct carrying powerful implications for his style of relating to both impersonal tasks and interpersonal relations. To be a scientist implied "knowing what was going on" rather than being a pawn of circumstances and further implied being a "leader" as opposed to a mere "sheep who followed the crowd." It also entailed expeditious mastery of tasks, which he contrasted with the sheepish tendency to "drag shit on" through procrastination. Up to this point in his hierarchy of constructs, Albert's value preferences were unequivocal: He uniformly preferred the "scientist" pole of the ladder and disdained everything implied in being "a product of the environment." At the fifth rung of his ladder, however, Albert showed his first sign of genuine conflict as he contrasted the advantages of businesslike efficiency (namely, to "work off anxiety") with the more straightforward "relaxation" associated with the contrasting stance. At this point, he reversed his pole preference and was unable to describe any superordinate implication of relaxation; it simply seemed to function as an ultimate goal for him. In personal construct terms, this tendency to lose the ability to articulate further higher order constructions suggests that the client has approached a core construct that is typically tacitly enacted rather than explicitly discussed in the course of daily life (Neimeyer, R., 1981).

In discussing the ladder with Albert after its elicitation (showing it to him in the pictorial form displayed in Figure 3.1), I asked him about his "slot movement" in preference at the fifth (top) rung (Kelly, 1955; Neimeyer, G., 1987). Visibly anxious, he described the tension associated with his scientific, businesslike stance and validated my interpretation of his ladder that such a stance seemed to entail a powerful need for cognitive, interpersonal, and instrumental control (at rungs 2, 3, and 4, respectively). When I asked how drinking related to his hierarchy of responses, he fell silent for a moment and then noted that it represented "an artificial way to relax," while still maintaining his "type A behavior." We then explored alternative "ways of relaxing" available to him at present and learned that these too were consistent with the demands of his central identity constructs. For example, he described activities such as "working like a dog at his cabin" and "planting 22 acres of pine seedlings, which would take 44 years to mature" as illustrations of ways to "unwind." With some sense of irony, Albert summarized his life with a further allusion to science. He remarked that "Newton's law applies to people as well: A body in motion tends to remain in motion." Only in the subsequent sessions were we able to examine the developmental roots of his overactivity and relentless need for control, as well as the dysfunctional extrapolation of this control orientation from the realm of inanimate objects to the realm of human beings, including himself.

TABLE 3.2 Facilitative Questions for Exploring Your Personal Construct Ladder

1. What are the superordinate values at the upper end of your ladder?
2. How are these values expressed in behaviors, traits, or roles at the lower end of the ladder?
3. What choices or alternatives are implied by your personal construct poles?
4. Did you ever hesitate in assigning a preference to one pole over the other? Why? Can you imagine ways of integrating both poles in such cases?
5. What life-style might someone have who made the contrasting pole choices?
6. What would be a positive connotation for the nonpreferred poles?
7. What people in your life would criticize your pole preferences? What people would support them?
8. How would someone 10-20 years older than you live out these preferences?

Although not all ladders show the slot movement pattern illustrated in Albert's preferences, virtually all provide powerful lenses for examining the problematic implicative structure of a client's choices. In using ladders in this clinical context, I have found selective use of various "facilitative questions" helpful in processing the meaning of clients' responses with them; they provide a point of entry into strategies of therapeutic change. Several examples of such questions are provided in Table 3.2.

Dialectical Laddering

It sometimes happens that an individual's sense of conflict about a basic life choice is so pervasive that a straightforward approach to laddering like that devised by Hinkle (1965) becomes unworkable; even at the first rung, the client may be unable to identify a clear value preference. In such cases, I have found it useful to modify the procedure to produce what might be termed *dialectical laddering*—that is, a ladder whose antithetical construct poles are reconciled in a higher order integration or synthesis. When such integration is successful, dialectical laddering provides not only an assessment of the structure of the client's current system but also a series of guideposts pointing toward new potentials to be explored in therapy and in daily life.

This procedure can be illustrated by its application in the case of Suzy K. At 33, Suzy was an accomplished concert pianist who toured widely with a major orchestra and who frequently was invited to give solo performances in the United States and abroad. Despite her accomplishments,

Suzy was a deeply unhappy woman, struggling almost constantly with a chronic sense of depression. She portrayed herself as a "cynical idealist" —cynical since the collapse of her religious faith in her teens but nonetheless an idealist in her propensity to retreat into a fantasy world populated by the characters of C. S. Lewis and J. R. R. Tolkien and to seek solace in the ethereal realm of her music.

Suzy's style of relating to other people soon emerged as a dominant theme in our sessions. As a young woman, she had studied for some years in Japan and in her words "carried over a Japanese composure to life in the United States." Even in therapy, Suzy retained a somewhat restrained, formal, and distancing demeanor, one that most of her associates and acquaintances interpreted as superiority. Spontaneous self-disclosure and emotional sharing were next to impossible for her, as she "needed to be beaten to death to show any emotion." Even when a moving sonata would begin to evoke tears, Suzy would act quickly to prevent them, feeling a keen internal pressure to protect her "image." Her only "real" relationship was with her lover, a married man with whom she had pursued a furtive affair for a few hours a month for the past 3 years. Despair over this "impossible" relationship and especially the "terror" of allowing herself to be known by anyone else (cf. Leitner, 1988) had brought her to the brink of suicide. She sought out therapy as a place to sort out the self-defeating beliefs or "underground ideas that she didn't recognize all the time" but that nonetheless regulated her present behavior.

As with Albert, I took this as a tacit invitation to explore more directly with Suzy those constructions that governed her ways of relating to other people. As we spoke about her interpersonal style, she described her difficulty in trusting others enough to open up to them, and I used this as the entry point into the laddering procedure outlined above. I first elicited from her the opposite of *trust*—*distrust*—and asked her which stance she preferred. She responded that although she found herself behaving in a distrustful way in virtually all relationships, both trust and distrust seemed to have painful disadvantages, so neither seemed viable in the long run. I therefore changed my pattern of questioning, asking, "What would be the implication for you of being 'trusting'?" She responded readily, saying it implied "burdening others," which she contrasted with "being controlled." Continuing this cycle of inquiry, I learned that burdening others further implied "relaxing control completely," as opposed to "not relaxing." Further recursive questioning suggested still higher order negative

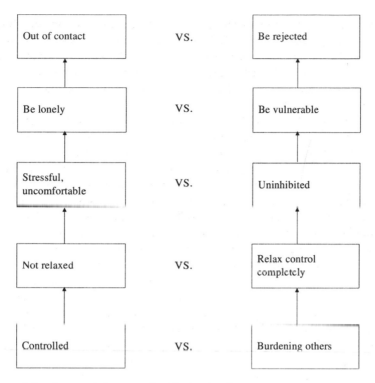

Figure 3.2a. Personal Construct Laddering for Suzy K.

implications of each construct pole, until Suzy was unable to identify any further superordinate constructs related to the issue of trust. This initial ladder is depicted in Figure 3.2a.

In Ryle's (1990) terms, what Suzy confronted was a basic dilemma, a "false choice" that led her to behave as she did because the only alternative she could imagine seemed as bad or even worse. To help her overcome the effects of this "polarized construing" (Neimeyer, R., 1985a), I asked her to return to her initial construct, trust versus distrust, and to try to find some "new alternative" that represented an integration or "some means of bringing together" the apparently antithetical construct poles. Thinking for a few moments, Suzy suggested that "realistic trust" might represent such an alternative, and I prompted her to say a bit more about how that would differ from the initially more extreme attitudes that it was designed to reconcile. I then moved on to the second rung of her construct ladder, requesting that she try to envision an integrative alternative to "relaxing control completely" versus "not relaxing." She tentatively suggested that it might be possible to relax control to some extent, as I recorded her responses on an elaborated ladder. We continued in this fashion until she had managed to articulate some kind of personally meaningful synthesis of each of the initially polarized dilemmas in her hierarchy of constructions. The results of this dialectical laddering procedure are presented in Figure 3.2b.

Suzy's spontaneous comments during this procedure suggested that the exercise of exploring her contrasting constructions and of trying to reconcile them, if only "cognitively," was genuinely therapeutic for her. For example, she noted that she "fought always being one extreme or the other in every relationship she was in" but that she could begin to see the possibility of "balancing" between the pain of being "lonely" and "out of contact" on the one hand and the fear of being "vulnerable" and "rejected" on the other. The cognitive shift involved in this recognition reflects what McWilliams (1988, p. 220) described as the evolution of a new "comprehensive construct" that "integrates various events and organizes them in terms of a higher-order principle. The incidental constructs precede, developmentally, the comprehensive constructs that integrate them, and they remain intact as essential elements" within the purview of the higher order construction. McWilliams went on to note that the development of such comprehensive constructs helps one "resolve what are apparent inconsistencies or lack of coherence within the context of a more superordinate structure" (1988, p. 220). This glimpse of integration was especially important in Suzy's case, as she struggled somehow to bring together her coolly professional public persona or "mask" and the deeply emotional "child" she was within. As she lamented, "I want to understand how the different pieces of me can be put together into one person. . . . I need some *meaning* to link them all up. . . . There is no one to whom the whole person matters." We then began to explore the development of her guarded and controlled style in the self-protective pseudomaturity that followed the death of her beloved father when she was 11 and the banishment of her childlike needs and emotions from the public domain. Eventually, returning to the signposts offered by the integrative possibilities in her ladder, we began to design "test tube experiments in intimacy" with select acquaintances and gradually invalidated many of the concerns

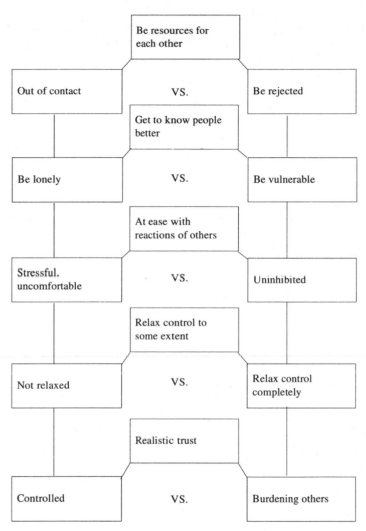

Figure 3.2b. Dialectical Ladder for Suzy K.

about rejection that she feared would accompany trust. This tendency to tack back and forth between understanding and behavior change is one hallmark of constructivist therapies, with their emphasis on "active insights and insightful actions" as two inextricably intertwined features of human change (Neimeyer, R. & Feixas, 1990).

Downward Arrow

Both variations on the laddering procedure described above help the counselor tease out higher order implications of a basic choice, which often has quite broad implications for the individual's life. Indeed the typical movement in laddering is from the specific to the general, from more circumscribed behavioral constructions to more abstract values. Although this is frequently valuable, it is often equally important to trace the client's implicit chain of inferences in a specific situation. When this approach seems useful, I often make use of the downward arrow technique, which is related to similar methods for exploring dysfunctional beliefs in a cognitive therapy format (Burns, 1980). My use of the method differs somewhat from that of most cognitive therapists, however, in the focus on deeper "schematic" processing of the meaning of an event and in the attempt to help the client revise the tacit rules embodied in the chain of inferences that the method elicits.

As an illustration of the downward arrow technique, consider the case of Lilly R., a patient in an inpatient psychiatric facility who was admitted following a deteriorating depressive course and increasingly hostile relations with several members of her nuclear and extended family. The evening before our scheduled group therapy for all patients in the Mood Disorders Program (Neimeyer, R., Robinson, Berman, & Haykal, 1989), Lilly received a phone call from her mother on the public phone in the unit to which all patients had access. Within minutes, the conversation had escalated into a loud verbal confrontation, whereupon a member of the nursing staff instructed Lilly to discontinue the call until she was able to handle it without resorting to a shouting match that was disturbing not only to herself but to other patients as well.

The next day Lilly came to group uncharacteristically sullen and remote. She had been placed on suicide precautions earlier in the morning after a concerned fellow patient confided to one of the hospital psychiatrists Lilly's growing impulses to injure herself. When I questioned her about her apparent withdrawal from the group, Lilly related the above facts but was unable to describe why the situation had had such a devastating impact on her. To explore her "problematic reaction" more fully, I used the downward arrow technique.

Like other cognitive therapy techniques (Beck, Rush, Shaw, & Emery, 1979), the *downward arrow* begins with an inquiry regarding the "automatic thoughts" that "flash through the person's mind" when confronted with a distressing situation. Rather than stopping with the conscious self-statements in immediate awareness, however, the technique involves asking a series of follow-up questions in the form of "Suppose that were true; what would that mean to you?" This technique has the effect of eliciting associated beliefs and conclusions that are reached at progressively lower levels of cognitive awareness but that nonetheless powerfully affect the individual's mood and behavior. In clinical applications, I sometimes liken this to peeling an onion, a metaphor that conveys the movement from thoughts directed toward external situations to those bearing on increasingly central issues. Clients also have compared the process tapped by the downward arrow to a domino effect, in which one conclusion triggers another in a chain reaction that sometimes can have catastrophic consequences.

In Lilly's case, she could recall only one thought flashing through her mind at the point of the nurse's initial instruction to end the call. This thought, "She's talking down to me," was followed by a wave of difficult-to-specify feelings, of which hopelessness was one. I therefore used this automatic thought as the point of entry into her construction of the event's meaning and asked, "Suppose the nurse were talking down to you. If so, what would that mean to you?" Lilly replied, "It would mean that I was being inappropriate." I continued by saying, "Okay, let's assume you were being inappropriate. What would that mean to you?" She responded, "That I can't control my emotions." Repeating this cycle of inquiry, she further elaborated (with increasing tearfulness) on the chain of implicit conclusions triggered by the nurse's apparent condescension. The complete downward arrow is portrayed in Figure 3.3, just as I had drawn it on the chalkboard in the group room to assist Lilly and others in visualizing her processing of the event.

Conducting this inquiry in a group therapy format proved valuable. Several group members were easily able to identify with her progressively more fatalistic conclusions, even if they had been unable to identify with the situation that initially triggered her distress. For this reason, I enlisted not only Lilly but also the other group members in deconstructing her pattern of "self-invalidation" by critically evaluating the meanings that she attributed to the event. As an initial approach, I segmented her

Situation: Depressed inpatient asked to discontinue emotional phone call to her mother by
   unit nurse.
Problematic reaction: Aware of thought flashing through her mind, "She's talking down to
   me." Felt extremely distraught and raised this as issue in group the next day.

Deconstruct this pattern of self-invalidation by:

   Identifying cognitive distortions at each level.
   Critiquing implicative link between each step.
   Discerning the Personal Rule for Living (PRL) that links first and last steps.

Figure 3.3. Downward Arrow for Lilly R.

responses into discrete steps or statements and asked the patients to spot
any of the dysfunctional thinking patterns or "cognitive distortions"
described by Burns (1980). In a spirit of supportive skepticism, patients
then began to point out how Lilly was twisting the evidence to reach a
whole series of unfair and dangerous conclusions about herself. For
example, they suggested that she may have been mind reading in conclud-
ing that the nurse was talking down to her, when it would be equally fair
to conclude that she was trying to be helpful or was merely enforcing unit
policy. They further questioned her labeling herself "inappropriate," a
popular psychiatric euphemism for *bizarre, hostile,* or *crazy.* Lilly then
joined them in recognizing that the inference regarding her inability to

control her emotions and others' desire to avoid her represented further examples of jumping to conclusions and mind reading, respectively. She also accepted the comment of another group member that the belief that she was "worthless" represented a compound of emotional reasoning and labeling that was deeply incapacitating. Finally the terminal conclusion that she should hurt herself seemed to stem from a kind of personalization, in which she attributed the entire incident to some basic "badness" in her that called for self-punishment.

Following this critique by the group, I then focused exclusively on Lilly and asked her to help me break the links in this chain of self-defeating inferences. Here, rather than focus on the content of each statement, we questioned the fairness of inferring subsequent beliefs from prior ones. This took the form of asking such questions as, "Just because someone talks down to you, does it mean that you are being inappropriate?" and "Even if you were being inappropriate, does that mean you can't control your emotions?" In each case, Lilly assertively responded no, recognizing with greater clarity the unfairness of her earlier conclusions. In a number of instances, she argued passionately against her prior inferences, particularly in response to my question of whether people who "feel worthless ought to be hurt."

Finally we attempted to gain an overall perspective on Lilly's "nonconscious algorithm" for responding to problem situations of this kind by deriving a personal rule for living (PRL) (Wessler & Hankin-Wessler, 1987) from her downward arrow. I pursued this by asking the group to formulate an "If . . . then" statement that captured the personal logic of Lilly's series of inferences, in some way linking her initial premises to her final conclusions. A few of these were offered, but the one that Lilly saw as best representing her unverbalized belief was, "If someone rejects me, then I am worthless and deserve to be punished." The exposure of this deep but tacit "attitude toward herself" (Guidano & Liotti, 1983) allowed us to move quickly into a closer examination of the history of this belief and toward a reappraisal of the effects of acting on such a basis in her adult life.

In conclusion, the downward arrow technique can be used to assess the often "unconscious" but nevertheless influential meanings that clients attach to events, which then provide a verbalized "text" for therapeutic "deconstruction" (cf. Anderson, 1990). Although in Lilly's case the articulation and dismantling of her problematic reaction were pursued in a group setting, the technique is equally viable to employ in an individual therapy context.

Repertory Grid

Of all the assessment techniques employed by constructivist psychologists, the repertory grid is perhaps the most frequently used. Devised in 1955 by George Kelly, the grid has become the workhorse of research in personal construct theory, being used in more than 1,000 published studies, the majority of which have appeared in the last 10 years (Neimeyer, R., Baker, & Neimeyer, G., 1990). Add to this the innumerable uses of the grid in clinical practice settings, and you have a method that might be considered the Rorschach or MMPI of constructivist assessment.

The comparison of the grid with the Rorschach and MMPI is instructive in a deeper sense as well. In many respects, it combines features of the projective tradition, which emphasizes elucidating the idiosyncratic perceptions of the individual subject with the tradition of standardized testing, which stresses quantitative comparison of subjects to one another or to established "norms." The amenability of the grid to both qualitative and quantitative analysis is one key to its popularity, along with its ability to be tailored to any of a number of specialized applications, from assessment of belief systems regulating different styles of parenting (MacDonald & Mancuso, 1987) to vocational counseling (Neimeyer, G., 1992).

What exactly is a *repertory grid?* From a statistical standpoint, Bell (1990, p. 26) defined it as "a set of representations of the relationships between the set of things a person construes (the elements) and the set of ways that person construes them (the constructs)." From a procedural standpoint, it represents a way of eliciting a respondent's construction of some domain of experience, typically by asking her or him to compare and contrast representatives of that domain (e.g., family members, possible careers) and then to describe systematically each of them on her or his own "repertory" of dimensions of evaluation, or personal constructs. The resulting "grid" of element descriptions across construct dimensions then can be analyzed formally or informally to suggest provocative patterns in the respondent's construing.

As an illustration of the use of the grid in the counseling context, consider the case of Andy W. At age 48, Andy sought help from me because he was deeply distressed about being "in love with two women." He had been married for 25 years to Sharon, an intelligent, attractive woman, and to all the world appeared to have the "ideal marriage." He described himself as "dedicated to his family rather than his job," although he had pursued a reasonably successful career for over two decades with a large equipment manufacturer. His two sons, Brian and Mike, both in their early 20s, were very much a part of his life both before and after the advent of his affair with Beth. Indeed his shared interests in his sons' athletic accomplishments provided one of the few diversions from the "torment and guilt" that had become almost a chronic part of his experience.

Andy's relationship with Beth had developed 2 years earlier, during one of Sharon's business trips connected with her work as a community organizer. Andy had "fessed up" to Sharon about his liaison with Beth within a week but subsequently found himself unable to extricate himself for more than a few weeks at a time from his relationship with the younger woman. He acknowledged some difficulties in his marriage, such as their "poor communication," but for the most part he found himself unable to speak very directly to his motives for either staying in the marriage or leaving it to build a life with Beth. Indeed he was aware primarily of his "fear that he would lose them both" and vacillated between one relationship and the other "several times a day." At the end of our first session, I suggested that we experiment with the repertory grid in the following meeting in order to understand some of the broader matrices of decision governing this critical area of Andy's life.

I administered the grid as a structured interview, both to enhance the personalism of the procedure and to permit me to intervene therapeutically if the task triggered any significant reactions that required immediate attention. This format required me to consider in advance what area of Andy's experience we would explore in more depth, which would then determine the elements that we would use in the grid procedure. Virtually anything can serve as an element in a grid, from types of leisure activities to aspects of oneself in different social roles; the only restriction is that all elements be drawn from the same domain of discourse in order to permit meaningful comparison (cf. Yorke, 1985). In Andy's case, I was concerned primarily with his constructions of Beth and intimate family members, including himself, and so included the names of each of these figures as elements on the grid. Secondarily I was interested in his implicit definitions of happiness and success and for this reason asked him to nominate the two people who came closest to achieving these goals. Finally, because I was attentive to his germinal working alliance with me as a therapist, I included my own name as the final element on the grid. In each case, I asked Andy to supply the first name of the figure to prompt him to consider the individual as a whole person rather than only in terms of his or her relationship to him.

Having elicited the elements and written down the names of each on small index cards, I then began the *construct elicitation* phase of the grid administration. Here again, several options are open to the counselor: You can (a) invite the client to provide these through systematic comparisons of elements, (b) provide them yourself by extracting relevant constructs from the client's laddering responses or session material, or (c) use standardized constructs to evaluate how one client might compare with others grappling with similar issues, such as incestuous abuse (e.g., Neimeyer, R., Harter, & Alexander, 1991). I chose the first option with Andy. I provided him sets of three figures and asked him to describe "some important way in which two of the figures were alike, and different from the third." For example, in the second row of the grid, he described his mother and the happiest person he knew as "lacking sensitivity" and contrasted both with his son, Brian, whom he considered "sensitive," providing me with one of the constructs I recorded on his grid (lack sensitivity vs. sensitive).

After eliciting 10 such constructs, I asked Andy to place each element on each construct dimension by assigning it a 1 if that figure were better described by the first pole, a 2 if it were better described by the second, and a 0 if neither pole appropriately applied to the element. Alternatively I could have asked him to rank order the elements on each construct or to rate them on Likert-type scales anchored by the two construct poles (Fransella & Bannister, 1977; Neimeyer, G. & Neimeyer, R., 1981), but I chose the simpler classification procedure because of its amenability to straightforward hand analysis in the clinical context. Andy's completed repertory grid, including elements, constructs, and element placements, appears in Figure 3.4.

Results of grid assessments can be interpreted at two basic levels, focusing on the content and structure of the client's constructions. At the content level, grids can be analyzed in an *impressionistic* or qualitative fashion by considering the unique constructions of specific figures on the grid and the idiographic meanings of particular constructs. (Table 3.3 provides a series of heuristic questions to guide such an analysis.) At a

Response Sheet

	Column 1	Mother	Father	Happy Person	Successful Person	Andy (self)	Brian (son)	Mike (son)	Sharon (wife)	Beth (lover)	Therapist	Column 2	
1	Someone I love	1	1	1	1	2	1	1	1	1	1	Someone I hate	1
2	Lack sensitivity	1	2	1	2	2	2	2	2	2	2	Sensitive	2
3	Committed to family	1	1	1	1	1	1	2	2	2	2	Independent	3
4	Understanding	2	1	1	1	1	2	1	2	1	1	Impatient	4
5	Bright	1	1	1	1	2	1	1	1	1	1	Just average	5
6	Very inward	1	1	2	1	1	1	1	2	2	1	Very outspoken	6
7	Child like inside	2	1	2	1	1	1	1	2	1	2	Get what you see	7
8	Have real communication	2	2	2	2	2	2	1	1	1	1	Aloof	8
9	Easy going	2	1	1	1	1	1	1	2	1	1	Emotional	9
10	Unaffectionate	2	2	1	1	2	2	2	1	2	0	Likes to touch	10

Figure 3.4. Repertory Grid for Andy W.

more *formal* level of analysis, constructs can be coded for their interpersonal content (e.g., whether they emphasize themes of morality, forcefulness, etc.; Landfield, 1971) or abstractness (suggesting the level of a client's sophistication in construing others; Applegate, 1990). (Table 3.4 provides a classification scheme for coding constructs on a continuum of concrete to abstract.) Because of space constraints, I will make only a few illustrative observations concerning the content of Andy's grid. More detailed analyses of grids across the course of therapy have been provided elsewhere (Neimeyer, R. & Neimeyer, G., 1987).

First, the content of Andy's constructs suggests that he is vigilant regarding the affective reactions of others, as terms such as *love, hate, sensitivity, impatient, emotional,* and *affectionate* occur with some frequency among his responses. This frequency could point to both a core emotional issue for Andy and a tendency on his part to experience strong feelings personally, especially in relation to his current conflicts. Second, most of his constructs represent socially communicable dimensions, although some capture more idiosyncratic distinctions, such as the construct

TABLE 3.3 Guidelines for Hypothesizing About the Content of Constructs (adapted from Landfield & Epting, 1987)

1. Assume that the poles of a construct represent contrasting alternatives in the person's system. What choices does this imply for his or her behavior?
2. Consider how the person describes social interaction. What are the major themes that he or she emphasizes in close relationships?
3. Observe the overuse of any given construct dimension. Might the repetition of a construct suggest an important but conflictual core issue for the person?
4. Does the individual make extensive use of self-referent constructs, describing others primarily in terms of their relationships to him or her?
5. What values are implied by the person's construct poles (e.g., as indicated by the placement of an "ideal" figure on each construct)?
6. Does the person tend to employ language or contrasts that are markedly idiosyncratic or obscure, suggesting a difficulty in being understood by others?
7. Has the individual used at least one construct suggesting openness to experience or change, and might this imply amenability to change in the context of psychotherapy?
8. If elements are rated on the various construct dimensions, what percentage are construed as positive, and what percent are construed as negative?
9. Imagine that the individual's construct dimensions were your own. What kind of a world would it be?
10. In what important ways does the person differentiate or fail to differentiate between self and relevant others (e.g., mother, father, spouse, therapist)?

TABLE 3.4 Abstractness Coding for Personal Constructs (adapted from Applegate, 1990)

Level 1: Physical qualities or social roles
     e.g., male, unattractive, college grad, aunt, Italian, teacher
Level 2: Specific behaviors
     e.g., drinks heavily, talkative, gives people a hard time
Level 3: Global evaluations providing no information about target person's perspective
     e.g., nice, mean, normal, terrific, good listener, outgoing
Level 4a: Specific attitudes or interests
     e.g., likes sports, politically conservative, hates TV
Level 4b: Attitudes or behaviors toward a specific other
     e.g., cares about me, good friend (of mine), takes advantage of her mother
Level 5: Dispositional qualities giving an "inside view" of target person
     e.g., secure in himself, shy, ambitious, generous, true Christian, lazy, intelligent

distinguishing between people who are "childlike inside" versus those for whom you "get what you see." Third, the dichotomies captured by certain constructs may imply problematic choices for Andy to the extent that he feels compelled to be either "committed to family" or "independent," to be "very inward" or "very outspoken," and to "lack sensitivity" or accept the pain that comes with being "sensitive." Moving him away from such "either/or" dilemmas toward a "both/and" integration of such contrasts represented one goal of his therapy. Finally, I was struck by the relative abstractness of his construing of others' internal states, although the virtual absence of behavioral descriptors in the grid raised questions about his ability to envision suitable actions that could be taken in light of his understanding of others.

Repertory grids also can be analyzed at a structural level, concentrating on the overall degree of differentiation within the client's construct system or among the figures rated on the grid, specific relationships between given constructs or elements, and a host of more subtle structural features that can be extracted by the current generation of computerized grid-scoring programs, many of which provide interactive feedback during the grid administration itself (Bringmann, 1992; Mancuso & Shaw, 1988; Sewell, Adams-Webber, Mitterer, & Cromwell, 1992). I will focus on only a few structural features of Andy's grid to exemplify this approach and concentrate on scoring procedures that can be conducted in a clinical context without the aid of a computer.

I began by visually scanning the completed matrix of ratings on Andy's grid to determine the number of times that he had used a zero rating, taking this as an indicator of his inability to meaningfully construe the figures in his life on either pole of a sample of his personal constructs. In this case, he had applied a zero only once (or 1% of the time in the set of 100 ratings), suggesting that he experienced little uncertainty or ambiguity in perceiving the inhabitants of his social world.

I then moved on to an examination of the interrelationships among the constructs implied by Andy's grid ratings. This analysis entailed computing the degree of match in the rating patterns of elements on each construct paired with every other construct, considering two constructs functionally similar if their ratings matched (as a 1, 2, or 0) on at least 8 out of 10 figures. This same algorithm was employed by Landfield and Cannell (1988) in their computer program for determining "functionally independent constructions," although this measure also can be derived through a straightforward visual comparison of rating patterns. In this instance, I compared construct rating patterns by simply copying rows of ratings on a thin strip of paper and then sliding it up and down the matrix of ratings shown in Figure 3.4, tallying the number of exact matches on pairs of constructs, a procedure that takes only a few minutes. For example, "easy-going" versus "emotional" met the 80% match criterion with "childlike inside" versus "get what you see"; that is, 6 out of 8 figures who were construed as "easygoing" were also seen as "childlike inside," and both of the persons construed as "emotional" were associated with "get what you see." Because constructs are bipolar, they also can be inverted in the course of this analysis. For instance, "easygoing" was inversely related to "lack sensitivity"; figures who were rated as one were rarely rated as the other. Thus instances of 80% exact mismatch (in which ratings of 1 on a given construct are paired with ratings of 2 on the other) also imply functional similarity but with the contrast pole of the second construct. In the above example, it would be equally correct to say that, for Andy, easy-going people are sensitive and to state that they tend not to lack sensitivity. For clarity, I have chosen to focus on implied linkages between the positive poles of his constructs, with the recognition that the same link-ages exist among their contrast poles by definition.

I have pictorially displayed the results of this matching procedure in Figure 3.5, which provides a semantic map of the construct interrelation-ships in Andy's system. On this map, Andy's constructs formed three clusters, the largest of which consisted of four constructs, and the other two of construct pairs. Two additional constructs (pertaining to inward-ness and affection) were relatively isolated from each other and from the rest of Andy's system. Interpretation of these relationships generated a number of clinically intriguing hypotheses. First, Andy frequently had used the term *easygoing* to describe himself during our first session, al-though at the time I took this as a relatively superficial reference to his interactional style. His semantic map suggested, on the other hand, that *easygoing* occupied a central place in his meaning system, insofar as it implied being "understanding," "sensitive," and "childlike inside," all characteristics he highly valued. Stated inversely, emotional people tended to be impatient, to lack sensitivity, and to be merely what you see ex-ternally. It was provocative to consider that whereas he described himself in terms of the positive poles of the constructs in this cluster, he tended to assign his wife to their contrasts.

A consideration of the construct pairs in his semantic map was also instructive, insofar as it suggested that his love for people was linked to his perception of them as bright. Did intelligence function for Andy as a

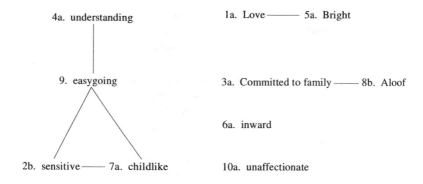

Figure 3.5. Semantic Map for Andy W.

NOTE: Constructs that are joined by lines are functionally similar in their classification of figures.

precondition for his positive regard? I was especially interested to discover that he associated only himself with the contrast poles of these constructs: He alone, among the figures he rated, was "just average" in intelligence and was "someone I hate." This cued me to the deep ambivalence that he experienced with respect to himself, something that we subsequently explored in greater detail in our sessions. It was also noteworthy that being "committed to family" implied being "aloof." In his present predicament, did his investment in his family paradoxically preclude his "have real communication" with them about his affair and the status of his marriage? Finally I was struck by the lack of implications of his remaining constructs, particularly that concerning affection. Was it difficult for him to see the relation between being affectionate and other important constructs having to do with love, understanding, sensitivity, and commitment?

It is also possible to "rotate" Andy's grid to examine functional similarities and contrasts among the figures that he rated, using an analogous procedure to that used to determine construct interrelationships above. In this case, I copied rating patterns for columns on slips of paper and slid them back and forth to compute matches in ratings of different pairs of figures across all 10 constructs. As with the construct pairings, pairs of figures also could be inversely related (such that when one figure was given a 1, the other was given a 2, on 8 out of 10 ratings). Pictorially representing these relationships among elements resulted in the "interpersonal map" presented in Figure 3.6.

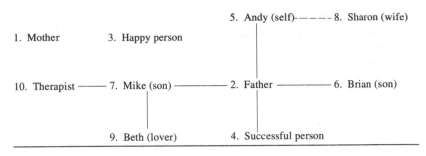

Figure 3.6. Interpersonal Map for Andy W.
NOTE: Figures that are joined by solid lines are functionally similar in the way they are rated on a sample of the subject's constructs. Figures joined by dotted lines are rated in a contrasting fashion.

The connections between pairs of figures in this map can be interpreted as reflections of the perceived similarity or identification of individuals with one another as construed by Andy. Seen from this perspective, several aspects of his interpersonal map were noteworthy. First, both his mother and the happiest person he knew were unidentified with any other figures on the grid; some inquiry into their unique roles in his life therefore seemed worthwhile in our future conversations. In contrast, his father was the most interconnected person in his system. Did his father serve as a kind of cognitive prototype for the perception of other male figures in Andy's life? Other figures by comparison were linked with only one or two others. For example, Beth (Andy's lover) shared with Mike (his favored son) most of the qualities that he prized—independence, an easygoing nature, understanding, a sense of being childlike, and a capacity for real communication—many of which he also glimpsed in me as a therapist. This helped explain for me some of Beth's appeal and also alerted me to the possible presence of a (positive) therapeutic transference, which could have implications for our working alliance as counselor and client (Kelly, 1955). Most important, Andy contrasted himself sharply with his wife, Sharon, whom he saw as dissimilar from all of the other figures rated on his grid. The tendency to construe one's partner as comprehensively in opposition to the self on one's core identity constructs is one hallmark of stable but negative relationships, in which one individual may reaffirm his or her own identity by contrasting him- or herself with the partner (Neimeyer, G. & Neimeyer, R., 1985).

In summary, the structural analysis of Andy's grid disclosed a number of patterns that merited further attention in our work together and helped him articulate some of the core concerns that motivated his pursuit of an extramarital affair. Although this analysis was accomplished solely through the use of hand-scoring procedures, a more refined depiction of the structural features of his grid (e.g., principal components plots, hierarchical cluster analyses) could be obtained from a variety of automated scoring programs designed for the personal computer (Bell, 1990).

Constructivist Assessment: Process-Oriented Methods

To this point, I have concentrated on methods that elucidate the structure or organization of personal belief systems and focused on a narrowly targeted area of the client's construing (laddering, dialectical laddering, downward arrow) or on a broader network of his or her constructions of self and others (repertory grid technique). To complement this approach, I will describe a second set of techniques for examining the *process* of construing over time by analyzing the more open-ended oral and written material provided by clients in response to various kinds of therapeutic tasks or invitations. This second approach has a fundamental affinity with the *narrative* model of psychological research and practice now being espoused by many constructivist authors (e.g., Bruner, 1990; Howard, 1989; Mair, 1989, 1990). As White and Epston (1990, p. 9) contended, a narrative model of clinical practice allows the therapist "to conceive of the evolution of lives and relationships in terms of the reading and writing of texts, insofar as every new reading of a text is a new interpretation of it, and thus a different writing of it." Therefore, by encouraging clients to explicitly formulate and analyze the "story they tell" about their lives, the counselor can assist them in "reauthoring" or revising the fundamental plots that they see themselves enacting on a daily basis. Indeed the "mere" formulation and confiding of a story that gives meaning to one's losses and pain is itself a powerful catalyst for healing, as the work of Harvey and his colleagues on "account-making" vividly demonstrates (cf. Harvey, 1989; Harvey, Orbuch, Weber, Merback, & Alt, 1992; Harvey, Weber, & Orbuch, 1990). The following constructivist techniques for promoting and revising such accounts vary in their degree of directiveness and specific objectives, but all help disclose inconsistencies and limitations in the client's current narratives and help foster an elaboration of such narratives in the direction of greater coherence and viability.

Self-Characterization

Kelly's (1955) refinement of *self-characterization* as an assessment device and *fixed role therapy* as a strategy for fostering client reconstruction may represent the quintessential examples of narrative means to therapeutic ends. Kelly began experimenting with both approaches in the late 1930s, synthesizing aspects of Korzybski's (1933) general semantics and Moreno's (1937) psychodrama into a distinctive method of brief psychotherapy (Neimeyer, R., 1985b; Stewart & Barry, 1991). Pilot research on these techniques conducted by Kelly's students during this period was based on the assumption that "a personality may be built up because of language" (Edwards, 1943/1982) and reconstructed through bold experimentation with a new role that was carefully written to "satisfy the case's inner needs, not merely modify his external behavior" (Robinson, 1943/1982). It is interesting that both students drew on the popular culture of their time, citing children's tendencies to "copy favorite movie and radio stars in speech and manner of dress," and the transformation of the scarecrow, tin man, and lion in the *Wizard of Oz* to argue for the plausibility of role enactment as a therapeutic technique. This early dissertation research suggested the promise of these methods in the treatment of various personality, academic, and social difficulties. In more recent years, these techniques have been applied in Europe (Bonarius, 1970) and North America (Adams-Webber, 1981) to such diverse problems as speech anxiety (Karst & Trexler, 1970), stuttering (Fransella, 1972), ego-dystonic homosexuality (Skene, 1973), and marital conflict (Kremsdorf, 1985).

As an assessment technique, self-characterization entails asking the client to "write a character sketch of ___ [client's name], just as if he were the principal character in a play. Write it as it might be written by a friend who knew him very *intimately* and very *sympathetically,* perhaps better than anyone really could know him. Be sure to write it in the third person. For example, start out by saying, '___ is . . .' " (Kelly, 1955, p. 323). Each clause in this instruction was chosen carefully to minimize the threat associated with drafting a more incriminating "self-analysis"; to encourage the client to present him- or herself in plausible, holistic terms; to prompt a novel, rather than habitual, perspective on the client's identity; and to elicit the unique organizing themes the client imputes to his or her life. As Kelly (1955, p. 324) noted, the overall "object of this kind of inquiry is to see how the client structures a world in relation to which he must maintain himself in some kind of role." Guidelines for the analysis of self-characterizations then can be used to bring to light this unique structure, providing a springboard for experimentation with alternative self-constructions in the context of fixed role therapy.

An example of this procedure is provided by my work with Brad J., a graduate student in counseling psychology who referred himself for therapy on the advice of a faculty member in his department with whom he had had a "personality conflict." To gain a broader view of Brad as a person, one less bound up with this initial "complaint," I asked him to complete a self-characterization (a blank sheet of paper on which I had typed the above instructions) as a homework assignment early in therapy. Brad returned the next session with the following character sketch:

Brad is a rather interesting fellow. To a number of people, he appears to be rather gruff. Loud, sarcastic at times, you know the type of person I'm referring to. To those who know him well, however, he is quite different indeed. I find him to be quite sensitive and caring (though he might deny it if you were ever to "accuse" him of those traits). He has experienced a great deal in his 32 short years and these experiences give him a strong desire to be a therapist. Why? Well, because he has experienced therapy himself and found that it changed his life very much for the better. He also wanted a profession that helped people live fuller lives, rather than one like law where people do nothing but attack and destroy one another. He hates lawyers, probably because of his ambivalent relationship with his father.

It is not only with his father that he has relationship problems. There are also problems with women. I think there is a real fear of getting close to a woman, a lot of which had to do with the fears of abandonment that his mother "gave" to him. He always tests the women he dates to see whether they can measure up to his (unreasonably high) standards and invariably they fail him. It's almost a "pre-emptive strike" against them. Why worry about them abandoning you when you can "nuke" them up front by having them fail your unreasonable standards. If you ask him about this, he will tell you he likes women a lot. But he really fears them.

As I had hoped, the self-characterization seemed to give Brad the latitude to raise important issues for therapeutic attention that might have been more intimidating to acknowledge directly in the therapy room at this early stage of our relationship. Among these were his deeply ambivalent relationships with his father, his mother, and women in general. Indeed a developmental analysis of these problematic attachment relationships and the client's corresponding self-knowledge would be entirely congruent with the objectives of long-term constructivist therapies (e.g., Guidano & Liotti, 1983; Liotti & Pallini, 1990). In keeping with Brad's preference for brief therapy, however, I opted to work on these relational difficulties obliquely, focusing first on the analysis and revision of his general social role and then extending his new "identity" to progressively more intimate relationships during the subsequent enactment phase of therapy.

Table 3.5 provides several guidelines for the analysis of self-characterizations, adapted from Kelly (1955) and my own experience with the procedure. As with the guidelines for interpreting the content of repertory grids presented in Table 3.3, these are meant to be suggestive rather than definitive and to assist the counselor in formulating some novel hypotheses about the client, based on an analysis of the character sketch that he or she provides. Like other hermeneutic methods, this analysis helps the reader grasp the deeper meanings implied by a text—in this instance, a narrative of the client's current life. In Brad's case, I employed six of these guidelines in analyzing his protocol, as detailed below.

What Does the World Look Like Through Brad's Eyes? It is a passionate, often painful place filled with strong emotions. It is a place inhabited by two "Brads" (at least), a boisterous, critical Brad—his persona—and a more tender, fearful Brad who is harder to contact.

Sequence and Transition. There is a progressive movement through the protocol from relatively superficial contexts of self-description (e.g., Brad as known by mere acquaintances) to allusions to deeper, perhaps more threatening relationships (e.g., friends in the abstract, therapist, father, mother, and women). This might provide a partial hierarchy of figures in relation to whom an enactment sketch might be rehearsed in therapy and pilot tested in daily life.

Organization. Brad's sketch is organized into two paragraphs, one portraying his hidden strengths, the second his hidden weaknesses.

TABLE 3.5 Guidelines for the Analysis of a Self-Characterization

1. Start with a credulous approach. Do not immediately start looking for the defense mechanisms, external contingencies, or cognitive distortions in the client's presentation, but instead try to answer the question, "What does the world look like through this person's eyes?"
2. Observe sequence and transition. Interpret the protocol as a flowing whole, assuming that apparent breaks are unexpected elaborations of similar or contrasting content.
3. Observe organization. Assume that the opening sentence of each paragraph has the greatest generality.
4. Reflect each statement against the context of the whole protocol. Do key terms take on somewhat different meanings in different settings?
5. Look for repeated terms with similar content. These may signify an important construct that is not adequately symbolized.
6. Shift the emphasis on different parts of the sentence. This may suggest alternative "readings" of its meaning.
7. Restate the essential theme in your own words to grasp its basic message.
8. Assume that the writer is working at the "growing edge" of his or her self-understanding. The areas that the person chooses to discuss should contain enough uncertainty to make exploration interesting and enough structure to make it meaningful.
9. Examine the client's attributional style. What cause-and-effect constructs does the client use?
10. What are the primary dimensions implied in the protocol? What are their implicit poles? These may suggest behavioral, emotional, or existential alternatives as the client sees them.
11. How does the client characterize him- or herself on these constructs? Does this change?
12. What are the idiosyncratic meanings attached to the terms?
13. Who are the person's validating agents, if any? Who invalidates the client in various roles?
14. What evidence does the person use to support her or his placement on given constructs? Which of these seems most amenable to change?

Reflection of Terms Against the Whole Protocol. *Sensitive* takes on two meanings against the context of the whole self-characterization: "attuned to others' feelings" and "easily hurt." Each reading is compatible with one of the two paragraphs in the protocol.

Repeated Terms With Related Content. *Sarcastic, attack, destroy, hate, ambivalent, pre-emptive strike, nuke*—all of these terms converge on a theme of anger and lashing out. This may signal a core issue that deserves further exploration, although the prominence of this theme is disguised somewhat by the subtlety with which it is woven throughout the text.

Dimensional Analysis. The following constructs (with inferred contrast poles) can be extracted from the text. The poles listed on the left are those with which Brad most aligns himself. He cautions, however, that two of them (gruff and sarcastic) are more descriptive of his surface personality than his deeper sense of self.

interesting vs. (boring)
gruff vs. sensitive and caring
loud vs. (unobtrusive)
sarcastic vs. (assertive)
insightful vs. (dull)
helping vs. destroying and attacking
hating vs. (loving)
fear and testing vs. (trusting)
close vs. (distant)
abandonment vs. (secure attachment)
unrealistic standards vs. (realistic standards)

Although analysis of a client's self-characterization can be valuable in itself, especially during the assessment phase of therapy or when counseling reaches an unexpected impasse, it also can be used to usher in fixed role therapy, as described more extensively elsewhere (Adams-Webber, 1981; Neimeyer, R., 1987). Pursuing this latter application, I used the results of the above analysis to draft an *enactment sketch* for Brad, portraying an alternative role that he would be asked to experiment with over a brief but intensive period of 2 weeks. In drafting this imaginary role, I tried to build enough bridges between it and his own self-characterization so that it would not seem completely alien, while at the same time introducing enough novelty to challenge him to grapple seriously with a somewhat different approach to life with others. In particular, I tried to construct the sketch around a central theme that was neither isomorphic with nor in opposition to his central identity constructs. This subtle balancing of "coherence" with and "orthogonality" to existing constructions is key to the success of the sketch, as it is to other constructivist interventions predicated on a "structure determinism" model (Efran, Lukens, & Lukens, 1990). My enactment sketch for this hypothetical character, Ed Venturous, was as follows:

Enactment Sketch for Ed Venturous

Ed likes to think of himself as a sort of Ripley of the mind—rather than collecting unbelievable curios from obscure parts of the world, he delights in discovering something unusual or remarkable about virtually everyone he meets. Like any true explorer, he is less interested in cataloging his discoveries than in "unearthing" them, and he is motivated more by the thrill of the quest than by the prospect of some terminal achievement. What makes Ed unique is that he extends this attitude even to people who seem mildly threatening or difficult to get to know. Like a "dark continent," someone with a strange or foreign outlook seems all the more intriguing to him, and he relishes the challenge of seeing what he might find at their interior.

If Ed were an anthropologist, he would definitely be a participant-observer in the cultures he was trying to understand, rather than an armchair theorist. However, he would definitely be an anthropologist rather than a social activist, since he is more interested in learning about the people and systems he interacts with than in changing them to fit any one idea of what would be considered "ideal." Indeed, Ed relishes idiosyncrasies in people, since they reflect the spirit of individuality that he values so highly. For this reason, Ed tends to fill his life with an improbable cast of characters, all of whom may be eccentric in their own way. This occasionally produces friction in Ed's social world, since he sometimes relates better to each of his friends individually than they do to each other.

If Ed has a weakness, it's that it's hard to know when to take him seriously. Of course, he laughs easily and genuinely, and at those times he may be easiest to "read." But he also relishes playing the "devil's advocate," playfully defending either side of a thorny issue just to see others' reactions. He sometimes describes himself as "testing" others through his own behavior, or by carefully observing how they react to each other. But for Ed, this "testing" has no right or wrong answers—like responses to a TAT, he finds them valuable simply for what they suggest about people's needs, motives and outlooks. In another person, this way of interacting might come across as detached or uncaring, but not in Ed. Although he is not quick to rush in with a solution to somebody else's problem, this stems more from his respect for the complexities of their unique situations than from any lack of involvement or sensitivity. Indeed, the difficulties he has encountered in his own life have taught him to distrust "simple solutions" to complicated problems. This tends to make his advice or reassurance, when it is given, all the more valuable.

Ed is also a complex individual. He once told me that he was like a mosaic of all the people he had ever known, as if he had fashioned his own personality out of pieces—some large, some small—taken from different sources. But there is no mistaking the individuality of his resulting character. Above all else, Ed is unique, integrating many passionate pursuits (love of travel, art, hiking, chess, mystery novels) that for some people might seem contradictory. In his private moments, Ed also enjoys exploring his own complexity, recording his own reactions as well as his impressions of others in a personal journal that he refers to as his "log book." This more interior, reflective side of Ed is every bit as lively as his more public side—both of them express his seemingly boundless curiosity.

To be useful, an enactment sketch need not portray an "ideal" person or a model of successful coping in whose image the client is asked to remake him- or herself. Indeed fixed role therapy is only complete at the point that the client explicitly *de-roles,* leaving behind the make-believe identity but carrying forward the lessons learned from temporarily living in a different assumptive world. For this reason, I attempted to give Ed some larger-than-life aspirations (being a "Ripley of the mind") but tried to play these out in the context of ordinary relationships and in a fallible rather than superhuman way. I also tried to make the sketch cohere with many of the self-constructions implicit or explicit in Brad's own self-characterization (like Brad, Ed was portrayed as interesting, insightful, passionate, and sensitive) and to reflect the general surface-to-depth organization of the original narrative. In other respects, I tried to introduce novelty by reframing constructions present in the original in a different light (testing, helping) and by building the entire sketch around an overarching theme (curiosity regarding others' outlooks) that was independent of or orthogonal to the dimensions present in his self-description. The central aim of drafting this alternative identity was to breathe life into a hypothetical character whom Brad might like to "get to know" over a brief period of intensive contact. I therefore conducted a "plausibility check" by presenting the written enactment sketch to Brad and by discussing the character with him. As a result of such discussion, the sketch can be modified to promote believability (Epting & Nazario, 1987), although in Brad's case, he found the character intriguing as described and did not request any modifications.

Once the client has accepted the enactment sketch, actual experimentation with the new role can begin. For Brad, this involved imagining that he had gone on vacation for 2 weeks, during which time Ed would live his life, do his work, and maintain his personal relationships. To promote Brad's adoption of this "as if" perspective, we rehearsed the role with one another, attempting to enact it in relation to a succession of increasingly challenging contexts ranging from his friendships, through his academic encounters with faculty and other students, to his relationships with his father, mother, and present girlfriend. These efforts were supported also by his adopting some of Ed's pastimes (e.g., taking a short trip, playing chess, reading novels, and keeping a personal journal). Thus we pursued not only a "top down" approach to role adoption (through daily reading of the sketch and an attempt to behave in accordance with Ed's "outlook") but also a "bottom up" strategy for taking up a new identity (by non-consciously inferring something of Ed's personality by behaving and even dressing as he would). Brad's earnest efforts to enact the new role led to an immediate improvement in the quality of relationships that he enjoyed with faculty in his department and set the stage for more fundamental changes in his understanding of women (including his mother) long after he formally had discontinued the "Ed Venturous" role and indeed psychotherapy in general. Interestingly he continued one aspect of the enactment, integrating it into his own life: the use of a personal journal to help him process his experiences in relation to others and to his own goals.

Although the idiosyncrasy of clients' self-characterizations and the resulting enactment sketches is perhaps most easily accommodated in individual therapy, it is worth noting that these same techniques have been employed successfully in recent years in a range of marital (Kremsdorf, 1985), family (Alexander & Neimeyer, G., 1989), and group therapy contexts (Beail & Parker, 1991; Epting & Nazario, 1987; Morris, 1977). Thus an emphasis on personal meanings and their reconstruction is not necessarily inimical to more interpersonal models of therapy.

Stream of Consciousness

As Mahoney (1991, p. 294) remarked, "One of the primary purposes of assessment is to refine our understanding of the felt experience of the person being served." This is particularly true in the case of assessment techniques having a *process* (as opposed to structural) orientation. Although self-characterizations suggest something of the sequence and organization of a client's self-construing, their formality tends to inhibit a more "on line" portrayal of the unpredictable shifts that characterize our spontaneous private experience. In contrast, the *stream of consciousness* technique developed by Mahoney (1991) "is an exercise in which the client is invited to attend to, and, as best one can, report ongoing thoughts, sensations, images, memories, and feelings" (p. 295). As such, it is related to *mindfulness meditation,* which Kenny and Delmonte (1986) conceptualized as a valuable method for "loosening" overly rigid constructions and for promoting greater self-awareness. "Streaming" is also closely related to Kelly's use of *chain association* (Neimeyer, R., 1980), as well as to Freud's method of free association, which he regarded as the "fundamental rule" of psychoanalysis. For example, Freud (1913/1963, p. 147) instructed the client:

> Your talk with me must differ in one respect from an ordinary conversation. Whereas usually you rightly try to keep the threads of your story together and to exclude all intruding associations and side issues . . . here you must proceed differently. You will notice that as you relate things various ideas will occur to you which you will feel inclined to put aside with certain criticisms and objections. . . . Never give in to these objections, but mention it even if you feel a disinclination against it, or indeed just because of this. . . . Never forget that you have promised absolute honesty, and never leave anything unsaid because for any reason it is unpleasant to say it.

Like this psychoanalytic method, streaming facilitates both the therapist's and client's access to experiences, associations, and meanings that are rarely articulated or publicly shared. The two methods differ, however, in two important ways (Mahoney, 1991). First, stream of consciousness work displays greater respect for the client's privacy and permits him or her to "edit" experiences to be shared with the therapist, while at the same time to make a mental note of important material for later reflection. This departure from traditional free association follows from the constructivist conceptualization of "defenses" as *self-protective* rather than *self-deceptive* maneuvers (cf. Neimeyer, R. & Harter, 1988). Second, streaming places much less emphasis on the therapist's interpretations of the client's material. This follows from the deeply held conviction of constructivist counselors that meanings are ultimately personal and that the client rather than therapist occupies the privileged perspective necessary to understand these meanings more fully.

The use of stream of consciousness as an assessment tool and therapeutic intervention can be illustrated by my work with Joan P. The initial psychiatric evaluation that accompanied the referral described her as "a very complicated patient" whose "clinical picture was not very clear," although a "chronic dysthymic disorder and underlying personality disorder of the borderline type" were the most probable diagnoses. Joan's formal contacts with the mental health profession reached back to her early 20s, when her struggle with bulimia had intensified, following her marriage to a man a few years her senior. Although her marriage—and with it, marriage counseling—dissolved within 3 years, she continued in therapy on an individual basis to deal with a growing number of troubling symptoms. Debilitating panic attacks eventually led to two lengthy hospitalizations of 6 months to 1 year, after which she returned to work in her family's automobile dealership and continued treatment on an outpatient basis. She had sought consultation with a psychiatric colleague at the point that she broke off this previous outpatient treatment because of "trust issues" and was referred for collateral treatment with me when it became clear that medical intervention to control her mood was in itself insufficient.

My first session with Joan added still further difficulties to the above list. Prominent among these were resentments toward several family members with whom she worked but on whom she was admittedly extremely dependent. She also reported increasing suicide ideation and escalating anxiety, accompanied by the breakdown of her "rituals of preparation," severely compulsive routines requiring her to arrange her wardrobe, toiletries, and breakfast service fastidiously before retiring for the evening.

At Joan's request, we met approximately twice per week through this turbulent period. Initially I responded to her request for immediate relief with behavioral interventions targeting her most pressing symptoms (e.g., relaxation training to reduce her debilitating anxiety, conflict management skills to employ with her family) but met with limited success. At this point, we backed away from strategies designed to "tighten" her construing through training her in specific new behaviors and began experimenting with nontraditional assessment techniques designed to "loosen" her construing regarding her habitual complaints. For example, Joan responded eagerly to an art therapy technique in which she used various colors of markers on a large tablet of paper to depict emotional transitions across her life. This was useful in illustrating phases of anger, depression, fear, and stress, each depicted in its own color over time.

This informal monitoring procedure was also helpful in alerting me to important emotional issues that were activated by her day-to-day life events. The most significant of these was signaled by a powerful anger "spike" on her chart while watching a television show on incest, although it was accompanied by similar spikes indicating confusion, guilt, and mistrust of other people. As I inquired into this network of feelings, a picture gradually began to emerge that made sense of her recurrent cycles of bulimia, her problematic sexual relationship with her ex-husband, her difficulties falling asleep, her rampant and unpredictable anger (especially toward family), and her undermined sense of trust in other people. Tearfully she related a history of abuse by her older brother, Gene, that began when she was 6 years old and continued until she was 10. During this time, Gene made her his "slave," making frequent humiliating sexual demands of her and threatening her with death if she were ever to disclose these to anyone. Between sobs, Joan related the guilt that she continued to carry, a guilt fueled by her "trying to make a game out of it" to gain some sense of control over the experience. She also confessed with embarrassment her own sadism, as was evidenced in childhood by her "murder" of her brother's pet snake and in adulthood by her delight in punishing a boy in her class during a brief period she worked as a classroom teacher.

The next few sessions were spent in a detailed exploration of the abuse experience and its aftermath. Initially Joan resisted my use of the word *incest* to describe her sexual relationship with her brother, protesting, "Whenever you use that word, it makes me feel sick. . . . But then I do get sick [referring to her bulimic vomiting]!" The intensity of her own reaction led Joan to acknowledge the severity of the abuse experience and to conclude that it had included coital intercourse, something she had "forgotten." Gradually she recovered traumatic memories of her brother's "sexual parties," in which she was repeatedly raped by several of his friends, and began to connect this with her current sexual preferences. Quietly she disclosed that her typical sensual contact was "without feeling" and that she "had to think of herself in the victim role during sex to halfway enjoy it." Joan connected this masochistic posture to her tendency to solicit abuse in a range of relationships because, as she noted, "At least when someone yells at me, I know that they care."

At this point in our counseling, Joan began expressing a persistent interest in the stream of consciousness technique, which I had mentioned to her several sessions before. I therefore began by explaining one intent of the exercise, namely to enable me to "understand more clearly what it was like to be her." I noted that streaming entailed her entering into a relaxed state from which she would simply allow her mind to wander to whatever associations seemed to draw her attention. I requested that she periodically reach into this current or stream of consciousness and "throw out a bucketful" to share with me. I gave her complete license, however, to "edit" the stream as much as she cared to and simply to note for her own later retrieval any images, thoughts, or feelings that provoked a sharp reaction.

When she expressed a willingness to continue, I asked her to recline in a comfortable chair as I reduced the lighting in the room to facilitate her therapeutic "loosening" (Neimeyer, R., 1988). We then used some progressive muscle relaxation techniques to induce the streaming state, after which I quietly invited her to begin sharing whatever came to her awareness whenever she was ready to do so. Over several minutes, Joan began by associating first to relationships, then to Gene, then to a strong feeling of anger, and then to a "knot" in her stomach, at which point she paused. I encouraged her simply to repeat the word *knot* aloud several times. As she did this, she seemed to become more angry, tensing her fists and feet until she suddenly fell silent. She expressed the feeling of being "stuck in the knot" and unable to enter it further. I then suggested that she simply allow her mind to wander once again to whatever drew her attention. She relaxed for a moment and then associated to Colorado, horses, riding horses, feeling free, wanting to be free, experiencing herself as not free, imagining herself behind bars, and then returned to the anger. Clenching her fists, she related an image of Gene sitting on his desk and making her kiss his feet as he repeated that she was his slave. Again she fell silent. After a few moments, I asked her to begin repeating the word *slave* aloud, which intensified her anger.

Because this drew us back to a similar impasse, and because our time was growing short, I requested that she leave the stream by gradually becoming aware of her breathing once again, the heaviness of her arms and legs on the chair, and gradually the sounds and light in the room. As she opened her eyes and resumed an alert posture, we briefly processed the 20-minute experience, avoiding any definitive interpretations of its meaning. We noted the compelling contrast of her image of herself as locked behind bars versus riding freely on a horse, which seemed to represent a powerful preverbal construct for her. We also described the tightness of the knot and her sense of being entrapped within it. She remarked that a part of her was screaming to get out of this prison and commented that this may have been the part of her that wanted to live. She contrasted this with the part of her that felt trapped, suffering, and wanted to die. Thus our first use of streaming in therapy seemed to yield useful understandings of the constructions that she continued to attach to the incest experience, setting the stage for our periodic use of the technique in future sessions.

In subsequent therapy, we made extensive use of *personal journal* work, yet another technique that has close affinities with a constructivist approach to assessment and counseling (Mahoney, 1991; Neimeyer, R., 1988). On the same large tablet on which she had depicted her feelings with different colors of pens, Joan began to "tighten," to summarize, evaluate, and reflect on the material brought to light by her streaming experiences. She wrote poignantly of her sense of abandonment by both parents, who treated her as a "plaything" but then left her to the predatory advances of her older brother. Her writing also allowed her to give voice to new insights about herself, such as her tendency to "slowly self-destruct" by smoking in bed, "accidentally" injuring herself, and binge eating. Finally her writing explored very sensitively her troubled sexual relationships ranging from her early encounters with Gene through her marriage and subsequent extramarital affairs. In summary, her journal seemed to continue the self-exploration facilitated by the streaming and provided a useful ally in integrating the meanings of her past in such a way that she could reach toward a more coherent and satisfying future.

Systemic "Bowties"

I have noted that many of the above techniques—including laddering, the downward arrow, the repertory grid, and self-characterizations—have been adapted to the assessment of individuals in marital, family, and group settings, although their focus of convenience is on personal meaning systems. Other measurement methods, however, are inherently systemic, elucidating the delicate interplay of perspectives that maintains a social construction of reality, whether functional or otherwise. In recent years, constructivists have made substantial progress in reconceptualizing family assessment and therapy, moving it away from a preemptive focus on behavioral exchanges and toward a focus on the shared or conflicting meanings with which painful or unsatisfying patterns of interaction are coherent (e.g., Alexander & Neimeyer, G., 1989; Efran et al., 1990; Hoffman,

1988). In particular, the work of Procter (1981, 1987) and Feixas (1990a, 1990b, 1992) explores the extensive interface of personal construct and systemic family therapies, offering a variety of novel assessment and intervention techniques for the practicing therapist.

One such technique is the *bowtie,* a conceptual tool for clarifying the position of each member of a relevant system, defined as the integrated stance that each person takes at the level of construction and action. An individual's position at the *construction* level includes one's construing about oneself and about the thinking of at least one other family member, complemented by several potential metaperspectives (e.g., what I think you think of me). The individual's position at the *action* level consists of behaviors that cohere with these constructions and that provide means of testing out the person's implicit hypotheses. At the same time, because all family members have corresponding positions, their behaviors provide validational evidence for one another's constructions as subjectively perceived by each other family member. The resulting feedback loops often function to maintain dysfunctional interaction cycles that become the focus of therapy.

As an example, consider the case of Dan and Deena T., a farming couple in their 40s with a 10 year history of marital distress. Deena first consulted me for help with her "depression" at the insistence of her team of physicians, who had run every conceivable form of sophisticated medical test but were unable to find a biological explanation for her chronic fatigue, generalized pain, and tendency toward anorexia. Our progress in treating her "mood disorder" was limited until we shifted from an individual to a systemic level and began examining seriously her perceptions of her family relationships. This approach opened the door to a litany of complaints, most of which centered around the neglect and verbal cruelty of her "alcoholic" husband, which only reinforced her depression. As a result, we invited Dan to join us for conjoint marital therapy, which he did only reluctantly when he was assured that he was being called in merely to "consult" on his wife's problems.

Not surprisingly, Dan's position was rather different. With genuine anguish, he described their desperate financial condition, trying to maintain a family farm in an era of declining subsidies, falling prices, and unpredictable weather. Deena confirmed his fear that foreclosure was a very real possibility unless the current soybean crop was successful, but with 4 months to go until harvest, rainfall had been seriously inadequate.

To make matters worse, Dan saw himself being undercut by a willful and helpless wife who kept accumulating thousands of dollars in medical bills for imaginary illnesses, forcing him to work alone on the tractor from sunup to sundown, only to return home to work on the financial management of the farm as well. Little wonder, in his view, that he drank to relieve his stress and had little time or inclination to spend "quality time" with a spouse whom he deeply resented.

Engaging in a kind of "zigzag" questioning (Procter, 1987), I elicited the meanings of each spouse's actions in the eyes of the partner, as well as the behaviors that fit with their respective positions. The resulting "bowtie" diagram is presented in Figure 3.7a. As illustrated graphically, the behaviors of each spouse were consistent with his or her interpretation of the marital situation and in turn provided apparent validation for the (problem-maintaining) constructions of the partner and so on in a seamless pattern of mutual validation with no clear beginning or end. Indeed the durability of this family construct system was evidenced by its pernicious persistence for nearly a decade with trivial variation. Interestingly the act of sharing this diagram with Dan and Deena was itself therapeutic, insofar as both felt understood on their own terms and were willing to consider, however fleetingly, how their own position might be viewed differently by the partner. The "bowtie" also provided a potential "road map" for future interventions, suggesting four potential targets for change corresponding to the constructions and actions of both spouses. This possibility evoked some optimism for the couple (and for me as a therapist!), insofar as the reframing of even one interpretation, or experimentation with even one new relational behavior, could destabilize and perhaps transform the problem-determining system.

Finally it is also worth emphasizing that the "bowtie" need not be limited in its application to two members of a given system. For example, in Dan and Deena's case, we found it useful to expand it to include the position of their 16-year-old daughter, Terri, who construed the conflict between her parents in terms of her father "bullying" her "helpless" mother, leading her to attempt to "draw off" his criticism, and literally enter their arguments to take her mother's part (see Figure 3.7b). (Of course, this "bowtie" could be expanded to represent both parents' constructions of Terri as well—including Dan's anger over being "ganged up on" and Deena's sense of vindication that her perception of her husband was being corroborated by an "objective" outsider.) Thus the "bowtie"

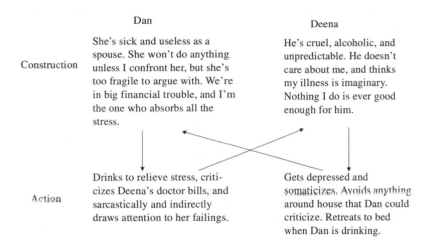

Figure 3.7a. "Bowtie" Linking Levels of Construction and Action for a Distressed Couple

technique proved useful in assessing the positions taken by each member of the family, that contributed to the creation and maintenance of their dysfunctional interaction.

Conclusion: You May Already Be a Constructivist!

In this chapter, I have presented several methods of assessment deriving from constructivist metatheory—the assumption that knowledge is a personal and social construction rather than a direct representation of the "real world" and that humans are best conceived of as proactive, goal-directed, and purposive beings rather than merely reactive organisms (see Mahoney, 1988, and Neimeyer, R. & Feixas, 1990, for elaboration). Although these epistemological and ontological assumptions have been adopted by a variety of psychological theorists (as the contributors to this volume illustrate), they are in fact more general expressions of a "postmodern" worldview. In the words of Anderson (1990), "Reality isn't what

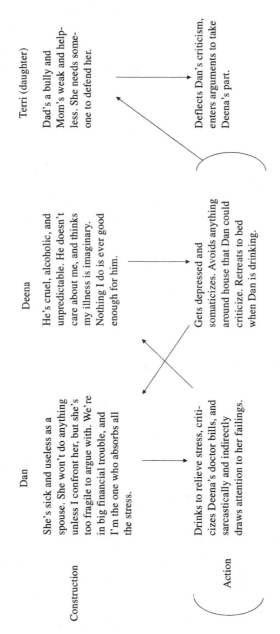

Dan

Construction

She's sick and useless as a spouse. She won't do anything unless I confront her, but she's too fragile to argue with. We're in big financial trouble, and I'm the one who absorbs all the stress.

Action

Drinks to relieve stress, criticizes Deena's doctor bills, and sarcastically and indirectly draws attention to her failings.

Deena

He's cruel, alcoholic, and unpredictable. He doesn't care about me, and thinks my illness is imaginary. Nothing I do is ever good enough for him.

Gets depressed and somaticizes. Avoids anything around house that Dan could criticize. Retreats to bed when Dan is drinking.

Terri (daughter)

Dad's a bully and Mom's weak and helpless. She needs someone to defend her.

Deflects Dan's criticism, enters arguments to take Deena's part.

Figure 3.7b. Expanded "Bowtie" Including Position of Daughter in Problem Determining Family Construct System

it used to be": We in contemporary Western societies are keenly aware of the relativism of cultural belief systems and (comfortably or uncomfortably) accept the responsibility for deciding what we choose to believe. As an approach to counseling, constructivism simply attempts to tease out the implications of this stance for psychological practice, and the resulting methods can be used intelligently by any helping professional who considers the exploration and transformation of personal and interpersonal meaning systems an important goal of psychotherapy.

Although a constructivist stance may be adopted implicitly by a majority of practicing counselors, inevitably there will be individual differences in therapist preferences and client needs that influence the selection of assessment and intervention techniques in any particular case. With this in mind, I have tried to present a range of methods that differ in their level of formality versus informality, structural versus process emphasis, and individual versus systemic focus. I hope that your experimentation with them enhances your work with clients and furthers your privileged participation in the process of human change.

References

Adams-Webber, J. R. (1981). Fixed role therapy. In R. J. Corsini (Ed.), *Handbook of innovative psychotherapies* (pp. 333-343). New York: John Wiley.

Alexander, P., & Neimeyer, G. J. (1989). Constructivism and family therapy. *International Journal of Personal Construct Psychology, 2,* 111-121.

Anderson, W. T. (1990). *Reality isn't what it used to be.* San Francisco: Harper & Row.

Applegate, J. L. (1990). Constructs and communication: A pragmatic integration. In G. J. Neimeyer & R. A. Neimeyer (Eds.), *Advances in personal construct psychology* (Vol. 1, pp. 203-230). Greenwich, CT: JAI.

Bannister, D., & Mair, J. M. M. (1968). *The evaluation of personal constructs.* London: Academic.

Beail, N., & Parker, S. (1991). Group fixed role therapy: A clinical application. *International Journal of Personal Construct Psychology, 4,* 85-95.

Beck, A. T., Rush, J., Shaw, B., & Emery, G. (1979). *Cognitive therapy of depression.* New York: Guilford.

Bell, R. C. (1990). Analytic issues in the use of repertory grid technique. In G. J. Neimeyer & R. A. Neimeyer (Eds.), *Advances in personal construct psychology* (Vol. 1, pp. 25-48). Greenwich, CT: JAI.

Bonarius, H. (1970). Fixed role therapy: A double paradox. *British Journal of Medical Psychology, 43,* 213-219.

Bringmann, M. W. (1992). Computer based methods for the analysis and interpretation of personal construct systems. In R. A. Neimeyer & G. J. Neimeyer (Eds.), *Advances in personal construct psychology* (Vol. 2, pp. 57-90). Greenwich, CT: JAI.

Bruner, J. (1990). *Acts of meaning.* Cambridge, MA: Harvard University Press.

Burns, D. (1980). *Feeling good.* New York: Signet.

Edwards, E. D. (1943/1982). Observations of the use and efficacy of changing a patient's concept of his role. *Fort Hays Studies, 3,* 1-49.

Efran, J., Lukens, R., & Lukens, M. (1990). *Language, structure, and change.* San Francisco: Jossey-Bass.

Epting, F. R., & Nazario, A. (1987). Designing a fixed role therapy. In R. A. Neimeyer & G. J. Neimeyer (Eds.), *Personal construct therapy casebook* (pp. 277-289). New York: Springer.

Feixas, G. (1990a). Personal construct theory and systemic therapies. *Journal of Marital and Family Therapy, 16,* 1-20.

Feixas, G. (1990b). Approaching the individual, approaching the system. *Journal of Family Psychology, 4,* 4-35.

Feixas, G. (1992). Personal construct approaches to family therapy. In R. A. Neimeyer & G. J. Neimeyer (Eds.), *Advances in personal construct psychology* (Vol. 2, pp. 217-257). Greenwich, CT: JAI.

Fransella, F. (1972). *Personal change and reconstruction.* New York: Academic Press.

Fransella, F., & Bannister, D. (1977). *A manual for repertory grid technique.* London: Academic.

Freud, S. (1913/1963). *Therapy and technique.* New York: Collier.

Guidano, V., & Liotti, G. (1983). *Cognitive processes and emotional disorders.* New York: Guilford.

Harvey, J. H. (1989). People's naive understandings of their close relationships. *International Journal of Personal Construct Psychology, 2,* 37-48.

Harvey, J. H., Orbuch, T. L., Weber, A. L., Merback, N., & Alt, R. (1992). House of pain and hope: Accounts of loss. *Death Studies, 16,* 99-124.

Harvey, J. H., Weber, A. L., & Orbuch, T. L. (1990). *Interpersonal accounts.* Oxford, UK: Basil Blackwell.

Hinkle, D. (1965). *The change of personal constructs from the viewpoint of a theory of construct implications.* Unpublished doctoral dissertation, Ohio State University, Columbus.

Hoffman, L. (1988). A constructivist position for family therapy. *Irish Journal of Psychology, 9,* 110-129.

Howard, G. S. (1989). *A tale of two stories: Excursions into a narrative approach to psychology.* Notre Dame, IN: Academic Publications.

Karst, T. O., & Trexler, L. D. (1970). Initial study using fixed role and rational-emotive therapy in treating public speaking anxiety. *Journal of Consulting and Clinical Psychology, 34,* 360-366.

Kelly, G. A. (1955). *The psychology of personal constructs.* New York: Norton.

Kenny, V., & Delmonte, M. (1986). Meditation as viewed through personal construct theory. *Journal of Contemporary Psychotherapy, 16,* 4-22.

Korzybski, A. (1933). *Science and sanity.* New York: International Non-Aristotelian Library.

Kremsdorf, F. (1985). An extension of fixed role therapy with a couple. In F. Epting & A. W. Landfield (Eds.), *Anticipating personal construct psychology* (pp. 216-224). Lincoln: University of Nebraska Press.

Landfield, A. W. (1971). *Personal construct systems in psychotherapy*. Chicago: Rand-McNally.

Landfield, A. W., & Cannell, J. E. (1988). Ways of assessing functionally independent construction, meaningfulness, and construction in hierarchy. In J. C. Mancuso & M. L. Shaw (Eds.), *Cognition and personal structure* (pp. 67-89). New York: Praeger.

Landfield, A. W., & Epting, F. R. (1987). *Personal construct psychology*. New York: Human Sciences.

Leitner, L. M. (1988). Terror, risk, and reverence: Experiential personal construct therapy. *International Journal of Personal Construct Psychology, 1*, 251-261.

Liotti, G., & Pallini, S. (1990). Lo sviluppo della conoscenza di se e la psicopatologia [The development of self knowledge and psychopathology]. In F. Mancini & A. Semerari (Eds.), *Le teorie cognitive dei disturbi emotivi* (pp. 55-75). Rome: Nuova Italia Scientifica

MacDonald, D. E., & Mancuso, J. C. (1987). A constructivist approach to parent training. In R. A. Neimeyer & G. J. Neimeyer (Eds.), *Personal construct therapy casebook* (pp. 172-189). New York: Springer.

Mahoney, M. J. (1988). Constructive metatheory II: Implications for psychotherapy. *International Journal of Personal Construct Psychology, 1*, 299-315.

Mahoney, M. J. (1991). *Human change processes*. New York: Basic Books.

Mair, M. (1989). *Between psychology and psychotherapy*. London: Routledge.

Mair, M. (1990). Telling psychological tales. *International Journal of Personal Construct Psychology, 3*, 121-135.

Mancuso, J. C., & Shaw, M. L. (1988). *Cognition and personal structure*. New York: Praeger.

McWilliams, S. A. (1988). Construing comprehensively. *International Journal of Personal Construct Psychology, 1*, 219-228.

Moreno, J. L. (1937). Interpersonal therapy and the psychopathology of interpersonal relations. *Sociometry, 1*, 9-75.

Morris, J. B. (1977). The prediction and measurement of change in a psychotherapy group using the repertory grid. In F. Fransella & D. Bannister (Eds.), *A manual for repertory grid technique* (pp. 120-148). London: Academic.

Neimeyer, G. J. (1987). Personal construct assessment, strategy, and technique. In R. A. Neimeyer & G. J. Neimeyer (Eds.), *Personal construct therapy casebook* (pp. 20-36). New York: Springer.

Neimeyer, G. J. (1992). Personal constructs and vocational structure. In R. A. Neimeyer & G. J. Neimeyer (Eds.), *Advances in personal construct psychology* (Vol. 2, pp. 92-119). Greenwich, CT: JAI.

Neimeyer, G. J., & Neimeyer, R. A. (1981). Personal construct perspectives on cognitive assessment. In T. Merluzzi, C. Glass, & M. Genest (Eds.), *Cognitive assessment* (pp. 188-232). New York: Guilford.

Neimeyer, G. J., & Neimeyer, R. A. (1985). Relational trajectories: A personal construct contribution. *Journal of Social and Personal Relationships, 2*, 325-349.

Neimeyer, R. A. (1980). George Kelly as therapist: A review of his tapes. In A. W. Landfield & L. M. Leitner (Eds.), *Personal construct psychology* (pp. 74-101). New York: John Wiley.

Neimeyer, R. A. (1981). The structure and meaningfulness of tacit construing. In H. Bonarius, R. Holland, & S. Rosenberg (Eds.), *Personal construct psychology: Recent advances in theory and practice* (pp. 205-213). London: Macmillan.

Neimeyer, R. A. (1985a). Personal constructs in clinical practice. In P. C. Kendall (Ed.), *Advances in cognitive-behavioral research and therapy* (Vol. 4, pp. 275-329). New York: Academic Press.

Neimeyer, R. A. (1985b). *The development of personal construct psychology.* Lincoln: University of Nebraska Press.

Neimeyer, R. A. (1987). An orientation to personal construct therapy. In R. A. Neimeyer & G. J. Neimeyer (Eds.), *Personal construct therapy casebook* (pp. 3-19). New York: Springer.

Neimeyer, R. A. (1988). Integrative directions in personal construct therapy. *International Journal of Personal Construct Psychology, 1,* 283-297.

Neimeyer, R. A., Baker, K. D., & Neimeyer, G. J. (1990). The current status of personal construct theory: Some scientometric data. In G. J. Neimeyer & R. A. Neimeyer (Eds.), *Advances in personal construct psychology* (Vol. 1, pp. 2-22). Greenwich, CT: JAI.

Neimeyer, R. A., & Feixas, G. (1990). Constructivist contributions to psychotherapy integration. *Journal of Integrative and Eclectic Psychotherapy, 9,* 4-20.

Neimeyer, R. A., & Harter, S. (1988). Facilitating individual change in personal construct therapy. In G. Dunnett (Ed.), *Working with people* (pp. 174-185). London: Routledge.

Neimeyer, R., Harter, S., & Alexander, P. C. (1991). Group perceptions as predictors of outcome in the treatment of incest survivors. *Psychotherapy Research, 1,* 148-158.

Neimeyer, R. A., & Neimeyer, G. J. (Eds.). (1987). *Personal construct therapy casebook.* New York: Springer.

Neimeyer, R. A., Robinson, L. A., Berman, J. S., & Haykal, R. F. (1989). Clinical outcome of group therapies for depression. *Group Analysis, 22,* 73-86.

Procter, H. G. (1981). Family construct psychology. In S. Walrond-Skinner (Ed.), *Developments in family therapy* (pp. 350-366). London: Routledge.

Procter, H. G. (1987). Change in the family construct system. In R. A. Neimeyer & G. J. Neimeyer (Eds.), *Personal construct therapy casebook* (pp. 153-171). New York: Springer.

Robinson, A. J. (1943/1982). A further validation of role therapy. *Fort Hays Studies, 3,* 51-90.

Ryle, A. (1990). *Cognitive-analytic therapy.* New York: John Wiley.

Sewell, K., Adams-Webber, J., Mitterer, J., & Cromwell, R. L. (1992). Computerized repertory grids: A review of the literature. *International Journal of Personal Construct Psychology, 5,* 1-23.

Skene, R. A. (1973). Construct shift in the treatment of a case of homosexuality. *British Journal of Medical Psychology, 130,* 174-176.

Stewart, A. E., & Barry, J. R. (1991). Origins of George Kelly's constructivism in the work of Korzybski and Moreno. *International Journal of Personal Construct Psychology, 4,* 121-136.

Wessler, R. L., & Hankin-Wessler, S. (1987). Cognitive appraisal therapy. In W. Dryden & W. Golden (Eds.), *Cognitive-behavioral approaches to psychotherapy* (pp. 196-223). New York: Hemisphere.

White, M., & Epston, D. (1990). *Narrative means to therapeutic ends.* New York: Norton.

Yorke, M. (1985). Administration, analysis, and assumption. In N. Beail (Ed.), *Repertory grid technique and personal constructs* (pp. 383-399). London: Croom Helm.

4

Listening to What My Clients and I Say: Content Analysis Categories and Scales

LINDA L. VINEY

C ONTENT scales and the categories on which they are based can be used effectively for assessment during psychotherapy. The first of these scales, measuring threat, that I will discuss was developed to answer a therapist's question: What is my client experiencing when her epileptic seizures start during our therapeutic session? (L. A. Gottschalk, personal communication, 1983). A range of available scales measure positive and negative emotions. I have used this method of assessment to answer other questions about clients' experiences during therapy, as well as the questions asked when monitoring the parallel experiences of therapists. Further it can be used to examine the ongoing processes of psychotherapy by applying it to units that combine the communications of client and therapist.

When I choose to use this method of clinical assessment, I make a number of assumptions that should be stated explicitly. They are assumptions about (a) the nature of the person (client and therapist), (b) the kind

AUTHOR'S NOTE: The work underlying this chapter was funded by the Australian Research Grants Committee. I would also like to thank Meg Smith, whose contribution to it has been invaluable, and "June," without whose bravery and permission it would not have been possible.

of science that is appropriate to those assumptions about the person, (c) the specific nature of this method, and (d) the psychotherapy that fits with this approach. I assume people to be basing their actions, both their successful and problematic ones, on the personal meanings that they give to events (Mahoney & Gabriel, 1987; Mahoney & Lyddon, 1988). They organize those meanings into a coherent system that they then use to interpret and predict events. Some of these meanings change in the course of adult development (Viney, in press); this process of change is accelerated during successful psychotherapy (Kelly, 1955).

Such a view of the person requires a science that favors assessment methods focused on people who are actively interpreting and predicting events and are capable of reflecting on those interpretations and predictions rather than dealing with a singular, stable, and fully knowable reality (Howard, 1986; Viney, 1987, 1988). The reflexivity involved in this approach implies that we therapists should assess our own contribution to therapy, together with those of our clients, using the same concepts and methods. My assumptions relating more specifically to the method of content analysis categories and scales are now provided. For therapists to work effectively with clients, we need to understand their personal meanings; some of those meanings will be found in what our clients say during psychotherapy.

Constructivist therapy is based on a number of key concepts (Kelly 1955). People use *constructs,* or personal meanings, to make sense of what happens to them. When people act, they experiment with their own construing, leaving it open to be supported or not supported by subsequent events. When their constructs receive support or validation, positive emotion, such as perceived competence, results; but it is when invalidation of them occurs that distressed emotion results (McCoy, 1980). *Anxiety,* for example, is experienced when people become aware that they do not have the constructs to make the interpretations and predictions about events that they need. *Hostility* occurs when people get no support for their predictions but try to extract such support anyway. It can be directed to the outside world, in the form of *anger,* or to the self, in the form of *depression.* *Helplessness* also occurs in invalidating circumstances, with power being directed to the world rather than the self. *Threat* involves invalidation of central constructs about self. Such invalidation is integral to change.

Personal construct therapy assumes that all constructs can be replaced by other interpretations or predictions. *Psychotherapy* provides a "protected laboratory, where hypotheses can be formulated, test tube size experiments performed, field trials planned, and outcomes evaluated" (Kelly, 1969, p. 229). Client and therapist then may be conceptualized as co-researchers. Emotions arising from invalidation, like threat, are considered to be integral to the clients' experience of this therapy. Psychotherapy consists of disconfirmations, as well as confirmations (Epting, 1984). Clients in personal construct therapy use their therapists as validators of their own construing, and their therapists test their clients' construct systems, both for predictive validity and for internal consistency (Neimeyer, G., 1987). The process of personal construct therapy therefore should involve some expressions of distressed emotions, such as threat, as well as positive emotion, such as perceived competence, that the therapist tries to anticipate.

I begin this chapter with an examination of this method of clinical assessment of content analysis and of the scales based on it. I provide a general description of these scales and then deal more specifically with the two scales (and sets of categories) that I shall use here. Then follows an account of ongoing assessment in psychotherapy that provides an example of the method in use, our goals, the course of our therapy, and its outcomes. In personal construct therapy, such ongoing assessment is at least as important as the assessment before therapy starts. "June" is the nom de plume, or should I say nom de parle, chosen by my colleague in this therapeutic enterprise. I shall show how I monitored June's expressions of threat to her during our therapy, as well as my references to her perceptions of threat with this method. I shall also show how I did the same for her expressions of competence, as well as my references to that competence. Finally I shall evaluate this method, first in its simple categorical form and then in its more complex scale form, acknowledging the advantages and disadvantages of both forms.

The Method of Clinical Assessment

Content Analysis

Content analysis of clients' verbal communications provides a way of listening to and interpreting people's communicated account of events. Such interpretation results in the identification of themes in such communication that then can be classified into categories (Krittendorf, 1980). A further step in this process may involve summaries of the frequencies of occurrence of those thematic categories after agreement between these independent interpretations is achieved. Then an important requirement of scientific endeavors—intersubjective agreement—is met (Popper, 1979). Content analysis was employed frequently with projective techniques and to monitor psychotherapy processes until the 1980s, when it became less common (Viney, 1983); but it is being reevaluated now. This revival has much to do with the range of techniques for such analysis that is becoming available for use with microcomputers (Richards, L. & Richards, T., in press; Viney & Porter, 1989). It provides assessment that is centered on the personal meanings of clients. And in its definition of the content of its categories, it acknowledges and articulates the role of the assessor in interpreting those meanings.

Content Analysis Scales

Content categories can provide the basis for content analysis scales with impressive psychometric qualities. An account of how such scales are developed may be useful here. The personal meanings to be assessed are described as precisely as possible and, if they involve multidimensional concepts, each of those dimensions is articulated. If this is not done well, then establishing interjudge consistency and evidence of criterion validity later can become difficult. Next, the size of the unit to be analyzed is defined; in this work, it has been defined as a *clause,* the language structure containing an active verb. Then the content of the verbal communication chosen to serve as cues for the application of the categories is specified, together with scoring examples. If differentiating scoring weights are employed, cues to their use also should be described. (These procedures will be provided later for the two scales on which I have chosen to focus.) A correction factor then is applied to take into account the differing lengths of verbal communications to be analyzed. Scores then can be calculated which may, depending on the shape of their distribution, need to be transformed. Comparative, or even normative, scale data then can be collected from samples of people and situations.

Scales measuring a wide range of personal meanings are available in addition to the scales assessing the meanings of threat and competence that I examine here. Scales are available for measuring the distress of uncertainty (which is very close to the constructivist concept of anxiety), depression, anger expressed both directly and indirectly, and helplessness, as well as the more enjoyable emotions of hope, sociability, and generally positive feelings (Viney, 1983). A set of scales is also available for measuring the personal meanings associated with different developmental tasks over the life span (Viney & Tych, 1985). All of these scales have shown acceptable intersubjective agreement, internal consistency, and variability over time. Their criterion validity has been demonstrated through correlations with self-reports, expert ratings, and physiological measures, and their construct validity by effective discriminations of samples and accurate predictions of outcome of laboratory-based and field-based experimental interventions (Gottschalk, 1982; Gottschalk, Lolas, & Viney, 1986; Viney, 1981).

These scales have been used successfully to assess the meanings of clients in psychotherapy to achieve a range of goals. For example, assessment of clients' meanings in order to better understand their problematic actions has occurred with drug addicts (Viney, Westbrook, & Preston, 1985), with clients who are dealing with serious illness (Viney, 1988, 1989), and with those who have been diagnosed as schizophrenic (Kinney et al., 1986). They have been assessed in order to predict outcomes of psychotherapy. It has been shown, for example, that clients who express considerable anger during therapy sessions show more gains than those who express little (de Abreu, 1986). This finding has been confirmed for the expression of anger by clients, while the reverse has been found for expressions of threat, relatively little proving more beneficial (Lolas, Kordy, & von Rad, 1986). The outcomes of psychotherapy also have been evaluated by use of these scales, with the greatest gains shown in terms of reduced references to depression, threat, and helplessness but increased references to competence (Viney, Benjamin, & Preston, 1989; Viney, Clarke, Bunn, & Benjamin, 1985).

Assessing Perceived Threat
by Use of a Content Analysis Scale

Those meanings of clients that indicate the distress of being under threat, as defined by personal construct therapists, will be assessed by a measure originally described as an Anxiety scale (Gottschalk, Winget, & Gleser, 1969). *Threat* is experienced when people become aware that they may need to change their most central constructs about themselves. The threat is to the construing of the physical self in the initial subscales of Death, Mutilation, and even some Separation Anxiety subscale categories, with the Guilt and Shame subscales focusing on threats to the construing of the psychological self, and the Diffuse Anxiety subscale categories dealing with the more general and less articulated responses to that threat, as can be seen in Table 4.1. I therefore have taken the liberty of renaming it the Threat Scale for this chapter on constructivist assessment. The definitions of each content analysis category of the Threat Scale are provided in Table 4.1, together with the weights advocated and some examples of scoring.

These categories for scoring the Threat Scale are applied carefully to transcriptions of the therapeutic sessions. A rough draft is first made, which includes all partial words and nonwords, nonverbal sounds, and pauses. Then the draft is checked for accuracy, preferably by another person working independently. In their final form, these drafts are triple spaced to allow space for the coding symbols. The transcripts then are claused, as shown in the example in which I have applied the Threat Scale (Table 4.2). This procedure is a very careful one. Each whole verbal communication is read once for meaning and then again to find themes to tally in each content category of the scale. Final tallies are arrived at only after at least one more reading. The raw scores are tallied in conjunction with the appropriate weights and are subjected to a square root correction, resulting in a total Threat Scale score. Such scaled scores can be calculated separately for each subscale. Learning to use the content categories is best done with others, for example, in therapy supervision, where it can provide a valuable training for the "listening ear" of the novice therapist.

The available information about the reliability and validity of this Threat Scale is highly encouraging (Gottschalk, 1982; Gottschalk et al., 1986; Viney, 1983). The most important form of reliability for this method is intersubjective agreement between independent assessors. Although the range of coefficients between them has been from .76-.96 over some 10 studies, the average has remained .90. Also the tests of differences in the means of the independent score distributions have revealed none. In terms of internal consistency, the Threat subscales intercorrelate differently for samples from different populations of clients, making separate contributions to the total score. Information about the consistency of the scores over occasions is also important, although for the continually changing people who are the clients and therapists of personal construct

TABLE 4.1 Definitions of Threat Scale Categories, Examples With Weights and Scoring Examples (after the Anxiety Scale of Gottschalk, Winget, & Gleser, 1969)

1. Death—references to death, dying, threat of death, or anxiety about death experienced by or occurring to:
   a. self (3), e.g., "The car was coming straight at me."
   b. animate others (2), e.g., "I went to her funeral last year."
   c. inanimate objects destroyed (1), e.g., "These flowers are beginning to die."
   d. denial of death anxiety (1), e.g., "Going to funerals doesn't bother me."
2. Mutilation (castration)—references to injury, tissue, or physical damage, or anxiety about injury or threat of such experienced by or occurring to:
   a. self (3), e.g., "I broke my leg doing it."
   b. animate others (2), e.g., "The cat bit the dog's ear."
   c. inanimate objects (1), e.g., "The vase was chipped."
   d. denial (1), e.g., "I never worry about their hurting themselves."
3. Separation—references to desertion, abandonment, loneliness, ostracism, loss of support, falling, loss of love or love object, or threat of such experienced by or occurring to:
   a. self (3), e.g., "My husband has left me."
   b. animate others (2), e.g., "My son was sent away."
   c. inanimate objects (1), e.g., "It was a desolate house."
   d. denial (1), e.g., "I don't mind that they don't talk to me."
4. Guilt—references to adverse criticism, abuse, condemnation, moral disapproval, guilt, or threat of such experienced by:
   a. self (3), e.g., "I drink too much."
   b. animate others (2), e.g., "My mother had no use for the man I married."
   d. denial (1), e.g., "That's not my fault."
5. Shame—references to ridicule, inadequacy, shame, embarrassment, humiliation, overexposure of deficiencies or private details, or threat of such experienced by:
   a. self (3), e.g., "I'm lost for words."
   b. animate others (2), e.g., "His mother shamed him into going."
   d. denial (1), e.g., "I'm not ashamed to admit it."
6. Diffuse or nonspecific—references by word or in phrases to threat and/or anxiety without distinguishing type or source of anxiety:
   a. self (3), e.g., "She had me frightened."
   b. animate others (2), e.g., "My mother was in a real state."
   d. denial (1), e.g., "I didn't worry about that."

therapy, high consistency of this kind would not be expected. In fact the generalizability coefficients calculated across occasions for the Threat Scale scores have shown low consistency over two occasions but higher consistency over five.

TABLE 4.2 Application of the Threat Scale Categories and the Calculation of Scores

---

Scaled Score = Total Raw Score (X Weights, if appropriate) X CF + ½ CF

where CF (the Correction Factor) = $\dfrac{100}{\text{Total number of words}}$

Example of a Client's Verbal Communication
(192 Words) Scored for the Threat Scale

"I worked up at the plant for 23 years / and I like it pretty much. / And a lot of the
       4a3   4a3

girls were jealous of me working, putting out so much work / and they made it pretty hard
                                                                  5a3

for me at times. But I stuck there anyway. / I don't know what to say. / Well, I got caught
   2a3   2a3

in one of the machines and got hurt. / My finger was mashed up./ And then, when the plant
       3a3   3a3

closed / everybody had to leave, put out. / And that kind of upset me too for a while. / I was
   6a4

really pretty afraid / when I first come in for these treatments / but then I found / it didn't
   6d1   6d1   6d1

bother me none at all. / So I've got over that, over that fear now. / I can take them every

time with no fear. / And I wish / my son would come up soon. / I been here three weeks
                       3u3   4b2

now / and he still ain't been out to see me. / He got into trouble with the law last year / and I
   6u3

worry some about him. /

Tabulation of Verbal Communication Coded for Threat
Correction Factor (CF) = 0.52

Subcategory	Total weight	Raw score
Death	0	—
Mutilation	6	3.12
2a3 x 2		
Separation	9	4.69
3a3 x 3		
Guilt	8	4.17
4a3 x 2		
4b2 x 1		
Shame	3	1.56
5a3 x 1		
Diffuse	10	5.21
6a4 x 1		
6a3 x 1		
6d1 x 3		
Total	36	18.75

Scaled score $= \overline{18.75 + \text{½ CF}}$
              $= 4.36$

The Threat Scale fulfills its purpose. It has validity, as indicated by a network of information about its scores based on empirical research that has been built up over the past 20 years. Although it has proved independent of gender, age, and educational level of clients, this scale is significantly correlated with reports of threat by self and expert assessors and with physiological measures of threat. The Threat Scale has discriminated effectively the threats involved in having relatives undergoing emergency medical treatment from people who did not (Bunn & Clarke, 1979) and predicted which patients would rehabilitate or recover well (Viney, 1990). They also have evaluated effectively the outcomes of psychotherapy, showing the predicted decline in experienced threat (Viney et al., 1985, 1989).

Assessing Perceived Competence by Use of a Content Analysis Scale

The Origin Scale (Westbrook & Viney, 1980) assesses the personal meanings that people ascribe to their actions as determined by their own choice, rather than by forces beyond their control. De Charms (1968) used the concept of *origin* to describe the first type of meaning, with *pawn* as the second. Because such perceptions, he argued, fluctuate from occasion to occasion, they are best tapped in accounts of clients' spontaneously spoken thoughts, so this constructivist method is more appropriate than the questionnaires that have been used for this purpose. The assessment of perceived competence is appropriately considered here in association with threat because it represents the degree to which people feel able to deal with threat. This concept is therefore similar to that of self-efficacy (Bandura, 1984). The "Origin" Scale is therefore also temporarily renamed the Competence Scale, and its content scale categories and scoring examples are provided in Table 4.3. Because competence must be expressed about the self only and not about others if it is to be effective, only first-person statements are scored for this scale. And no weights are considered useful. Otherwise the process of applying these content categories and calculating the scaled score is the same as for the Threat Scale. The content categories of Intention, Exertion, Ability, Influence, and Cause all contribute to a total Competence Scale score.

The evidence for the reliability and validity of this scale is similarly encouraging (Viney, 1983; Westbrook & Viney, 1980). The intersubjective agreement between independent assessors has ranged from .90-.94,

TABLE 4.3 Definitions of Competence Scale Categories, Examples With Weights and Scoring Examples (after Westbrook & Viney, 1980)

A person is considered to perceive her- or himself as an origin if:

1. *Self-expresses intention* (says that she or he intended, planned, decided; mentions plans, purposes, goals, e.g., "I planned the party," "We decided to have a child.")

2. *Self-expresses exertion or trying* (describes her or his efforts to achieve some stated or implied result, e.g., "I'm trying to find out," "It took quite a bit of energy to load the boxes.")

3. *Self-expresses ability* (comments on her or his skill, competence, e.g., "I became school champion," "I'm managing very well.")

4. *Self-describes overcoming or influencing others or the environment* (e.g., "I didn't let them stop me," "The hill was steep, but I managed to climb to the top.")

5. *Self-perceived as cause or origin* (e.g., "I took control during labor," "I produced the play.")

with an average of .92, and also with no distinguishable differences between sample score means. In terms of consistency of scores over occasions, the generalizability coefficients even over five occasions were low. Perceptions of competence, as measured by these content analysis scales, seem more likely to vary over time than perceptions of threat. The validity of the Competence Scale also has a confirmatory network of information established about it. Like the Threat Scale, its scores are independent of gender and age but, as predicted, are correlated with occupational status. Its scores also have been associated with scores on other measures of these perceptions, with measures of other positive states, and with use of appropriate coping strategies showing criterion validity. They discriminated people in uncontrollable situations from those who were not, as well as youth workers from their clients, and predicted rehabilitation or recovery from physical illness, thereby showing construct validity (Viney, 1990).

A Psychotherapy Case: June W.

June's Initial Psychological Functioning and Our Therapeutic Goals

June came to a university-based clinic asking for help. Her main concerns at the age of 55 were her problems in her 30-year-old marriage, her alienation from her two adult children who were by then starting families of their own, and her internal confusion of feelings. Her personal meanings for her marriage were "30 years of frustration and hell," and even during her pretherapy assessment session with me, she was ridden with emotions such as frustration, anger, suspicion, as well as depression. Her depressive feelings were linked to feelings of rejection and loneliness and, when her depression welled up to despair, led her to explore a range of ways of committing suicide, none of which she had so far put to the test. The confusion of which she complained appeared to result from the plethora of strong emotions that she was experiencing, which were linked with her incapacity to interpret and predict many events in her life, especially those involving other people. Her anger at the people close to her showed her last ditch stands to force from them confirmation for her invalidated ways of construing.

Such were the more problematic aspects of June's functioning from my perspective. However, I also saw her as having a number of abilities that would be useful in psychotherapy. The first was her unusual ability to use words to express her personal meanings and to test her understanding of mine, combined with a down-to-earthness that seemed very practical. The second was her courage, which I saw in her accounts of several events in her life, but also in the very act of her coming to the clinic from an Anglo-Saxon community that clings fast to the idea that people should be able to manage without help. The third was her strong and sustaining religious beliefs, even though she did not, at that time, see her church community as supportive of her. Finally she demonstrated her sense of humor early, a capacity that requires ability to take a perspective on construing very similar to the perspective of constructivist psychotherapy. For example, as we began our first therapy session, she offered: "I'm trying to work out who needs the psychological attention, Job or his confidants."

June and I negotiated a list of therapeutic goals, which she began with providing order in her confusion and building better relationships, especially with her family, to whom she wished to be closer. Both of us then added to our list that she would come to have more sense of personal control and choice. I also wanted to help her see herself as both a creator of her own personal meanings and as being able to discard them in favor of new ones—that is, to see herself as both construer and reconstruer. Because she was not as yet thinking constructively, she probably did not fully understand this goal when we set it initially. Nor did she have the same confidence that I had that her accepting and experiencing more fully some of her feelings would be useful. Of course, at that stage, her experience of those feelings was that they seemed likely to overwhelm her. After the initial assessment interview, we decided on four weekly sessions of brief psychotherapy that she consented to have taped, on the condition that she could wipe out anything that she wanted to at the end of those sessions. She later released all of the tapes for my use.

The Course of Psychotherapy With June

After some initial anger and suspicion, June moved quickly into a trusting relationship with me in which her ability to work therapeutically proved most impressive. For example, during the first therapy session, I was able to help her reconstrue whatever was invalidating her construing by using our relationship to show what was happening. With most clients, I would explore tentatively such transference only much later in the therapy. By transference, I mean June's transfer of earlier construing to me, without testing whether it was appropriate.

Linda	I feel that you still, that you're carrying around some anger from other kinds of experiences. Certainly nothing you've told me about your husband endears him to me. But um, I also remember that you had a fair amount of anger for me the first time we met. And you didn't. . . . You were very polite and didn't actually express it; but it was there; and you didn't know anything about me at that point.
June	Pretty unfair of me, wasn't it.
Linda	It doesn't matter if it was fair or unfair.
June	See it's probably not you personally. It's um what you represent.
Linda	To you.
June	To me.
Linda	And that's what I mean, that it's the tapes that you recorded earlier in your life somewhere which you still keep playing when you come into new situations.
June	Yeah, probably peers, school teachers. Forgive me for that. You don't really look like a school teacher. Mmm. Of course.
June	I don't want to hurt you. It's the last thing I want to do. Um, I'm trying to think. Well, OK, why was I angry at you? I mean, if you hadn't said so, I wouldn't have noticed. So it wasn't that high on me. Um, ministers, doctors, everybody who has hurt me, I suppose. I've got another doctor coming up tomorrow who's going to talk

	me into a hysterectomy. You know, he's my enemy emotionally; mentally, he's my friend.
Linda	A lot of those people are authority figures.
June	Oh, I said peers, my parents. I hate being continuously told submit ourselves to your husband. That went out with straw hats.

She also responded eagerly to my suggestion in our first session that looking at the meanings of dreams might be helpful to getting in touch with her less verbalized personal meanings by reporting a dream at the beginning of the second session. To make sense of this dream, I provided the Gestalt interpretation technique. I find this technique easy for clients to use after formal therapy has finished to continue to conduct their own therapeutic tests of their construing and its implications for their actions.

June	Twice this week I've dreamt a similar type of dream of being falsely accused. If people tell me I'm a murderer when I'm a murderer, well hallelujah! But if they tell me I'm a thief when I'm not a thief, well, you know, that bugs me! I don't know why, tell me why.
Linda	Well, you tell me about the dream.
June	Oh well, the first one was um, there was a lady there. And she said, "You've done so and so." I just forget who it was. It wasn't terribly important what she'd accused me of; but I suppose it bugs me. The next thing, her husband stood behind her and said, "No, June didn't do that." So one for June, you know. And then of course in the dream I was still standing there and she, this woman, had a cow with great huge horns and this cow was trying to gore me; and I was sort of dodging around the . . . some sort of a building apparatus ah to keep the cow from attacking me. That was all that that dream was about.
Linda	Mmm.
June	A couple of nights later . . . do you want to say something?
Linda	Well, let's just deal with one at a time. Do you have any ideas about what the dream means to you?
June	Well, the first thing is false accusation, you know. I don't know where people dream up these things, you know. It's my dream, but why people think I'm guilty of such and such, you know, um. Is it me that gives a false impression, or are they jealous of me and just want to put a label on me?

Linda	Mmm, there are . . . Some of the people who are interested in interpreting dreams consider that because it's your dream, then it's you that's in every part of the dream.
June	Yes, I'm the wife and the husband and the cow.
Linda	Right.
June	Yes. Ah.
Linda	Just take one at a time.
June	Yes, I don't know how I . . . This woman is dead now as a matter of fact. I don't know how I relate to her.
Linda	Could she be some part of you?
June	I hardly know her. Used to speak to her over the phone. I met her once. Saw her a couple of times in the street from a distance. I don't um, you know, know that I relate particularly to her. I relate more to her husband.
Linda	Um, even the way you describe her as not feeling that you relate particularly to her. That could still mean it's a part of yourself that you dreamt about, couldn't it? Because you could be dreaming about part of yourself that you don't know very well.

This led off into our exploring her constructs of rejection, and then our dream interpretation was resumed.

Linda	Now what about the next figure in the dream, her husband? Um, what um . . . you said that you felt you knew the husband, when you looked a bit better. What other association do you have?
June	Oh that's rather involved. His wife is now gone; and he cares about me. But um, we're not that close. Could've been but . . . that's probably why he stuck up for me. Then how does that relate to me, as he is me?
Linda	Yes, think about that.
June	Well, I could understand more, him being me than the wife being me, uh, probably because we're two peas in a pod. We've probably both got the same hang-ups so, you know, that's probably what our relationship is based on. But there must be another part of me, one who accuses me at the emotional level and another part of me who stands by me. Sort of I'm at the top, like a triangle.
Linda	Oh, that's not all there is to you yet, but you know, you can only explore a couple of facets at a time, I think.

June   So in actual fact, I've got two people within me arguing against
            myself.
Linda   One against you, and one for you.

June also was able to use metaphors, not only to express her personal
meanings but to reconstruct them. She enjoyed this, and so did I, and this
mutual enjoyment, together with her sense of humor, added a quality of
playfulness to some of our more therapeutic interactions. Her metaphor
of ship and crew in our last session serves as an example.

Linda   Well, as you say, the process of self-exploration has certainly be-
            gun, and it's certainly not confined to what goes on between the
            two of us; it's going on in between our meetings. So I'm wondering
            whether you feel that you need me to help the process along or
            whether you'd like to take off as captain of your own ship?
June   I would like to try and think as the captain; but I know when I get
            into rough seas I'm going to need a good navigator.
Linda   (laughs)
June   See, it's alright while I'm in port. But now I'm heading out . . . and
            I don't know of anybody else who, um with enough qualifications
            to be able to truthfully (pause) assist me and get to where I'm going.
            I mean we've got so many quacks . . . ah oh this is what you need
            or that's what you need and I've tried them all; none of them will
            work.
Linda   I don't uh, I'm not suggesting that you should see somebody else
            at this stage or indeed that we should stop having these sessions;
            but the end result of the sessions, that I want to see, is you out there
            as captain of your own ship.
June   Well, I think I'm ready for it. When I get into rough seas, I'll feel
            the need of some support. Will I be able to phone and make an
            appointment?

There was another humorous use of this metaphor at the end of this session

Linda   Well, about all I can say to you is, "Safe journey."
June   Thank you. I'll send you a cablegram.
Linda   (laughing) OK. Well, um. . .
June   "Captain and ship doing well!"

The Achievements of June's Therapy

Many of our joint goals for this therapy were achieved. June began to experience some order in her confusion, but this was tempered realistically by her recognition that she would always find her personal meanings highly complex. She opened our last session with this comment.

June   I thought I had all the answers last Friday morning; but I'm not sure and I wanted to see what you thought. It was just something that you said last week that triggered off a whole train of thinking about why I chose my husband.

That relationship also improved as she reconstrued it. As she was able to share her own perspective with her husband more openly, he was able to see things a little more from her point of view. She also reported being approached by the daughter from whom she had been estranged.

June   My daughter rang me up yesterday, and she said, "Mum, I love you" (crying). Oh, she said it, but I haven't heard from her. She also said to me, "Mum, I've felt so terrible to think that you haven't seen our baby grow up, growing up." She's only 7 months old. I missed about 3 months. (pause) I just said, "Look, Love, I love you too," and she burst into tears (crying).

Linda   And you burst into tears. (laughing)

June   Well, something's happened. Something's triggered off this. I didn't expect to see that child. I bought a doll for her last Saturday and, silly me, I said, "Here's this doll, but I may never be able to give it to her 'til she's 21. It will be no use then." The hardest thing is faith for me. The biggest thing is doubting.

Linda   Well, you went ahead and bought it though.

June   I did. And I can give it to her today.

June also came to acknowledge that she herself had created her own construct of rejection or acceptance by others in relationships and that she could choose to apply it quite differently.

June   Maybe I'm getting rid of my great big sign that says "Please Reject Me."

And she could do so in ways that would give her more sources of validation and enjoyment.

Monitoring June's Perceptions of Threat and Her Therapist's References to Them Using Content Analysis Categories and Scales

This example of assessment of client and therapist using the content analysis scales and categories focused on June's perception of threat and competence, together with her therapist's references to these perceptions. The extent of the expression of threat and competence by June is measured by the content analysis scales and categories, and their course over therapy sessions is plotted. Then their variations over session segments, regardless of session, are examined. The same procedure is followed for my references to her perceptions of threat and then competence. Then I apply the content analysis categories that form the basis for these scales to clarify whether certain patterns of comment and response can be found, first for the client's comment followed by the therapist's response, and then for the therapist's comment followed by the client's response. The frequency of these patterns is examined, together with whether they vary over sessions. Examples of the client's and therapist's contributions (scored separately) are provided, followed by examples of the patterns containing comment and response. I then consider what has been learned about June and our therapy from this application of the method. Here I have had the luxury of applying the content analysis categories and scales after our therapy was complete. They can be used, however, to assess the contributions of client and therapist, as well as the processes of therapy, at any time while the therapy continues.

June's Perceptions of Threat

June was unfortunately expressing many perceptions of threat. In her first therapy session, almost half of her verbalized meanings were of this kind, and this number decreased very little over the four sessions (Figure 4.1). Some excerpts from this first of four sessions of our therapy show

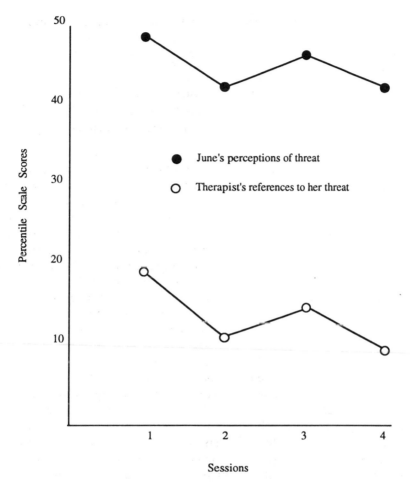

Figure 4.1. Threat Percentile Scale Scores Over Sessions Assessing Both June's Perceptions of Threat and Her Therapist's References to Them.

the kinds of threat that she was sharing with me. They involved her perceived failure to meet the standards of others, her apparent isolation from them, and her emotional exhaustion. The first such excerpt comes from a long monologue on which June had embarked, part of which is reproduced here.

June   Yesterday someone phoned me, crying for help. It was obvious
            from the desperation in her voice, you know . . . and I said, "What's
            wrong?" and she said, "I feel terrible." I said, "Do you want me to
            come and get you?" With that, she passed out at the other end of
            the phone. . . . So I rang the Assistant Pastor's wife, who said to
            leave her there. I said, "Look, I wouldn't do that to a dog." She said,
            "She's only using you. Leave her there." And then she got stuck
            into me, "The trouble with you, June, is that you never forgive."

This excerpt showing the threat of her isolation comes from a later interaction between us.

June   I can't see anything wrong with the person I am inside. She's
            helpless, yes, but what's the great sin about that?
Linda   Hmm . . . I guess what I really can't understand is why you need
            to protect yourself so much from other people if you feel comfort-
            able with yourself.
June   Because I'm lonely, I suppose, I'm comfortable with me but there's
            that loneliness that, well . . . Do you relate to people? If you be
            what they want you to be, you're not yourself. If you be yourself,
            then they misunderstand you.

And later again her emotional exhaustion from having dealt with so much
threat was apparent.

Linda   I'm getting the impression today that there is a great gulf between
            your head and your heart.
June   Oh, that's for sure.
Linda   Is there a particular reason why the gulf is bigger than usual today?
June   (sighs) I probably have to divide myself to ease the pain. I am in
            emotional pain at the moment. Not as far as suicidal or anything.
            I'm just looking for a means of, oh well, let's get on with doing some-
            thing and forget about it. But I don't forget. It's tormenting me.

   It would have been useful not only to know about the course of June's
perceptions of threat over therapy sessions but also over segments of those
sessions. When her Threat Scale scores were plotted over four equal time
interval segments of our sessions, they showed that she tended to express
somewhat less threat as she approached the middle of each session,
compared with at the beginning or second half of it (Figure 4.2).

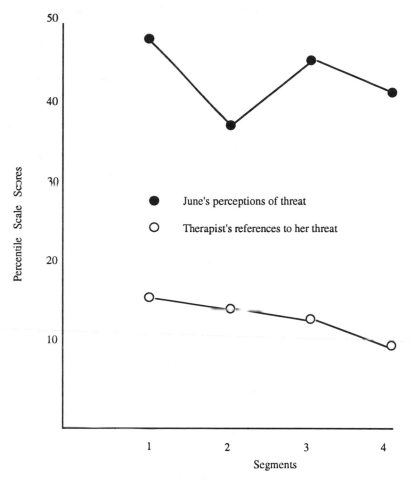

Figure 4.2. Threat Percentile Scale Scores Over Session Segments Assessing Both June's Perceptions of Threat and Her Therapist's References to Them.

June's Therapist's References
to Her Perceptions of Threat

As June's therapist, I both intended to and proved to have been highly selective in referring to only about a quarter of her expressions of threat, and this proportion decreased only slightly from the early sessions to the later ones (Figure 4.1). Some further excerpts from our first session show the kinds of threats she expressed that I chose to acknowledge. These too dealt with her perceived failure to meet others' standards, her isolation through rejection, and the often quite violent self-rejection that she sometimes experienced as a result.

Linda	Didn't we just establish that you are not offensive to everyone else, only some people?
June	It takes a little while to get through my mind because, even though I can accept it emotionally, the wounds are causing me to say, "Hey, you're not, you know." The emotions are arguing back with me.
Linda	And that's really why you keep your covered wagon covers down.
June	Ooh, yes, I mean, I allow my mental washing to be aired.
Linda	What you are really thinking behind those canvasses is, you know, if people really knew me, then they wouldn't want to be close to me.

I responded to her self-blame in this excerpt.

Linda	The question you need to answer for yourself is whether these problems with people occur because they have a strange set of beliefs about human beings and maybe you need a new set of friends? Or is it because somehow in your relationship this kind of thing comes up; in which case, it has more to do with you than them.
June	OK . . . If the whole class fails an examination, the teacher's at fault, not the class. If half the class fails, it's the pupils' fault. Right?

The final excerpt showing my references to June's perceptions of threat focuses on her identification with the smelly poor of Charles Dickens's day toward the end of our first therapy session.

Linda	You said you are, said you are somebody with the stench of the gutter on you. Tell me more about that.
June	I don't know. I guess it's the difference between the two types, you know in, you know, the total opposite of June, a clean person who lives in a nice home, and a miserable person that's . . . I feel pushed in that regard, I don't feel that I'm laying down there because I want to lay down there. That's part of the trap I suppose.

Linda	And the stench?
June	I thought I just answered that question. Maybe I haven't.
Linda	It's the feeling that I'm still wanting you to flow with.
June	I'm trying. I don't feel as though I smell. It's also related to rags. You know, the beggar and the rich man, the rich glutton. I'm sure you know the story in the Bible.

My references to June's perceptions of threat varied little over the segments of our sessions (see Figure 4.2).

June's Perceptions of Threat
Followed by Her Therapist's References to Them

The analyses that I have reported so far have used the content analysis scale to look at the contributions to therapy of client and therapist separately. I now apply content analysis scale categories to the text of our client-therapist dialogue to units that include both of our references to June's perception to threat. Some 12-15% of changes from June's floor holding to mine contained this emotional expression of June's threat followed by my references to it, and this percentage changed little over the four therapy sessions. This pattern proved to occur significantly more often than by chance (see Table 4.4). When its occurrence over adjacent and later floor holdings was monitored, it was completed significantly more often later than in the adjacent one (see Table 4.4). I acknowledged June's experience of threat, but only certain examples of it. I then encouraged her to explore and expand on her construing of these examples. The kinds of units scored are now described.

In our second therapy session, this interchange occurred.

June	I really wasn't wanted.
Linda	You feel your parents didn't want you; but why do you blame yourself for being born?

And this interchange occurred at the beginning of our third session.

| June | There's more to be done in this area, that's going on deep down within me. |

TABLE 4.4 Results of Chi Square and Hierarchical Log Linear Model Tests of Association Between Patterns of June's and Her Therapist's Use of the Threat and Competence Categories

THREAT

Client, then Therapist
  Occurrence of pattern in adjacent floor holdings (chi square)
    $\chi^2 = 5.04$, $df = 1$, $p < .02$.
  Frequency of pattern over adjacent and later floor holdings (hierarchical log linear models[*])
    $\chi^2 = 6.12$, $df = 3$, $p < .01$, log linear parameter estimate (lambda) = 1.40, $S.E. = .41$, so $Z = 3.33$, $p < .01$.
Therapist, then Client
  Occurrence of pattern in adjacent floor holdings (chi square)
    $\chi^2 = 13.85$, $df = 1$, $p < .01$.
  Frequency of pattern over adjacent and later floor holdings (hierarchical log linear models[*])
    $\chi^2 = 10.65$, $df = 6$, $p < .01$, Lambda = .81, $S.E. = 39$, so $Z = 3.10$, $p < .01$.

COMPETENCE

Client, then Therapist
  Occurrence of pattern in adjacent floor holdings (chi square)
    $\chi^2 = 8.99$, $df = 1$, $p < .01$.
  Frequency of pattern over adjacent and later floor holdings (hierarchical log linear models[*])
    $\chi^2 = 1.68$, $df = 3$, $p < .01$, Lambda = .81, $S.E. = .39$, so $Z = 2.10$, $p < .01$.
Therapist, then Client
  Occurrence of pattern in adjacent floor holdings (chi square)
    $\chi^2 = 12.52$ $df = 1$, $p < .01$.
  Frequency of pattern over therapy sessions (chi square)
    $\chi^2 = 8.52$, $df = 3$, $p < .05$.
  Frequency of pattern over adjacent and later floor holdings (hierarchical log linear models[*])
    $\chi^2 = 6.64$, $df = 6$, $p < .01$, Lambda = .74, $S.E. = .26$, so $Z = 2.29$, $p < .01$.

[*]Two-way, 2 x 2 or 2 x 4 contingency tables were used for all the analyses reported in this table except these. See Tabachnik and Fidell (1989) for details of this multiway frequency analysis.

Linda   There is obviously something important there and is taking a long time to come up to the surface, so it would be surprising if we could deal with it in just one session.

Both of these interchanges involved June's therapist referring immediately to her perception of threat, but sometimes this occurred later in the session, as in these excerpts.

June   My one brother and my three sisters you know: "Hole," they used to call me. "Little Hole's no good."

Linda   (several exchanges about June's anger at this treatment were then followed by this) You do still have part of yourself that's inside of yourself, that respects yourself.

This one was from our second session.

June   I used to think my house was a pig sty.

Linda   (later, after a description by June of her guilty fears about house-keeping, this acknowledgment by her therapist occurred) You don't quite know what you feel now, but at least you don't feel the bad things you used to feel.

June's Perceptions of Threat
Following Her Therapist's References to Them

Content analysis categories can be applied to the therapy text in the same way to examine the unit of June and her therapist's speech in which her perceptions of threat occurred after my reference to them. They too proved more frequent than by chance occurrence but also more prevalent over later floor holdings (see Table 4.4). In the first session, as much as 80% of changes from my floor holding to June's contained these units, although this declined severely to 40% in the second session. It rose then to the fourth session (see Figure 4.3), but the increase was not statistically significant.

The type of adjacent floor holdings scored will be described with some examples, and then more examples with delayed responses will be examined. Those in which June's reply followed immediately included her focusing on her hurt and fear. In the second session, her therapist started this interchange.

Linda   You're crying because you feel hurt.

June   Yes, I'm hurt, lonely but (continues to cry) but why? (sighs) I'm in turmoil in my stomach. But why? It's locked in down there isn't it? (sighs again) I have spiritualism (crying). Some terrible things happened to me as a kid. Yet when I really analyze this, I guess they wouldn't seem so terrible. Like pictures falling off walls, little

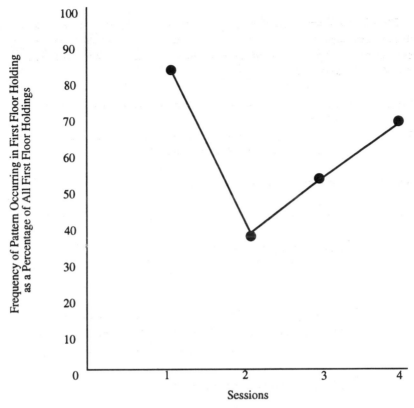

Figure 4.3. Percentage of June's Perceptions of Threat Following Her Therapist's References to Them Occurring in the First Floor Holding Over Four Therapy Sessions.

> blue lights around the room, my mother going off in a trance. (continues crying)

And in the third session, this exchange involved her fear.

Linda   Is this brutality part of what you are frightened of then, or is the most important thing the possible supernatural element in your relationship with your husband?

June   The supernatural. I mean, this is where I was last week. My mother's spiritualism—I'm scared of it.

Then in some units the therapist's references to June's perceptions of threat came some time before her eventual acknowledgment of them. Both examples come from the third session, and they deal with her more hidden threats and frustrations.

Linda   Sometimes it seems hard for you to understand what is going on within you.

June   (10 minutes passed before she picked this up) I'm just a little thick, you see. It takes a while to get through to me.

And then the frustration came.

Linda   I think that what I don't hear so much of is that frustration that you were thinking about before.

June   (after considering some of her recent achievements for a minute or two) I get upset when people criticize me and say, "June, you don't get up and do anything." And I know inside I can.

Monitoring June's Perceptions of Competence and Her Therapist's References to Them Using Content Analysis Categories and Scales

June's Perceptions of Competence and Helplessness

June's reported perceptions of herself as competent proved to be encouragingly as frequent during the first session of therapy as her references to sources of threat had been. They were fewer in the second session, but they then increased to a peak in the last session (see Figure 4.4). Some excerpts from this first session are now provided. They deal with her initial statements of helplessness that contradict her perceptions of competence. Then some of her expressions of competence from the last session are presented.

The first two examples of helplessness that were identified with the parallel Pawn Scale (Westbrook & Viney, 1980) dealt with her early attempts to understand the emotional implications of her construing and actions.

June   I feel crazy mixed up today.

Linda   Tell me about how it feels, not what it thinks like but what it feels like.

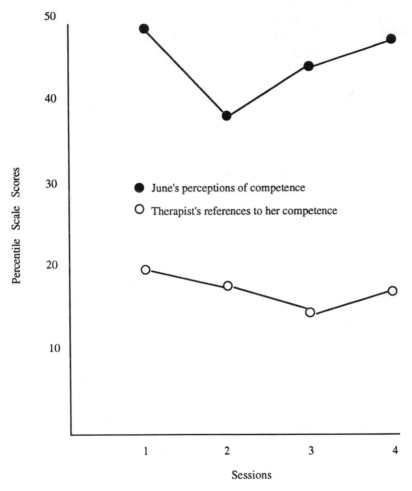

Figure 4.4. Competence Percentile Scale Scores Over Sessions Assessing Both June's Perceptions of Competence and Her Therapist's References to Them.

June   Blough! You want a better explanation than that. (sighs) Probably like a lot of razor blades, sharp!

This was followed soon by this example.

Linda   You can't think of anything else but being sad.

June	That's about it. Yeah!
Linda	And even when you seem to be feeling something else, it's often just a facade.
June	That's right, I mean you've got to smile. You can't wear your heart on your sleeve. But I don't know how to do it.

Some of her perceptions of competence expressed in the last session, however, were in considerable contrast to these expressions of helplessness. Both examples have to do with her getting in touch with her own power. In the first of these, it was during a reflective monologue.

| June | When I really get to grips with myself, I really feel that, OK, I am a person. I just think, I am a person, I have every right to be here. I can say, "Now look, Mother, if you say that I shouldn't be here, and, Father, if you say I shouldn't be here . . . God said I should be here. He has predestined us." |

And here is another example from later in this last session.

| June | If I can get right before I start my studies, I'll do those much more easily. And I'll be able to give my whole being to achieve what I'm after. I've always felt like a six-cylinder motor car that is only operating on two, maybe four cylinders and never gets to full power. |
| Linda | So you are beginning to accept for yourself that you are a woman of very special strengths and capabilities. |

June's perceptions of competence were examined also by plotting her Competence Scale scores over segments of sessions. She tended to express more competence in the second segment of each session, although she expressed less at the end of the session (see Figure 4.5).

June's Therapist's References
to Her Perceptions of Competence

While I proved to have responded very selectively to June's perceptions of threat, I provided about half as many references to her competence as she did. This proportion decreased slightly in our second and third therapy sessions but increased slightly in our fourth (see Figure 4.4). Excerpts from our first session show the areas of helplessness, of feeling controlled

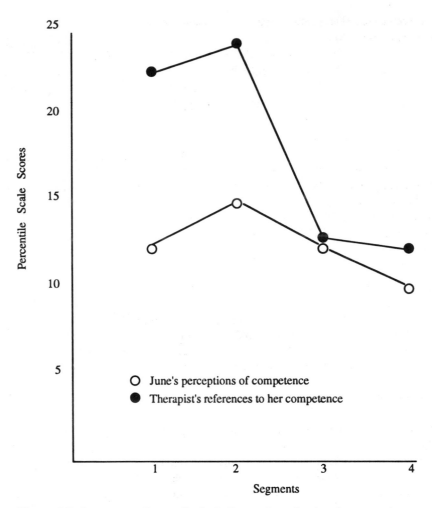

Figure 4.5. Competence Percentile Scale Scores Over Session Segments Assessing Both June's Perceptions of Competence and Her Therapist's References to Them.

and frustrated, in which I sought to acknowledge her construing. I have included also some excerpts from our last session, in which I tried to confirm her construing of her improving relationships with others.

In our first session, I referred to these statements of helplessness by June:

June   They're pushing me to the point where I don't want to get up.
Linda   Who's pushing you?

And this was another statement that I apparently considered important too.

June   I don't know. I'm so confused. What's the use.
Linda   It's all part of the helpless, frustrated feeling.
June   I guess so. Because what good do I do? Where am I going to get?

In our last session, one of the main areas of construing of her own competence that was supported for June proved to be her ability to relate positively with others.

June   This morning I'm beginning to think I'll turn my back on the church.
Linda   Well . . . there are other churches.
June   That's right. I'm a little inclined to think that they'll all be bad.
Linda   But you're pretty sure about the question I've been asking. You do feel that you can receive love from other people?

The same theme occurred in this excerpt.

Linda   It's important for you to be able to say about yourself, "I am honest and outspoken."
June   Not particularly. It gets me into trouble. But I like honesty in other people, in friends. So maybe it's alright.
Linda   It's a part of your view of yourself then, that you are honest and outspoken.

The references to June's competence by her therapist occurred most often in earlier segments of our therapy sessions—in fact, the end of its first half. It was in the second half of our sessions that my references to her expressions of competence strongly decreased to parallel her own (see Figure 4.5).

June's Perceptions of Competence
Following Her Therapist's References to Them

Both of our references to June's perceptions of herself as competent, with her references preceding mine, will be dealt with here. Some 35% of changes from her floor holding to mine during the first therapy session contained June's expression of competence that was followed by my reference to it. This percentage was relatively constant over the four therapy sessions. This pattern proved to occur significantly more often in adjacent floor holdings than by chance, and it was completed even more often in later than adjacent floor holding (Table 4.4). I acknowledged June's experiences of competence, but only selected examples of it. The kinds of units scored, with examples of both immediate and later responses from me, are now described.

In our second therapy session, this interchange about her own psychological functioning occurred.

June   I am self-critical.

Linda   But then there is another part of you who knows that June is a worthwhile person; and these are two antagonistic forces in your own personality.

June   And how do I bring reconciliation to those two?

Linda   Being aware of them is the first step.

Later in the same session, another example deals with June's recent baiting of her husband.

June   I just wanted him to realize that I am there.

Linda   Well, what if you tried to tell him how you feel?

Other examples but with my response occurring later are now given. The first comes from our second session.

June   I try to find out what is going on about June. . . . (and this response occurred a few units later)

Linda   Do you feel you understand more about yourself now?

And in the next session, this example occurred.

June	Well, OK, I've climbed the mountain and got to the top, and now I can see my way clear down the valley.
Linda	(and a few interchanges later) You seem much more . . . relaxed, self-possessed, more comfortable with yourself today.

June's Perceptions of Competence
Following Her Therapist's References to Them

When the units of analysis consisted of the therapist's references to June's perceptions of competence followed by her own perceptions of competence, 75% of the changes to new floor holdings contained these units. This pattern occurred significantly more often than by chance and was completed more often in later rather than adjacent floor holdings (see Table 4.4). The frequency of the pattern declined sharply from the first to the second session but increased in the third and fourth sessions, with the increase over sessions proving statistically significant (see Figure 4.6 and Table 4.4).

The kinds of adjacent units that were scored are described now, with some examples; more delayed examples will be examined later. Those in which June's reply followed immediately included both personal and interpersonal themes, as in examples of earlier patterns in the therapist-client dialogue.

Linda	So you feel it may be one of those old tapes we were talking about last week which you keep playing to yourself, even though it's not relevant now. It was something, you, you know, laid down as a tape when you were a child and now you're still playing it.
June	Yeah, there's probably a little girl inside of me still who is wanting to be heard.

And this example concerning her husband occurred in the same session.

Linda	What is it you want from him?
June	I just want to be loved and accepted. And he's beginning to love me now.

Both delayed examples come from our third session, with the first focusing on June's ability to accept people who are different from her.

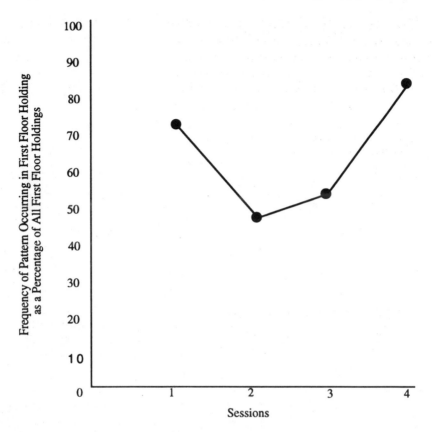

Figure 4.6. Percentage of June's Perceptions of Competence Followed by Her Therapist's References to Them Over Four Therapy Sessions.

Linda   It's one of your strengths that you can take that kind of attitude in that situation.

June   (a few minutes later) I relate better to men than to women. Although I think I have related pretty well to you, because you're not a talker that goes on and on.

The second had to do with her own interpretation of future dreams.

Linda   When we dream, we use our own symbols that are based on the experience we have had.

June   (a few minutes later also) I am looking for a white horse, with my knight in shining armor.

What Has Been Learned About June's Psychotherapy Using Content Analysis Categories and Scales

The application of just two of the available sets of content analysis categories and scales has revealed much about June and our psychotherapy. The acuity of the method of content category analysis in identifying qualitatively significant aspects of my client's construing and her interaction with me has been demonstrated in many of the examples I have given. It provided me with awareness of many aspects of June's and even of my own contribution to our therapy to which I had not previously had access. In this summary, however, I want to focus on what has been achieved by the application of content analysis categories and scales to provide quantitative information and how it fitted with the goals, progress, and outcomes of our therapy.

June's perceptions of threat— and there is evidence that they interfere with therapeutic movement—proved initially to be common and appeared to become somewhat less common over the four sessions of therapy. They were initially much associated with her confusion of feelings and poor interpersonal relationships. The tendency was for her to prefer to deal with them during the middle periods of any session. My references to these contributions of threat from June proved to be highly selective, and they became less common as our sessions went on. I tended to make more references to them toward the end of our sessions. When our contributions to therapy concerning threat to June were considered together, first with hers preceding mine, they proved relatively rare but more frequent than by chance. They were more often completed later rather than immediately after June's comment and varied little in frequency over our sessions. With my references to threat preceding hers, these patterns were significantly more common than chance. Although they decreased somewhat over sessions, this decrease was not statistically significant. The initial analyses of the quantitative data were graphical, but those that followed involved the testing of nonparametric statistical models.

June's perceptions of her own competence, which have been demon-strated to be related to therapeutic gains, proved different from those for her perceptions of threat. The percentage of her statements of this kind was actually quite similar to that for threats, but it increased over sessions. These comments were associated with her gradual establishment of per-sonal control and choice, together with beginning to see herself as a con-struer and so able to reconstrue. She made most of her relevant comments toward the middle of sessions rather than the end. As her therapist, I re-ferred to her competence about half as much as she did; my frequency changed little over our therapy sessions. I tended to provide such com-ments toward the beginning of sessions. When our joint contributions to therapy were considered with hers preceding mine, they proved more common than for threat and more common than by chance. They were more often completed in my later floor holdings rather than in the first one after hers and were constant over sessions. With my references to com-petence preceding hers, these patterns were more frequent than by chance. Although they decreased over sessions, that decrease was not statistically significant.

Evaluation of the Use of Content Analysis Categories and Scales in Constructivist Psychotherapeutic Assessment

In this chapter, I have attempted to show how content analysis catego-ries and scales can be used to assess the personal meanings of clients and, reflexively, of therapists too during psychotherapy. The underlying as-sumptions are either constructivist assumptions or compatible with those assumptions, as I have shown for content analysis categories alone and for content analysis scales. Both can be used to listen to meanings that have been constructed, especially those negotiated between client and therapist in the context of psychotherapy. They also can be applied re-flexively so that the same constructivist assumptions can be made not only about client and therapist but also about assessors from outside that relationship.

Two sets of content categories and scales to assess the personal mean-ings of client threat and competence were examined in some detail. Then I introduced an account of my psychotherapy with June. My initial construing of her, our negotiated goals, and the course of our therapy were described, together with our outcomes and an overview of how the content analysis categories and scales were applied to illuminate our therapy. The extent of my client's perceptions of threat to herself and of her own competence, with how and when they occurred, were assessed, as were my references to both of these perceptions. Then the patterns of our combined references to them, hers first and then mine, were also considered in terms of how and when they occurred. A summary was provided of the therapeutically useful information about June and her therapy with me that has been supplied by this application of the method. In this example of therapy, it was supplied after therapy had concluded, but this methodology can be used during therapy.

It remains for me to consider the advantages and disadvantages of this method of assessment, by first examining the content analysis categories and then the content analysis scales. The content analysis categories proved adept at identifying some of the most important personal meanings expressed by clients and therapists; they provided this information in a form readily accessible to others. I also found that employing these *content analysis categories* can provide a useful training for those inexperienced in clinical assessment or even in therapy, because doing so provides useful training in listening to exactly what clients (and therapists) say. For the same reasons, it provides a viable way to monitor the progress of therapy. Some current developments in the programming of personal computers suggest that much of the organization of this kind of qualitative information will be accelerated in the future. In terms of disadvantages, however, applying these categories alone results in somewhat problematic evidence of reliability and validity, and the categories are limited to, at best, a form of categorical measurement that makes even simple comparisons cumbersome and that allows only the use of nonparametric statistics.

The *content analysis scales* were developed to answer these criticisms of the content analysis categories. They provide measurement of demonstrated interjudge reliability and criterion-based and construct validity with which comparisons both within and between clients and therapists are made relatively easy. The level of measurement that they achieve also makes possible the testing of complex parametric multivariate statistical models. Like the categories, the scales have potential for increasing use at this time with microcomputers. For me, their main advantage lies in the way that they can be used, if needed, for quantitative assessment but can be complemented easily by employing their categories alone for qualitative assessment.

The major disadvantage of both content analyses categories and scales is that they can deal only with verbal communications and not with nonverbal communications; such nonverbal communications cannot be ignored in psychotherapeutic assessment. Of course, many influential constructs of clients are preverbal and so unarticulated, and many remain so even during successful psychotherapy. Constructivist psychotherapy, however, like most other psychotherapies, is based essentially on what clients say and what therapists then say, and what clients then say, and so on. Psychotherapy is essentially a verbal enterprise, so it seems appropriate to use, together with other techniques, an assessment method of content analysis categories and scales that is essentially verbal.

References

Bandura, A. (1984). Recycling misconceptions of perceived self-efficacy. *Cognitive Therapy and Research, 8,* 231-255.

Bunn, T. A., & Clarke, A. M. (1979). Crisis intervention: An experimental study of the effects of a brief period of counseling on the anxiety of relatives of seriously injured hospital patients. *British Journal of Medical Psychology, 52,* 191-195.

de Abreu, P. B. (1986). Aggressiveness in psychotherapy and its relationship with the patient's change. In L. A. Gottschalk, F. Lolas, & L. L. Viney (Eds.), *Content analysis of verbal behavior* (pp. 69-74). Berlin: Springer Verlag.

DeCharms, R. (1968). *Personal causation.* New York: Academic Press.

Epting, F. (1984). *Personal construct counseling and psychotherapy.* Chichester: John Wiley.

Gottschalk, L. A. (1982). Manual of uses and applications of the Gottschalk-Gleser Verbal Behavior Scales. *Research Communications in Psychiatry, 7,* 273-327.

Gottschalk, L. A., Lolas, F., & Viney, L. L. (Eds.). (1986). *Content analysis of verbal behavior in clinical medicine.* Heidelberg: Springer.

Gottschalk, L. A., Winget, C. N., & Gleser, G. C. (1969). *Manual of instructions for using the Gottschalk-Gleser Analysis Scales.* Berkeley: University of California Press.

Howard, G. S. (1986). *Dare we develop a human science?* Notre Dame, IN: Academic Publications.

Kelly, G. A. (1955). *The psychology of personal constructs* (Vols. 1 and 2). New York: Norton.

Kelly, G. A. (1969). Personal construct theory and the psychotherapeutic interview. In B. Maher (Ed.), *Clinical psychology and personality* (pp. 123-139). New York: John Wiley.

Kinney, D. K., Jacobsen, B., Bechgaard, B., Jansson, L., Farber, B., Kassell, E., & Uliana, R. C. (1986). Content analysis of speech of schizophrenics and control adoptees and their relatives. In L. A. Gottschalk, F. Lolas, & L. L. Viney (Eds.), *Content analysis of verbal behavior* (pp. 102-106). Berlin: Springer Verlag.

Krittendorf, K. (1980). *Content analysis*. Beverly Hills, CA: Sage.

Lolas, F., Kordy, H., & von Rad, M. (1986). Affective content of speech as a predictor of psychotherapy outcome. In L. A. Gottschalk, F. Lolas, & L. L. Viney (Eds.), *Content analysis of verbal behavior* (pp. 76-86). Berlin: Springer Verlag.

McCoy, M. (1980). Positive and negative emotions: A personal construct theory interpretation. In H. Bonarius, R. Holland, & S. Rosenberg (Eds.), *Recent advances in the theory and practice of personal construct psychology* (pp. 212-220). London: Macmillan.

Mahoney, M. J., & Gabriel, T. J. (1987). Psychotherapy and the cognitive sciences: An evolving alliance. *Journal of Cognitive Psychotherapy, 1,* 39-59.

Mahoney, M. J., & Lyddon, W. J. (1988). Recent developments in cognitive approaches to counseling and psychotherapy. *Counseling Psychologist, 16,* 190-234.

Neimeyer, G. J. (1987). Personal construct assessment strategy and technique. In R. A. Neimeyer & G. J. Neimeyer (Eds.), *Personal construct therapy casebook* (pp. 217-225). New York: Springer.

Popper, K. R. (1979). *The logic of scientific discovery*. New York: Basic Books.

Richards, L., & Richards, T. (in press). The transformations of qualitative method: Computational paradigms and research processes. In N. Fielding & R. Lee (Eds.), *Using computers in qualitative research*. New York: Russell Sage.

Tabachnik, B. G., & Fidell, I. S. (1989). *Using multivariate statistics*. New York: Harper & Row.

Viney, L. L. (1981). Content analysis: A research tool for community psychologists. *American Journal of Community Psychology, 9,* 269-281.

Viney, L. L. (1983). The assessment of psychological states through content analysis of verbal communication. *Psychological Bulletin, 94,* 542-563.

Viney, L. L. (1987). *Interpreting the interpreters: Towards a science of construing people*. Melbourne, FL: Krieger.

Viney, L. L. (1988). Which data collection methods are appropriate for a constructivist psychology? *International Journal of Personal Construct Psychology, 1,* 80-92.

Viney, L. L. (1989). *Images of illness* (2nd ed.). Melbourne, FL: Krieger.

Viney, L. L. (1990). A constructivist model of psychological reactions to physical illness and injury. In G. J. Neimeyer & R. A. Neimeyer (Eds.), *Advances in personal construct psychology* (pp. 423-442). New York: Pergamon.

Viney, L. L. (in press). Can we see ourselves change? Towards a constructivist model of adult psychosocial development. *Human Development*.

Viney, L. L. (in press). Can we see ourselves changing? A constructivist model of adult psychosocial development. *Human Development*.

Viney, L. L., Benjamin, Y., & Preston, C. (1989). An evaluation of personal construct therapy for the elderly. *British Journal of Medical Psychology, 42,* 55-63.

Viney, L. L., Clarke, A. M., Bunn, T. A., & Benjamin, Y. N. (1985). Crisis intervention counseling: An evaluation of long-term and short-term effects. *Journal of Counseling Psychology, 32,* 29-39.

Viney, L. L., & Porter, A. (1989). *The computer-based analysis of content analysis scales.* Unpublished paper, University of Wollongong, Australia.

Viney, L. L. & Tych, A. M. (1985). Content analysis scales to measure psychosocial maturity in the elderly. *Journal of Personality Assessment, 49,* 311-317.

Viney, L. L., Westbrook, M. T., & Preston, C. (1985). The addiction experience as a function of the addict's history. *British Journal of Clinical Psychology, 24,*73-82.

Westbrook, M. T., & Viney, L. L. (1980). Scales measuring peoples' perceptions of themselves as origins or pawns. *Journal of Personality Assessment, 44,* 167-174.

5

Convergent Lines of Assessment: Systemic and Constructivist Contributions

GUILLEM FEIXAS

HARRY G. PROCTER

GREG J. NEIMEYER

CONSTRUCTIVIST epistemology emphasizes the active participation of personal and social processes in the construction of reality. Attention to these processes has been at the heart of personal construct and family systems theories since their inception, each placing greater weight on features of the knowing system than on the objective aspects of "reality" itself. Assessment that follows from these traditions accordingly has been concerned primarily with describing the structure and processes of the knowing system.

In this regard, both family systems and personal construct approaches have aligned themselves more closely with the second of two major orientations toward assessment distinguished by Hampson (1982). The first is centered in the person administering or directing the assessment. In this

AUTHORS' NOTE: The first author thanks the Department de Personalitat, Avaluacio i Tractaments Psicologics, Universitat de Barcelona, SPAIN 08028, for the support given for the writing of this chapter. This chapter is an adaptation of an earlier unpublished manuscript titled, "Constructivist Assessment of Couples and Families," by G. Feixas and H. Procter.

orientation, clinicians propose a set of dimensions relevant to their theoretical assumptions (e.g., extroversion-introversion), devise instruments to measure the concepts that they have invented, and apply those instruments to people to classify them according to theory-derived categories. According to the second orientation, however, assessment is centered on the client's "lay perspective," focusing its struggle on devising procedures to help articulate and investigate categories that people use when classifying other people and events. Researchers in this latter approach are interested in eliciting meanings from clients rather than in imposing their own meanings on clients. Assessment emanating from the client's perspective seeks to preserve and articulate the unique structure and process of that perspective, objectives that largely constitute the aim of constructivist assessment.

This aim has been endorsed broadly by a growing number of individuals working at the interface of personal construct and family systems theories. Given its continuing development, we cannot write this chapter as if it were a consolidated domain. Rather we will present our view of the emerging domain of constructivist family assessment as it is taking shape and form within the contemporary crucible of professional practice. Central contributors to this movement have been systemic constructivism (SC) and personal construct theory (PCT), and this chapter explores their developing interface.

Although they share basic constructivist assumptions, these two traditions developed independently, and their points of convergence have been explored only recently. Procter (1978, 1981) initiated a theoretical integration, and work has continued to develop that interface (Alexander & Neimeyer, G., 1989; Dallos & Procter, 1984; Procter, 1985a, 1985b; Feixas, 1990a, 1990b, in press a). Understanding this integration relies on understanding the independent traditions reflected in systemic constructivism and personal construct theory.

Systemic Constructivism

In earlier systemic formulations still regarded as central for many family therapists (e.g., Haley, 1963; Watzlawick, Beavin, & Jackson, 1967), the presenting problem was considered in the context of a behavior sequence of the family members in which the symptom had a homeostatic function that in some way was designed to preserve and perpetuate the existing system. For example, intergenerational coalitions (e.g., Haley, 1965; Minuchin, 1974) or the actual solution itself that was attempted by the family in order to solve the problem were considered to be key segments of the behavioral pattern that perpetuated the problem (Watzlawick, Weakland, & Fisch, 1974). In the last decade, however, systemic therapists have begun to draw from constructivist orientations, mainly following from the influence of epistemologists working within the fields of biology (Maturana & Varela, 1980) and cybernetics (von Foerster, 1981).

Bateson's (1972, 1979) thoughts were particularly influential in this regard. As a forerunner of modern family systems theory, he greatly increased the sensitivity of systemic therapists to the importance of knowing processes and their relevance for clinical practice. Together with Bateson, other constructivist authors, such as von Glasersfeld (1984), von Foerster (1981), and Maturana and Varela (1980), are among the most quoted sources of theoretical and clinical inspiration in the systemic literature of the past decade.

The accretion of constructivist ideas into systemic practice is increasingly evident. A recent special issue of *The Family Therapy Networker* was dedicated to constructivism, in which Efran, R. Lukens, and M. Lukens (1988) articulated constructivist principles; this issue was followed by a sequel welcoming the family therapist to clinical practice in a postmodern world (O'Hara & Anderson, 1991). Hoffman (1985, 1989) likewise has narrated the evolution of the systemic movement toward constructivism. Other relevant examples are Watzlawick's (1984) edited book and Keeney's (1983) conceptualization of change, both of which develop constructivist themes as linchpins of professional practice. The earlier focus on behavior sequences within the family therapy literature has shifted toward the investigation of meanings, with particular emphasis on the ways in which behaviors are construed by different family members. Problems are now explained in terms of family myths, premises, or shared belief systems that are coherent with symptomatic behaviors.

The role of assumptions in governing both individual behaviors and family interactions was suggested by Bateson (1972, 1979) and has been a central tenet in constructivist family therapy. Cecchin (in Boscolo, Cecchin, Hoffman, & Penn, 1987) asserted that "the biggest shifts in family therapy come when you succeed in operating at the level of deep premises" (p. 89). Penn (1985) also considered premises as central issues for the system's change because a premise is an "inclusive contextual idea in a system that seems to organize or constrain behaviors linked to a problem" (p. 302). Thus most of the procedures employed by those therapists (known as proponents of the Milan approach—circular questioning) are devised to explicate and challenge those family premises.

The constructivist view assumes that change in therapy is aimed at changing the system's knowing structures, meanings, or premises. Thus Sluzki (1985) ascribed to the therapist the role of a "constructor of realities" whose role is in part to represent more viable alternatives for the family. Minuchin also viewed change from this perspective, asserting that "patients come to therapy because reality, as they have constructed it, is unworkable. All types of therapy, therefore, depend on a challenge to their constructs" (Minuchin & Fishman, 1981, p. 71). For Goolishian and Anderson (1990), change in therapy implies a reconstruction of the story that the system has created around the problem. Thus the conversation is maintained until a new "narrative" is created (see also Loos & Epstein, 1989).

This position is also congruent with Bogdan's (1984) elaboration of Bateson's (1972) "ecology of ideas" in the sense of a system in which a reciprocal confirmation of ideas occurs so that "the ideas of each member lead him to behave in ways that confirm or support the ideas of every other family member" (Bogdan, 1984, p. 376). Moreover other models have been proposed by family therapists that are consistent with this emphasis on meanings, as distinct from the traditional focus on behavioral interactions. The notion of family paradigms, proposed by Reiss (1981), is one of the more elaborate proposals that develop the role of meaning systems in families:

> The central idea around which our model is built is that the family, through the course of its own development, fashions fundamental and enduring assumptions about the world in which it lives. The assumptions are shared by all family members, despite the disagreements, conflicts, and differences that exist in the family. Indeed, the core of an individual's membership in his own family is his acceptance of, belief in, and creative elaboration of these abiding assumptions. When a member distances himself from these assumptions . . . he is diluting his own membership and begins a process of alienation from his family. (p. 1)

> We now speak of the family paradigm as a central organizer of its shared constructs, sets, expectations, and fantasies about its social world. Further, each family's transaction with its social world is guided by its own paradigm,

and families can be distinguished . . . by the differences in their paradigms.
(p. 2)

Other authors have supported Reiss's notions with their own work (see
e.g., Constantine, 1986). For example, in a specific clinical application,
Constantine (1986) pointed to the crucial role that the paradigm developed by the couple plays in the treatment of jealousy and extramarital
relationship problems. Kantor and Lehr (1975) had already noted the
important role of the family's model of reality as an explanatory system.
Kantor and Neal (1985) not only affirmed that the conception of family
paradigms "is perhaps the most important idea for family therapists"
(p. 17) but also suggested that "models of reality inform our personal and
shared meanings, affective reactions, behavior patterns, and thematic
concerns" (p. 16). In his works, Kantor pointed to the relevance of the
interaction between individual premises or beliefs and those held by the
family as a whole.

This interest in the family's shared meanings (family paradigms, myths,
premises, etc.) comes in the company of an increasing interest on individual dynamics and personal meanings (see Doherty, 1988). Personal construct theory (Kelly, 1955) represents a long tradition in this regard, extending its range to the area of shared meanings and social constructions
in a way that complements the growing edge of systemic therapies.

Personal Construct Approaches
to Families and Couples

The original focus of personal construct theory (PCT) was the individual and individual therapy (see, for example, Bannister & Fransella, 1986;
Feixas & Villegas, 1990; Kelly, 1955; Neimeyer, G. & Neimeyer, R.,
1981, for an introduction to PCT). Kelly (1955), however, was careful to
extend the application of his theory from the individual to the interactional level. Although the person is unique and has an idiosyncratic system
of construing and understanding the world, these understandings are
forged against broader patterns of interpersonal, social, and cultural
interaction. As a result, human beings share some commonalities in their
construing of the world, and it is these shared referents that constitute
cultural and societal worldviews. On the basis of the potential commonality of meaning among diverse people, we can think of models of communal systems of construing—that is, shared meaning systems. These

pathways between the individual and the social domain are provided by Kelly's (1955) individuality-commonality dimension.

The sociality corollary adds a new dimension to social construction of meaning in pointing to the nature of relationships. If an individual is able to understand the other's construing processes, he or she can develop a role relationship with that person; the construing processes become interconnected in a way that spawns an emergent relational quality to their shared interaction. This pattern of ongoing activity that follows from interactants' understandings of one another was called a *role relationship* by Kelly (1955). In a role relationship, each member recognizes the other as a validating agent (Landfield, 1988), with one person's behavior becoming (in)validational evidence for the other's core constructions, and vice versa (a notion close to the views presented by some of the abovementioned systemic constructivists, such as Bateson, Bogdan, and Kantor).

Personal construct theorists have developed Kelly's social ideas in several ways. Duck and his colleagues studied the development, maintenance, and dissolution of personal relationships (Duck, 1973, 1983; Duck & Condra, 1990), and R. Neimeyer and G. Neimeyer (1985) elaborated an account of disordered relationships based on Kelly's theory.

G. Neimeyer (1984, 1985; Neimeyer, G. & Hudson, 1985) has been working on a personal construct model for marital relationships that is derived from the study of close relationships. According to this viewpoint, relationships are pursued for the elaboration of the personal construct system—that is, for the improvement of the predictive capacity of the individual. In other words, this model asserts that marital relationships are pursued for the extension and elaboration of the partner's anticipatory system, and satisfactory relationships are those that enrich and extend the personal meaning in one's life. Thus G. Neimeyer (1985) proposed that the development and maintenance (and potential problems and breakdowns) of marital relationships are subordinated to the individual's leitmotif for anticipation postulated by Kelly (1955). The choice of a partner therefore is governed by the anticipated elaboration of one's construct system, reflecting the expectation that "through marriage the world will become more meaningful, predictable, and understandable" (Neimeyer, G. & Hudson, 1985, p. 127).

Other personal construct theorists have broadened the theory to accommodate phenomena arising from wider social processes (Procter, 1978; Procter & Parry, 1978). For example, Procter (1978, 1981) formulated the notion of family constructs as an extension of Kelly's personal constructs. He described family constructs as shared distinctions used by all of the members of the family in a way that is characteristic of that family. Procter based his claim for the existence of shared family realities on the appreciation that the family is the main validating agent of the child's growing personal construct system. This fact has been noted also by Guidano and Liotti (1983), who studied the evolution of construction systems in the context of early affectional bonds. These authors assert that "at least during infancy, reality almost coincides spatially with the family" (pp. 32-33).

Procter saw family constructs as organized into a family construct system (FCS), which "governs the sequences of contingent choices that constitute the interaction patterns of the family members" (Procter, 1981, p. 355). Thus some family constructs, premises, or myths play a superordinate role in organizing the thinking and behavior of the family members. The FCS evolves through (usually implicit) negotiation between the foundational members (usually the couple). The negotiation of a common family reality includes views about the world, about the actual and potential family members, and about ways of relating one member to another. The origins of a FCS can be traced in two different but connected forms. First, its negotiation entails the personal interpretation that each member of the couple has of the construct system of their families of origin. Second, the FCS arises as a particular (and potentially idiosyncratic) interpretation of a much broader (sub)cultural system of construing related to the culture(s) to which the couple belong.

The FCS model can interface effectively with many systemic notions, such as interactional patterns, boundaries, enmeshment, alliances, and myths (see Procter, 1981). From this perspective, conflicts arise when the family's constructed reality is not working well for everybody. The FCS evolves through negotiation (usually implicit) in moments of perceived invalidation. The family life cycle itself can provide some invalidating situations. When one member acts in an unusual and unexpected way, this can become an invalidation of others' constructs. Because such innovative pathways are inherent to personal growth and development, the tendencies of the other members to return to older ways are potential sources of conflict in family development. In those conflicts, one member often must make a choice between his or her own personal growth and adapting to others' expectations. Symptoms often are compromised solutions to that conflict; negotiation does not lead to an agreement that allows for a certain level of mutual anticipation. Then someone usually starts labeling the situation or a segment of it in problematic or pathological terms. Procter (1981) considered these problems to be "disorders of negotiation" (p. 356) and suggested how some systemic and personal construct interventions can be used to generate a reconstruction of the FCS not demanding a symptomatic solution.

Recent work has elaborated these central themes. For example, Procter (1985a) proposed the notion of *position* to represent the construing and action of a given family member in relation to the others; its usefulness for assessment will be developed later in this chapter. In related work, Dallos (1990) and Dallos and Aldridge (1985, 1987, 1988) studied the choice of a family member adopting a given position in relation to the formation of symptoms, and they addressed the intergenerational transmission of family constructs as well.

An Integrative View

PCT and the systemic approach remained for many years two different traditions; PCT focused on the individual's construction processes, while the systemic approach viewed problems in terms of family system dynamics. The evolution of constructivism, however, has begun to build a bridge between these two orientations, broadening the application of PCT to interpersonal and social arenas, and focusing systemic theories on issues of personal meaning.

As a result of these developments, the way in which many systemic therapists approach their clients' problems is perfectly compatible with PCT and vice versa. Several common traits have been described elsewhere (Feixas, 1990b) and can be summarized as follows:

1. Personal construct systems can be described as having the cybernetic properties of totality, feedback, equifinality, and feedback describing open systems.
2. Both approaches acknowledge the central role of anticipation (or "feedforward") in the organization of behavior.
3. Both approaches acknowledge the role of labeling (even "diagnosis") in the creation and maintenance of problems.

4. Both approaches advocate the understanding and use of the client's language and worldview, even when conveying an alternative view or construction.

5. Both approaches view "resistance" as a therapist's construction in response to the clients' efforts to preserve current systemic organization.

6. Both approaches may use pragmatic suggestions as a way to experiment with alternative meanings.

7. Both approaches view therapy as a process oriented toward the reconstruction of the meanings ascribed to events.

This convergence follows in part on a shared grounding in constructivist epistemology. Certainly both PCT and the systems approach share the assumption that knowledge results from an active process of co construction rather than from a direct representation of reality. Because knowledge of the external world is construed actively by the subject (observer) in a given social context, the idea of having "true" or authorized knowledge about reality vanishes. Thus Kelly's (1955) assertion that reality can be interpreted in a variety of ways is shared by many constructivist thinkers (e.g., Bateson, 1979; Feixas & Villegas, 1990; Kenny & Gardner, 1988; Mahoney, 1988; Maturana & Varela, 1980; von Foerster, 1981; Watzlawick, 1984). Given their epistemological commonality, systemic and personal construct approaches can be integrated in a way that permits the joint presentation of their contributions to the assessment of couples and families. Although technically eclectic, the methods of assessment discussed below share common assumptive frameworks that make them compatible at theoretical levels.

Interview Methods

The interview is a process that enables the (co-)creation of information. For Bateson (1972), information is a "difference that makes a difference," and differences are the primary data of experience (Bateson, 1976). Rather than viewing information as "data to be collected" or pieces of knowledge passed from one individual to the other, this view of information is related to the context in which it is generated and to the system that receives it. As Deissler (1987) suggested, information has a confirmatory or novelty effect on the family system, depending on the family's previous structure.

During the interview, the family's construction of their reality (their FCS or family myth) is displayed. But this is not a neutral process. Rather, it has an effect both on the interviewer and on the family. This information about the organization of the family not only helps the interviewer develop a "therapeutic myth," or theory about the family, but also has a confirmatory effect on their members and in turn on the family's organization. The "return-effect" of the family's description makes this process a recursive one. Thus Deissler (1987) considered the questioning-answering process as a recursive creation of information. In sum, the family's description of their reality is an "invention" that follows from their basic premises and that creates a self-confirmatory effect on those premises or constructs.

Interviewing several people in the presence of others is a powerful co-creative process that has diverse effects. By answering the interviewer's questions in the presence of others, family members implicitly define their relationships to the others. This interaction creates an interpersonal spread of effects (Deissler, 1987)—that is, a set of reactions coming from the other members that in turn generates new reactions both in the family and the interviewer. Deissler (1987) suggested that a question addressed to one member of the family sets off a "subconscious search" (Erickson & Rossi, 1979; Procter, 1985a) within other members of the family as well:

> The therapist, through the questions which he directs to the son, at the same time indirectly encourages the parents to reflect on the subject, to generate internal scenes, visual and auditory memories, feelings, and the like. The subconscious search processes are evoked on the parents too, although the question is directed "only" to the son. The son's answer then occasions the parents to make the comparisons with the answers which they have found. Perhaps the mother expresses her agreement with the answer her son has given ideo-motorically, by nodding her head, while the father may express himself explicitly by denial. (Deissler, 1987, pp. 28-29)

From the constructivist point of view, the therapist participates in a recursive co-creation of meaning from the very moment he or she interacts with the family system. Therefore the boundaries between "assessment" and "intervention" become blurred because these are only approximate distinctions. In fact many of the procedures considered in this "assessment" chapter may have substantial therapeutic effects (Neimeyer, G. &

Neimeyer, R., Chapter 1, this volume), as is clear in the use of such procedures as circular questioning.

Circular Questioning

Circular questioning has become one of the most popular forms of interviewing among systemic family therapists. Since its introduction into the therapeutic arena by Selvini-Palazzoli, Boscolo, Cecchin, and Prata (1980), this method has undergone further elaborations (e.g., Deissler, 1987; Fleuridas, Nelson, & Rosenthal, 1986; Penn, 1982, 1985; Tomm, 1985). *Circular questions* are those devised to reveal relationships and differences among relationships (Bateson, 1972). They typically invite family members to describe the relationship between two other members (often present in the therapy room) or to speculate on how another member may react to a given problem and what reactions are likely to be generated in other members in response to that reaction. This "gossiping" in the presence of others initiates a vortex of reactions in the family, providing rich information about relationships. *Circular* refers to the complex, mutual networks of effects, as opposed to a linear conception of cause and effect. As Tomm (1985) said, "To understand the system is to understand the coherence in its circular organization. Thus, it is the circular connectedness of ideas, feelings, actions, persons, relationships, groups, events, traditions, etc. that is of interest to the systemic therapist. The questions are circular in that they attempt to elucidate these organizational connections" (pp. 37-38).

Many typologies of circular questions have been described (e.g., Deissler, 1987; Penn, 1982; Tomm, 1985), but one system, proposed by Fleuridas, Nelson, and Rosenthal (1986), is particularly useful for the sake of illustration. This typology consists of a factorial matrix defined by crossing four purposes (problem definition, sequence of interaction, comparison/classification, and intervention) with three temporal orientations (present, past, and future/hypothetical) and three types of investigation (difference, [dis]agreement, and explanation/meaning). This matrix yields a total of 36 different types of questions. Selected examples of these appear in Table 5.1. In our adaptation, we omitted the fourth of the purpose types, "intervention," because all of them might be regarded as "interventions" insofar as they each may register an impact on the family's construction of experience.

TABLE 5.1 Types of Circular Questions and Selected Examples (adapted from Fleuridas, Nelson, & Rosenthal, 1986)

I. PROBLEM DEFINITION
   A. Present   "What is the problem in the family now?"
      Difference   "Does the child eat so little when Dad is at home?"
      Agreement   "Do you agree with your son's view of the problem?"
      Explanation "Why do you think this problem occurs?"
   B. Past   "How was this problem before? How did it start?"
      Difference   "How was John's problem before his sister was born?"
      Agreement   "Who agrees with Dad that this was the major concern of the family then?"
      Explanation "Why do you think that was so relevant at that time?"
   C. Future   "How would the problem be in the family if things were to continue as they are?"
      Difference   "What would be different if Ann would leave home?"
      Agreement   "If you make a decision, would your mother agree with it?"
      Explanation "If Joe killed himself, who would miss him the most?"

II. SEQUENCE OF INTERACTION
   A. Present   "When your mom and brother are fighting, what does your dad do?"
      Difference   "Do your parents react the same when you fail your exams?"
      Agreement   "Who agrees with you that Mother yells at Dad every time he stomps out of the house?"
      Explanation "How do you explain Dad's tendency to leave home when that situation occurs?"
   B. Past   "Has your mom always mediated between your sister and Dad?"
      Difference   "Has your mom reacted any different than Dad when you were sick?"
      Agreement   "Did you agree with your parents when they decided to move your grandmother to a residence?"
      Explanation "How do you explain your mother quitting the job when your dad started drinking?"
   C. Future
      Difference   "How would your parents' relationship be different if your mom were to return to school?"
      Agreement   "Do you think your mom would agree that they would probably get divorced if she were to return to school?"
      Explanation "Dad, why do you think your daughter and wife both agree that a divorce is likely should your wife return to school?"

III. COMPARISON/CLASSIFICATION
   A. Present   "Who is most convinced that something is wrong with his behavior? Who next?"
      Difference   "How does his behavior bother you differently than it bothers Mom?"
      Agreement   "Who disagrees with Dad the most?"
      Explanation "Who do you think has the best explanation for this problem?"

TABLE 5.1 Continued

B. Past	"Before Mary left home, who was closest to Dad? Then who?"
Difference	"Was Peter also the closest to Mom before the problem began?"
Agreement	"Do you agree with Mom that they got along better before you moved out?"
Explanation	"How do you explain the distance Mom and Dad experienced at that time?"
C. Future	"Who will be closest to Mom when all of you children have grown up and left home?"
Difference	"What would you do differently if Mom and Dad got along?"
Agreement	"If your grandma were here with Mom, with whom would she agree the most?"
Explanation	"Mom, why does Dad think that Jill will be the closest to you when the children grow up?"

The first aspect for us to consider refers to the area to be explored with the questions. The first of these, Problem Definition, carries obvious interest for the constructivist interviewer because the main focus is on how family members define and explain the nature of the presenting problem in their own terms. Sequence of Interaction ("who does what when") is a traditional area of interest for systemic therapists focused on the pragmatic effects of family members' interaction, and it also reveals organization patterns governed by the family's meaning structure. Comparison/ Classification questions provide qualitative information about the family members' constructions of themselves in terms of their perceived similarities and differences (the basic components of the construing process); they also illuminate organizational patterns such as coalitions and alignments among family members.

Time-oriented questions investigate an essential axis on the story the family tells to themselves (and to the interviewer). This led Penn (1982) to define *circular questions* as a search for information regarding "differences in relationships the family has experienced before and after the problem began" (p. 272), thus tracing the "chronological arc" or the development of the symptom over time. Also important is the projection of the present construction system into future or hypothetical circumstances, which conveys relevant information about the family's organization and the solutions that therefore would be possible. Penn (1985) pointed to the interest of investigating future anticipations or maps and proposed the cybernetic term *feed-forward* to expose the potential of future-oriented questions: "Pragmatically, future questions, in combination with positive connotation, promote the rehearsal of new solutions, suggest alternative actions, foster learning, discard ideas of predestination, and address the system's specific change model" (Penn, 1985, p. 299). She considered these questions to be one of the most remarkable types of reflexive questions, and she stressed the advantages of their use when she noted that "families with problems are sometimes so preoccupied with present difficulties or past injustices that, in effect, they live as if they 'have no future'. . . . By deliberately asking long series of questions about the future, the therapist can trigger family members to create more of a future for themselves" (p. 173).

Differences and (dis)agreement questions point to the contrasts and similarities of views within the family. The previous pragmatic emphasis on behavioral interactions precluded the use of "why" questions in favor of "what for" questions. As Furman and Ahola (1988) noted, however, interest in the explanation of the problem from the client's point of view now has become central to any constructivist formulation. The theory that the family has constructed around the problem may or may not contain the possible keys for its solution. If the problem is explained in a way that does not allow for solutions (e.g., "genetic predetermination") the theory may have to be challenged or circumvented in order to achieve change.

The potential for change in circular questions led Selvini-Palazzoli et al. (1980) to wonder whether this type of interview is such a powerful therapeutic tool that it obviates further intervention. In a more recent formulation, Cecchin (1987) suggested that "circular questions undermine the family's belief system" and by doing this "creates opportunities for new stories" (p. 412). It is hoped that these new stories will allow for alternatives in which the problem is no longer coherent or central.

Cognitive Marital Therapy

Another interview technique for assessing and articulating family constructions is *cognitive marital therapy* (CMT; Waring, 1980). Emphasizing the empowering process of nonjudgmental sharing, CMT directs family members toward developing, exchanging, and understanding one another's private constructions of their relationships and experiences. The technique calls for family members to discuss their theories and accounts of their relationships and difficulties with one another. The therapist serves primarily as a host or consultant to partners in this time-limited therapy, serving to prompt, facilitate, and guide them in their process of mutual inquiry. "What is your theory about the cause of your fights?" for example, might serve as a therapeutic prompt for each person in turn to articulate his or her own personal theory as to the origin of their arguments. Ambiguous disclosures are brought into sharper focus by asking partners to trace the implications of their thinking. Questions such as "What does that mean to you personally?" or "If you were to boil down your thoughts to their essence, what is your basic belief here?" can help partners focus their theories and deepen their disclosure in a relatively nonthreatening environment. Attention is redirected periodically, primarily through the use of open-ended questions, to prevent partners from drifting into storytelling or character assassination. This method actively encourages and promotes the formulation and discussion of family constructions without directly challenging or disputing the validity of those constructions, and for that reason it provides family members with therapeutic reassurance. "If the task of therapy were always to disrupt the use of faulty constructs as soon as possible," noted Kelly (1969, p. 86), "then one might say that reassurance should never be used. However, the task of therapy is to prepare the client for achieving long-range goals, and not simply to perform surgery on his misconceptions." Cognitive marital therapy can be a useful tool in this regard. It can function successfully as part of a larger therapeutic objective aimed at what Kelly (1955) termed *controlled elaboration,* a process marked by the systematic articulation and development of a set of presenting problems in relation to the larger personal and interpersonal contexts that support them.

Exploring the Family Construct System

Any type of conversation or activity that the family or couple engage in will reveal their construing. For example, one can use such structured tasks as planning a holiday or discussing a certain topic to elicit family constructs. Reiss (1981) designed a variety of problem-solving tasks in formal research designs that are used to tease out family construing.

In a therapeutic context, however, it is important, especially in initial interviews, to be congruent with the expectations and purpose of the interview, and we commonly will use the brief therapy categories (problem, attempted solutions, goals, theories about the problem, and expectations about treatment) to focus the investigation and to help define the context as being concerned with change (Procter & Walker, 1988).

It is important to remember that a question implicitly will provide direction to the family's thinking. To ask, "What does your mother make of your problem?" presupposes that there is a problem and that the mother's thinking is relevant to it. Of course we often will use this fact deliberately to steer the conversation to apparently fruitful areas and to provide the family's own topics and distinctions in subsequent questions.

In investigating the family's construing, we have a wide choice of topics to explore. For example, we may want the family to look at events, such as problematic or traumatic episodes. We may wish to learn more about how they see individuals, both within and outside the family, relationships between these individuals, symptoms, pleasurable times, leaving home—the list is endless. We provide the opportunity to discuss these, keeping a careful eye on the way in which distinctions and similarities are drawn by the different members. Alternatively we may focus on one salient construct, such as frightening versus calming, and invite the family to consider people or events that fall under one or the other side of this dimension.

An example is the use of the *conversational grid* (Feixas, 1990a), named by virtue of its similarity to the more structured pencil-and-paper repertory grid technique (see Neimeyer, R., Chapter 3, this volume; next section, below). This form of interview consists of first identifying a relevant characteristic referred to by the family (for instance "nervous"). To begin the procedure, the therapist asks the family to make a list of the most important people in their lives. Typical "grid" questions may be asked of the members of the system:

1. What would be the opposite of "nervous"?
2. Who is the most "nervous" in the list of people? Who is the next most "nervous" after him or her? and so on until getting a rank ordering of all people according to this construct.
3. Who would be a good example of "calm" (elicited opposite for nervous)?
4. Are other people in the extended family or outside the family good examples of "nervous" people or "calm" people?

In the course of this interchange, the family probably will disagree or discuss these questions, invoking other people or constructs that can be included in further investigation:

5. Are all the "nervous" people also considered "sick"? Can you find someone who is "nervous" but not "sick"?

This line of questioning also might have a therapeutic effect because it challenges the existing lines of implication of these two constructs, thus facilitating a context for loosening this implication. Further therapeutic action could be considered along the lines of what Kelly (1969) termed altering the meaning of the construct, or rotating "the reference axes" (p. 231), which has been considered a major strategy for psychotherapeutic change (Feixas & Villegas, 1990; Neimeyer, R., 1987).

As we proceed with the interview, the positions of the members gradually will become clearer. Kelly emphasized the importance of contrast poles of constructs as providing a context of meaning to the emergent pole. In families, construing among the members is in dialectical interdependence. Thus, in one current case, to the extent that Father sees his daughter Joan as obstinate, Mother sees her as not being able to help it. This is what we mean by the term *family construct,* as opposed to a personal construct. Interviewing can be seen as a progressive "unpacking" of their mutually dependent positions. Thus we might ask Father for a fuller explanation of the word *obstinate* or for other obstinate people he knows. In progressively clarifying and elaborating his position, we will ask him for evidence of why he holds a particular view: "What makes you say that she is obstinate? What was she doing that you would describe as obstinate?" As he describes an episode, his wife (and daughter) will recall it, construing it through the constructs of her position. As she applies her position to the evidence that he has isolated through his, the opportunity for reconstruction and negotiation of meanings between them becomes possible. Further elements will be invoked in the form of events or examples that are then open to construction and reconstruction by all the members present. We have called this the "zigzag" interviewing technique as we return the family from the level of construing to the level of evidence and back again ("And what did you make of that situation, Joan?") in a way that is both investigative and therapeutic. In this particular example, Joan was able to make more sense of her parents' disagreement, thus modifying her potential actions in relation to their conflicts and silences.

Gradually the interviewer will assemble a clearer and more elaborate picture of the system of positions within the family construct system. Questioning should be interspersed with summaries and recapitulations given to the family to check accuracy and to elicit error-correcting feedback. "Let me see if I've got you right, Mrs. Jones. The way you saw that Tuesday evening was . . . " The interviewer may test the hypothesis more actively by introducing new topics or by asking questions in a different area of the family's life.

Hinkle (1965; see also Fransella & Bannister, 1977; Neimeyer, R., Chapter 3, this volume) devised the *laddering technique* for gaining access to superordinate structures. By starting at a given construct level, this technique allows the interviewer to "ladder" up to investigate the family's core value system. This method consists of asking the family which of the two poles of a construct they would prefer to be and why they would prefer to be this. For example, once an important family construct used to distinguish a wife from her husband and children (sensitive versus matter-of-fact) was established, it was possible to "ladder" with the couple up to a core value of belief in God versus atheist; ultimately sensitivity was valued because sensitive people have strong religious convictions, whereas atheists are more matter-of-fact. This construct had a different cleavage line in this family, with the children and the wife anchoring one side of the construct (Christian belief) and the father anchoring the other (atheist). These superordinate constructs can give a good understanding of how particular beliefs have been governing particular family conflicts and processes. Laddering allows one to understand the construct system hierarchy. Having understood the various positions in the system and how they are interlinked, one then can determine how they are governed by superordinate value constructs that probably originate in the traditions of the family and the wider subculture (school, work, religion, etc.).

Writing Methods

Writing methods can be used to develop further the interview process described above. Each member of the family may be asked to write a response to a particular instruction, and these may be shared later to reveal differences and commonalities among family members.

Family or Couple Characterization

Alexander and G. Neimeyer (1989) presented the *family characterization sketch,* an adaptation of Kelly's (1955) self-characterization technique (see Neimeyer, R., Chapter 3, this volume for an extended illustration). The couple or family is asked to take about 15 minutes to write a brief sketch of themselves according to the following instructions:

> Write a brief character sketch of this family. Write it from the perspective of someone who knows the family intimately and sympathetically, perhaps better than anyone else really knows the family. You should write it in third person. For example, begin by saying, "I know the Smith family . . ." (Alexander & G. Neimeyer, 1989, p. 13)

Encouraging them to consider the family itself elicits constructs that they use to distinguish themselves as a group from other families. This method can give valuable insight into processes occurring between them and figures in the outside world such as in the extended family, at work, and at school. It is also of relevance to periods of transition within the family, as in courtship or leaving home for a young person, adoption of a new member, or the blending of stepfamilies. The resulting commentaries that emerge from a family characterization sketch also can provide a glimpse of their areas of convergence and divergence in terms of distinctions made within the family. Thus the family characterization sketch is a way to enable the family members to make explicit their (usually implicit) view of themselves as a family group through their own writings and comments, with minimal influence by the therapist.

Autobiographical Table of Contents

To increase the partners' perspectives on themselves as a couple, G. Neimeyer (1985) suggested using a *relationship chronology technique.* Partners are invited to consider that they are writing their autobiography as a couple. Because writing the entire autobiography would take too long, they are asked individually to write only the chapter headings of the autobiography, along with a brief summary for each chapter. These chapters may be used as elements in a grid for which each partner may provide constructs. Particular chapter headings and elicited constructs provide information about the construction of their relationship. By sharing and discussing each other's view, differences and similarities appear. It often usefully highlights the different perceptions each holds about themselves as a couple (Neimeyer, G., 1985). Important turning points in the history of the couple and the different ways in which each partner interprets these may be unearthed by this technique. The details can be used to help them elaborate and negotiate construing in areas that have been associated with conflict.

Family or Couple Metaphors

Metaphors have received increasing attention in the area of psychotherapy for a long time but recently have been given added emphasis (Erickson & Rossi, 1976; Mair, 1977). They can be useful in articulating unspoken constructions that otherwise would be difficult to express in words. People use metaphors far more often in their discourse than is usually apparent to them. They are another extremely useful indicator of a family's or couple's construction. As G. Neimeyer (in press) suggested, metaphors can serve as useful windows onto the systems that individuals use to interpret and anticipate their familial interactions. Each metaphor simultaneously highlights and hides certain features of the family expectations.

Family members can be encouraged to share their metaphors about the family by asking them to complete sentences such as "Families are like ___ ," and then to write what they mean. In one case, for example, a teenage girl offered that "A family is like a blanket. They are there when you need them. You can uncover when you get too hot, or pull them closer when you get too cold. The blanket is security; it will always be there no matter what happens. Blankets can be tugged and pulled, but well-made blankets always remain intact." The potency and power of metaphorical constructions such as this give force to each person's family constructions and serve as a vehicle for further discussion and elaboration.

The discussion of each member's family metaphor often reveals commonalities and divergences among them. These points of contact and divergence may be used by the therapist to encourage sociality—that is, mutual understanding of each other's view. One creative means to facilitate this shared construction is to encourage family members to "stretch or shrink" each person's metaphor. For instance, family members might extend the blanket metaphor by noting that families, like blankets, protect you when you feel insecure, fit the particular contours of each and every person, and so on. Such metaphorical extension helps family members feel validated and understood by one another in a supportive and creative enterprise. In addition to extending the family metaphor, some of the aspects of the metaphor may be challenged by other family members or by the therapist, highlighting the fact each person's constructions have blind spots or limitations, as well and that no single perspective has a corner on the market of truth.

Grid Methods

Repertory grids, proposed by Kelly (1955) for the investigation of personal meanings, have become an established assessment method among personal construct practitioners. An increasing number of research findings, variations in the method, and creative applications and computer programs for their analysis have developed over the years. Readers who are unfamiliar with basic repertory grid technique should first read R. Neimeyer's description and illustration of the method in this volume (Chapter 3). In this section, we will focus on extensions of the grid method for family and couple evaluation. The schematic presentation and the following discussion presuppose familiarity with applications of basic grid methods and the basic grid technique (see G. Neimeyer, 1993, for a videotape illustration of repertory grid technique).

Some of the applications depicted in Table 5.2 are derived conceptually from PCT, while others have adapted the grid method to tap specific concepts coming from other conceptual backgrounds. For example, Ryle's *dyad grid* (Ryle & Breen, 1972a) was designed initially for testing psychoanalytically oriented hypotheses. Hartmann (1988) and Sanchez (1988) produced grid designs to test systemic notions. Some authors who designed grid methods to extend PCT to the family assessment intended to develop their methods as an operationalization of their theoretical elaborations (e.g., Neimeyer, G. & Hudson, 1985; Procter, 1978, 1985b). Others (e.g., Mancuso & Handin, 1980; McDonald & Mancuso, 1987) adapted grid methods to assess particular construct subsystems and to design an adequate treatment plan according to this analysis.

One main conceptual issue needs to be taken into account when extending grid methods to couples and families. Repertory grids were designed

TABLE 5.2 A Schematic Presentation of Grid Procedures for Families and Couples.

Author(s)	Type of element	Type of construct	Procedure	Measures
Ryle & Breen (1972b)	Dyadic. Relationships between the couple, with parents, and between both sets of parents, other couples	Relational constructs elicited conjointly or supplied (Ryle, 1985)	Each partner completes his/her own grid and another one predicting the other's responses	Similarity. Accurate empathy. Clinically useful plots
Wijesinghe & Wood (1976)	Simple (members of the couple's psychotherapy group) (total: 8)	Four supplied (relevant to group interactions) and four elicited separately by the triadic method	Each partner completes his/her own grid and another one predicting the other's responses	Predictive accuracy. Clinically useful plots
Procter (1978, 1985b); Feixas, Cunillera, & Villegas (1987)	Simple (family members and others) and meta-perspectives (family members) (total: 16)	Elicited for individual grid and supplied for family grid (total: 16)	Family grid pooling constructs from the individual grids	Perceived similarity. Commonality, Sociality, Perceived Commonality, Meta-commonality, Self-concept Comparison
Mancuso & Handin (1980); McDonald & Mancuso (1987); Mancuso (1988)	Supplied child-rearing statements	Supplied parent role descriptions	Separate individual completion by each parent	Clinically useful plots For the assessment of parent role construction systems
Childs & Hedges (1981)	Simple (couple members and ideal selves), meta-perspectives, and meta-metaperspectives (total: 12)	Elicited separately from each member by the triadic method, combined to form a single set of constructs (total: 25)	Separate individual completion	Similarity. Comparison of (meta)perspectives. Actual/ideal discrepancies
Karastergiou-Katsika & Watson (1982, 1985)	Simple. Family members	Supplied. Derived from a text completion method (total: 20)	Separate individual completion	Similarity. Clinically useful plots

Reference	Elements	Constructs	Administration	Measures
Neimeyer, G. & Hudson (1985)	Simple. Couples and parents (total: 6)	Elicited separately from each member by the triadic method (total: 6)	Exchange grid method (Thomas, 1977)	Content similarity. Functional similarity. Predictive accuracy.
Gale & Barker (1987)	Simple. Family members	Supplied. Derived by judges on the Kantor & Lehr (1975) dimensions (affect, power, meaning) (total: 52)	Separate individual completion	Similarity. Clinically useful plots
Jolly & Vetere (1987)	Elicited problematic situations	Supplied. Derived from (a) observers' scenarios diaries, (b) key words in family video-tapes (total: 16)	Separate individual completion	Similarity. Clinically useful plots
Willutzki, Grzempowski, & Goohs-Kammler (1987)	Elicited problematic situations	Elicited separately from each couple member	Exchange grid method (Thomas, 1979)	Clinically useful plots
Sanchez (1988, 1990)	Simple. Family members	Supplied. Behaviors and interactions conceptually derived from systemic concepts (total: 37)	Separate individual completion	Similarity. Clinically useful plots
Hartmann (1988)	Simple (family members, ideal self, ideal parent, ideal child)	Elicited separately from each family member by a modified version of Orlik's method	Separate individual completion	Element distances interpreted in terms of conflicts and coalitions
Harter, Neimeyer, R., & Alexander (1989)	Relational real, ideal, and metarelational (total: 16)	Supplied (from Neimeyer, G., 1987 research) (total: 10)	Separate individual completion	Actual similarity. Ideal similarity. Sociality. Predictive accuracy. Actual-ideal discrepancy
O'Loughlin (1989)	Simple (couple, parents, ideal self, ideal partner) (total: 3)	Supplied (from G. Neimeyer, 1987 research) (total: 8)	Each partner completes his/her own grid and another one predicting the other's responses	Similarity. Perceived similarity. Level of understanding of each partner

initially for the evaluation of personal meanings. When adapted to couples and families, certain grounds for comparison must be provided. Although providing identical elements to the different members may be a relatively problem-free strategy, the comparison among constructs raises more serious conceptual concerns. Several different research strategies have been adopted to solve this problem.

Eliciting the Constructs Separately. This strategy simply implies eliciting constructs individually from each family member and then assembling them together, with no grounds for statistical comparison. This conservative option limits some possibilities of the conjoint analysis of the individual grids but has the advantage of remaining close to each person's view. Some studies have attempted to mitigate the limitation of conjoint analysis. For example, the use of the *exchange grid* design (Thomas, 1979) involves the completion of four grids: (a) rating the elements along one's own constructs, (b) rating the elements along one's partner's constructs, (c) predicting the way that the partner would rate the elements along one's own constructs, and (d) predicting the way that one's partner would rate the elements along his or her constructs. This design allows for the analysis of the predictive accuracy of each partner and also of the functional and content similarity (see, e.g., Neimeyer, G. & Hudson, 1985). Moreover, extremely useful simple plots can be extracted from this design (Willutzki, Grzempowski, & Goohs-Kammler, 1987). This solution increases substantially the administration time, however, and should be limited to dyads (couples). The exchange of multiple grids among more than two members can be an exhausting process, although group applications have demonstrated the grid's flexibility and utility (Neimeyer, G. & Merluzzi, 1982).

Another tactic is that of Hartmann (1988), who bases his comparison on the analysis of the elements only, allowing for the fact that constructs may not be shared in the various grids. The distances provided by the statistical analysis of the individual grids of family members might depict their overall perception of proximities and boundaries, information that could be very useful for grasping family coalitions and conflicts (Minuchin, 1974).

Supplying the Constructs. Many authors (Gale & Barker, 1987; Harter, Neimeyer, R., & Alexander, 1989; Jolly & Vetere, 1987; Karastergiou-

Katsika & Watson, 1982, 1985; O'Loughlin, 1989; Ryle, 1985; Sanchez, 1988, 1990) have adopted the strategy of simply supplying the constructs in their research. Although it bears serious conceptual drawbacks, the methodological advantages of supplying constructs are clear. When using the same constructs, grids can be compared easily in many ways because both constructs and elements are common. Supplying the constructs, however, has serious limitations (Yorke, 1985). The same construct labels do not guarantee the same personal meanings. Another issue concerns the meaningfulness of supplied constructs and the homogeneity of their range of convenience. Several studies (see Bonarius, 1977) have demonstrated that supplied constructs are less meaningful than elicited ones, both in terms of extremity of ratings and according to the individual's ranking of importance (see also Neimeyer, G., Leso, Marmarosh, Prichard, & Moore, 1992).

In sum, the main concern with supplied constructs has to do with its compromise regarding the assessment of idiosyncratic constructions. This remains a polemic issue, however. For example, Fransella (1981) argued for the fairness of using supplied constructs on the basis of the commonality corollary. She asserted that, given a common sociocultural context, the degree of overlap allows for the use of common constructs because most of the participants will be able to find a meaning for the construct label. Fransella (1981) suggested that this research strategy should be complemented with adequate pilot studies to select the construct to be supplied in order to ensure its representativeness and homogeneity.

This suggestion is certainly in line with some of the grid studies presented in Table 5.2. Although some derived their set of supplied constructs from previous research (Neimeyer, G., 1987; Ryle, 1985), others intended to operationalize theoretical concepts (Gale & Barker, 1987; Mancuso & Handin, 1980; Sanchez, 1988, 1990). Another creative and ecological solution is to derive the constructs from the observer's diaries and videotaped recording of family life (Dallos & Aldridge, 1987; Jolly & Vetere, 1987). In any case, it seems advisable to perform a formal pilot study to control the psychometric qualities of the different constructs, as advocated by Sanchez (1988, 1990).

Combining the Constructs. This is a moderate option that retains the advantages of individual elicitations, while still enabling comparisons among grids. It consists of adding the constructs elicited by one partner to the ones elicited by the other and having both rate the elements, using the combined list of constructs. Childs and Hedges (1981) used this strategy and added a variety of twists to provide additional information. Among these were instructions to use several levels of metaperspectives (e.g., "The way in which I view my wife's view of me") in completing the grid ratings. The obvious drawback of this option is its limitation to dyads. When comparing more than two members, the list of constructs would be too large and the complexity of the metaperspectives would quickly become complicated.

Eliciting the Constructs Conjointly. This is a rarely used alternative (Ryle & Breen, 1972a) that bears some potential benefits. The couple or family members decide conjointly which constructs will be included in the common grid. Thus the participants are most responsible for the constructs to be used. The weakness of this strategy is apparent: The elicitation of construct is left to the hazards of the conjoint interview. The very interactional dynamic of the interview influences the construction of the grid itself, and it is hard to capture these dynamics in the grid analysis. The influence of the interviewer is also particularly evident here. Some additional form of observational analysis could be added to the grid design to counterbalance these influences. Also present is the danger that the purpose of the task (the selection of representative constructs) might be misunderstood or seem irrelevant to the members.

An interesting combination of "combining the constructs" and "eliciting the constructs conjointly" is that used by Bannister and Bott (1973). They first elicited constructs from each spouse, rated them independently, and then combined those constructs in a larger grid that the couple completed conjointly. The therapists therefore were able to observe the relative importance (dominance) of each partner's view in determining the couple's network of shared meanings. This strategy partially addresses some of the critiques expressed above.

Selecting Individual Constructs for a Family Grid. This is one of the most sophisticated grid designs for the study of families. It accrues the advantages of most of the previous designs, with the single disadvantage of its complexity. In its original application (Procter, 1978; 1985b), subjects were asked to complete a 16×16 individual grid to elicit the constructs from triadic comparisons among the elements (family members plus external positive and negative figures). Then four constructs of each family member were selected to be included in a family grid common to all the members. Therefore, in a family of, say, four members, the family grid would include four constructs from each member for a total of 16 constructs. The elements for the family grid included the four family members themselves and their metaperspectives (e.g., "How Mom sees Dad," four metaperspectives for each of the other three members), resulting in a total of 16 elements.

The key issue of this design is the selection of individual constructs. Procter (1978) proposed a generic rationale for this selection process— that is, to get a good "spread" of constructs which at the same time accounts for much of the variance in the individual grids. He first suggested several criteria for the exclusion of constructs and then proceeded to suggest using the constructs most highly linked to each of the separate factors in the grid. This strategy was aimed at selecting constructs that are reasonably independent (Landfield, 1977). In a study presented by Feixas, Cunillera, and Villegas (1987; see also Cunillera & Feixas, 1990), the criteria for the selection/exclusion of individual constructs were defined following a series of ordered priorities. First the excluding criteria were applied to reduce the individual constructs to a useful set. Then inclusion criteria were applied for the selection of the four constructs from among the remaining constructs. So, for a given grid, 6 of the 16 constructs might first be excluded, and then the application of the inclusion criteria might narrow these down to the selection of 4 of the remaining 10 constructs. These criteria are presented in a revised form in Table 5.3.

This design is consistent with the idea of a shared set of constructs among the family members, as proposed by Procter (1978, 1981). Moreover it allows for a very complete analysis. Aside from the information derived directly from the individual grids, the other measures derived from this design (see Table 5.2) give it additional analytic power. Its main disadvantage is its complexity with families of more than five members.

Another set of objections comes from the conceptual side. Some of the concerns shown for the strategy of supplying constructs can apply here (and for the "combining constructs" strategy) as well. There is no guarantee that selecting and pooling constructs will provide a meaningful grid form for every member. Neither is it possible to guarantee that the members ascribe the same meanings to a given construct label. Even if one accepts the idea of a shared set of family constructs, it is still possible for

TABLE 5.3 List of Exclusion and Inclusion Criteria for the Selection of
Individual Constructs to Be Pooled in a Family Grid

Exclusion criteria:

1st   *Nondiscriminating constructs.* Exclude those constructs rating with the very same
       score across family members.

2nd   *Excessively concrete constructs.* Exclude those constructs that appear to be too
       specific (e.g., "plays in brass band vs. not in band"), or physical (e.g., "muscular vs.
       weak") or situational ("worker vs. supervisor"). This criterion was proposed in this
       very same form by Procter (1978).

Inclusion criteria:

1st   *Explicit commonality.* Include those constructs representing the grid label(s) two or
       more members spontaneously used in their individual grids.

2nd   *Discriminating power.* Include those constructs that discriminate more among the
       family member elements of the individual grid. This notion is similar to that of
       Landfield's (1977) ordination but is considered here because of the construct's
       capacity to draw distinctions among family members. In doubtful cases, the greater
       the discriminating power of the construct among the family elements, the higher the
       chance of being selected.

3rd   *Orthogonal explicative power.* Include those constructs accounting for the greater
       percentage of variance within the principal components or factors resulting from the
       statistical analysis of the individual grids. A mostly representative set of individual
       constructs is acquired when selecting the most relevant ones (in terms of variance)
       for each of the three first factors, although this varies according to the structure of
       every grid.

---

an individual member to use a construct not in the others' repertories. But
Fransella's (1981) arguments are generally instructive in this regard. In
the context of a family, we usually have sufficient grounds (although no
certainty) for assuming reasonable levels of commonality.

   In considering which of these repertory grid strategies to adopt in any
particular family assessment, several issues must be taken into account.
For example, the study of couples allows for more complex and lengthy
designs. Conversely, the larger the number of members, the greater the
limitation on the designs available. The purpose of the assessment is also
a determining issue. Research studies usually seek the testing of specific
hypotheses. Clinical studies also pursue definite though different goals,
with the therapist searching for specific information that bears on his or
her hypotheses about the family and its dynamics. The population is also
different in research and clinical settings, the latter being more anxious
and willing to obtain quick answers. As a general strategy, it is advisable

to choose an approach that elicits the needed information with minimal procedural complexity.

Another important issue to be considered in selecting a grid method for couples or families is the type of elements to use (see Feixas, 1988, for a general classification). Simple elements (people or situations) are direct. Relational elements (the way A relates to B) may involve a higher level of abstraction. They also imply the use of relational constructs; that is, constructs that describe interaction (e.g., "A depends on B") inferred from many behaviors between those persons are usually expressed through relational verbs (e.g., *loves, hates, admires*). These relational constructs, though abstract, provide clinically rich information. On the other hand, the use of metaperspectives (inspired by the work of Laing, Phillipson, & Lee, 1966) is a fair operationalization of Kelly's sociality included in most grid designs, either in the form of metaelements (e.g., "My view," "My mother's view," "My father's view") or asking the subject to predict the other's response (e.g., exchange grid method).

It must be noted that the methodological developments presented in this section allow for the assessment of therapeutic change in a process orientation of psychotherapy research (cf. Greenberg & Pinsof, 1986). Several studies already have used these grid designs to assess the family's change across a therapy course by including re-administration of the grid following a therapeutic intervention (Childs & Hedges, 1981; Neimeyer, G., 1987; Ryle & Breen, 1972b; Wijesinghe & Wood, 1976) or a simplified session-by-session recording (Ryle & Lipshitz, 1975). Ryle (1985) also outlined some implications of the dyad grid design for psychotherapy research. It should also be mentioned that most of these grid methods can be (and some have been) applied for the investigation of the client-therapist relationship, although this is outside the scope of this chapter.

In spite of its complexity, the grid offers a rich and provocative set of data about a couple or family. Moreover, it well may provide the best available basis for operationalizing many of the family processes described at a clinical level by family researchers and therapists.

Some Concluding Remarks

Despite its novelty, constructivist assessment of couples and families represents a fruitful and growing area of interest. Not only has it been fertile in providing creative and sophisticated assessment tools but also in furnishing therapists with methods for the development and elaboration of further methods aimed at articulating personal and family meanings.

The emerging interface of two different traditions—PCT and the systemic approach—allows for multiple cross contributions from the one to the other. Their common epistemological stance—constructivism—warrants the coherent utilization of their methods. Despite developing from different traditions, the assessment procedures presented in this chapter are directed toward the same goal: the investigation of the family's meaning system. They all assume that the way the system (either personal or familial) construes reality deserves a primary focus, and they provide the therapist with multiple inroads into exploring these constructions.

By exploring commonalities and differences in construing processes, the constructivist assessment methods presented in this chapter examine the way personal meanings interact within broader familial and social constructions. Sometimes family members share a common reality. At other times, they locate themselves in opposite positions within the family's shared avenues for construing events. Finally they may use largely independent ways of construing events and experiences. Conflicts arising from this multiple universe can be better understood by assessing the family's construing process.

Although this chapter has presented specific applications of constructivist assessment in pragmatic terms, it is complemented by related work that more adequately addresses conceptual (Alexander & Neimeyer, G., 1989; Feixas, 1990b; Loos & Epstein, 1989) and empirical (Neimeyer, G. & Hudson, 1985; Neimeyer, R. & Neimeyer, G., 1985) aspects, as well as work that further details the application of constructivism to marital and family assessment (Dallos, 1990; Procter, 1987). The interview, writing, and repertory grid techniques reviewed here, however, illustrate three common features of constructivist assessment: (a) its emphasis on the primacy of personal experience, (b) its concentration on developing and transforming meaning through language, and (c) its reflexive awareness of the co-constructed nature of psychological issues. According to this view, family members join with therapists in forging a shared and shifting view of presenting problems. This serves as an apt reminder that whatever we do as therapists to "assess" personal and family meanings, those efforts themselves become interlaced into a larger social fabric jointly woven by everyone involved in the process of family therapy.

References

Alexander, P., & Neimeyer, G. J. (1989). Constructivism and family therapy. *International Journal of Personal Construct Psychology, 2,* 111-121.

Bannister, D., & Bott, M. (1973). Evaluating the person. In P. Kline (Ed.), *New approaches in psychological measurement.* London: John Wiley.

Bannister, D., & Fransella, F. (1986). *Inquiring man: The psychology of personal constructs* (3rd ed.). London: Routledge.

Bateson, G. (1972). *Steps to an ecology of mind.* New York: Ballantine.

Bateson, G. (1976). Foreword. In C. E. Sluzki & D. C. Ranson (Eds.), *Double bind: The foundation of the communicational approach to the family.* New York: Grune & Stratton.

Bateson, G. (1979). *Mind and nature: A necessary unity.* New York: E. P. Dutton.

Bogdan, J. (1984). Family organization as an ecology of ideas. *Family Process, 23,* 375-388.

Bonarius, H. (1977). The interaction model of communication: Through experimental research towards existential relevance. In A. W. Landfield & J. K. Cole (Eds.), *Nebraska Symposium on Motivation, 1976: Personal construct psychology* (Vol. 26). Lincoln: University of Nebraska Press.

Boscolo, L., Cecchin, G., Hoffman, L., & Penn, P. (1987). *Milan systemic family therapy: Conversations in theory and practice.* New York: Basic Books.

Cecchin, G. (1987). Hypothesizing, circularity, and neutrality revisited: An invitation to curiosity. *Family Process, 26,* 405-413.

Childs, D., & Hedges, R. (1981). The analysis of interpersonal perceptions as a repertory grid. *British Journal of Medical Psychology, 53,* 127-136.

Constantine, L. (1986). Jealousy and extramarital sexual relations. In N. S. Jacobson & A. S. Gurman (Eds.), *Clinical handbook of marital therapy.* New York: Guilford.

Cunillera, C., & Feixas, G. (1990). Acuerdos and desacuerdos en el sistema de constructors familiares [Agreement and disagreement in the family construct system]. *Cuadernos de Terapia Familiar, 13,* 35-44.

Dallos, R. (1990). *Family belief systems: Therapy and change.* Milton Keynes, UK: Open University Press.

Dallos, R., & Aldridge, D. (1985). Change: How do we recognize it? *Journal of Family Therapy, 8,* 45-49.

Dallos, R., & Aldridge, D. (1987). Handing it on: Family constructs, symptoms, and choice. *Journal of Family Therapy, 9,* 39-41.

Dallos, R., & Aldridge, D. (1988). Choice of pathology and systems of construing. *Journal of Strategic and Systemic Therapies, 7*(1), 27-41.

Dallos, R., & Procter, H. G. (1984). *Family processes: An interactional view. Unit 2 of D307 Social Psychology course.* Milton Keynes, UK: Open University Press.

Deissler, K. (1987). *Recursive creation of information: Circular questioning as information generation.* Marburg, Germany, InFam.

Doherty, W. J. (1989). Oil and vinegar or oil and water? The quest for mutuality in individual and family therapies. *Journal of Family Psychology, 2,* 386-395.

Duck, S. W. (1973). *Personal relationships and personal constructs.* London: John Wiley.

Duck, S. W. (1983). Sociality and cognition in personal construct theory. In J. Mancuso & J. Adams-Webber (Eds.), *Applications of personal construct theory*. Toronto: Academic.

Duck, S. W., & Condra, M. (1990). To be or not to be: Anticipation, persuasion, and retrospection in personal relationships. In G. J. Neimeyer & R. A. Neimeyer (Eds.), *Advances in personal construct psychology* (Vol. 1). Greenwich, CT: JAI.

Efran, J., Lukens, R., & Lukens, M. (1988, September-October). Constructivism: What's in it for you? *Family Therapy Networker*, pp. 27-35.

Erickson, M., & Rossi, E. (1976). Two-level communication and the microdynamics of trance. *American Journal of Clinical Hypnosis, 18*, 153-171.

Erickson, M., & Rossi, E. (1979). *Hypnotherapy*. New York: Irvington.

Feixas, G. (1988). *L'analisi de construccions personals en textos do significacio psicologica* [Personal Construct Analysis of Autobiographical Texts]. Doctoral dissertation on microfilm (n. 328). Barcelona: Publicacions Universitat de Barcelona.

Feixas, G. (1990a). Approaching the individual, approaching the system: A constructivist model for integrative psychotherapy. *Journal of Family Psychology, 4*, 4-35.

Feixas, G. (1990b). Personal construct theory and the systemic therapies: Parallel or convergent trends? *Journal of Marital and Family Therapy, 16*, 1-20.

Feixas, G. (in press a). Personal construct approaches to family therapy. In R. Neimeyer & G. Neimeyer (Eds.), *Advances in personal construct theory* (Vol. 2). Greenwich, CT: JAI.

Feixas, G. (in press b). Personal constructs in systemic practice. In R. A. Neimeyer & M. J. Mahoney (Eds.), *Constructivism in psychotherapy*.

Feixas, G., Cunillera, C., & Villegas, M. (1987, August). *PCT and the systems approach: A theoretical and methodological proposal for integration*. Paper presented at the Seventh International Congress on Personal Construct Psychology, Memphis, TN.

Feixas, G., & Villegas, M. (1990). *Constructivismo and psicoterapia* [Constructivism and psychotherapy]. Barcelona: Promociones and Publicaciones Universitarias.

Fleuridas, C., Nelson, T., & Rosenthal, D. (1986). The evolution of circular questions: Training family therapists. *Journal of Marital and Family Therapy, 12*, 113-127.

Fransella, F. (Ed.). (1981). *Personality*. London: Methuen.

Fransella, F., & Bannister, D. (1977). *A manual for repertory grid technique*. London: Academic.

Furman, B., & Ahola, T. (1988). The return of the question "Why": Advantages of exploring pre-existing explanations. *Family Process, 27*, 395-409.

Gale, A., & Barker, M. (1987). The repertory grid approach to analyzing family members' perception of self and others: A pilot study. *Journal of Family Therapy, 9*, 355-366.

Goolishian, H., & Anderson, H. (1990). Understanding the therapeutic process: From individuals and families to systems in language. In F. Kaslow (Ed.), *Voices in family psychology*. Newbury Park, CA: Sage.

Greenberg, L. S., & Pinsof, W. (1986). *Psychotherapeutic process*. New York: Guilford.

Guidano, V. F., & Liotti, G. (1983). *Cognitive processes and emotional disorders*. New York: Guilford.

Haley, J. (1963). *Strategies of psychotherapy*. New York: Grune & Stratton.

Haley, J. (1965). Toward a theory of pathological systems. Reprinted in Haley, J. *Reflections on therapy*. Washington: Triangle.

Hampson, S. (1982). *The construction of personality*. London: Routledge.

Harter, S., Neimeyer, R., & Alexander, R. (1989). Personal construction of family relationships: The relation of commonality and sociality to family satisfaction for parents and adolescents. *International Journal of Personal Construct Psychology, 2,* 123-142.

Hartmann, A. (1988). *Repertory grid technique in family research: Diagnosis of conflicts and coalitions.* Unpublished manuscript, University of Heidelberg.

Hinkle, D. N. (1965). *The change of personal constructs from the viewpoint of a theory of implications.* Unpublished doctoral dissertation, Ohio State University, Columbus.

Hoffman, L. (1985). Beyond power and control: Toward a "second-order" family systems therapy. *Family Systems Medicine, 3,* 381-396.

Hoffman, L. (1989). A constructivist position for family therapy. *Irish Journal of Psychology, 9*(1), 110-129.

Jolly, C., & Vetere, A. (1987). Repertory grids, interviews, and films. In A. Vetere & A. Gale (Eds.), *Ecological studies of family life.* London: John Wiley.

Kantor, D., & Lehr, W. (1975). *Inside the family: Towards a theory of family process.* San Francisco: Jossey-Bass.

Kantor, D., & Neal, J. (1985). Integrative shifts for the theory and practice of family systems therapy. *Family Process, 24,* 13-30.

Karastergiou-Katsika, A., & Watson, J. P. (1982). A new approach to construct elicitation for a grid test. *British Journal of Clinical Psychology, 28,* 67-68.

Karastergiou-Katsika, A., & Watson, J. P. (1985). A comparative study of repertory grid and clinical methods for assessing family structure. *Journal of Family Therapy, 7,* 231-250.

Keeney, B. (1983). *The aesthetics of change.* New York: Guilford.

Kelly, G. A. (1955). *The psychology of personal constructs* (2 vols.). New York: Norton.

Kelly, G. A. (1969). Personal construct theory and the psychotherapeutic interview. In B. Maher (Ed.), *Clinical psychology and personality: The selected papers of George Kelly.* New York: John Wiley.

Kenny, V., & Gardner, G. (1988). Constructions of self-organizing systems. *Irish Journal of Psychology, 9*(1), 1-24.

Laing, R. D., Phillipson, H., & Lee, A. (1966). *Interpersonal perception: A theory and a method of research.* New York: Springer.

Landfield, A. W. (1977). Interpretive man: The enlarged self-image. In A. W. Landfield (Ed.), *Nebraska Symposium on Motivation.* Lincoln: University of Nebraska Press.

Landfield, A. W. (1988). Personal science and the concept of validation. *International Journal of Personal Construct Psychology, 1,* 237-249.

Loos, V. E., & Epstein, J. R. (1989). Conversational construction of meaning in family therapy: Some evolving thoughts on Kelly's sociality corollary. *International Journal of Personal Construct Psychology, 2,* 149-168.

Mahoney, M. J. (1988). Constructive metatheory: I. Basic features and historical foundations. *International Journal of Personal Construct Psychology, 1,* 1-35.

Mair, M. (1977). Metaphors for living. In A. W. Landfield (Ed.), *Nebraska Symposium on Motivation, 1976* (pp. 241-290). Lincoln: University of Nebraska Press.

Mancuso, J. C. (1988). Analyzing cognitive structures: An application to parent role systems. In J. C. Mancuso & M. L. Shaw (Eds.), *Cognition and personal structures.* New York: Praeger.

Mancuso, J. C., & Handin, K. H. (1980). Training patients to construe the child's construing. In A. W. Landfield & L. M. Leitner (Eds.), *Personal construct psychology: Personality and psychotherapy.* New York: John Wiley.

Maturana, H., & Varela, F. (1980). *Autopoiesis and cognition.* Boston: Riedel.

McDonald, D. E., & Mancuso, J. C. (1987). A constructivist approach to parent training. In R. A. Neimeyer & G. Neimeyer (Eds.), *Personal construct therapy casebook.* New York: Springer. (Trad. cast. en DDB, Bilbao, 1989)

Minuchin, S. (1974). *Families and family therapy.* Cambridge, MA: Harvard University Press. (Trad. cast. en Ed. Gedisa, Barcelona, 1977)

Minuchin, S., & Fishman, H. C. (1981). *Family therapy techniques.* Cambridge, MA: Harvard University Press.

Neimeyer, G. J. (1984). Cognitive complexity and marital satisfaction. *Journal of Social and Clinical Psychology, 2,* 258-263.

Neimeyer, G. J. (1985). Personal constructs and the counseling of couples. In F. Epting & A. Landfield (Eds.), *Anticipating personal construct psychology.* Lincoln: University of Nebraska Press.

Neimeyer, G. J. (1987). Marital role reconstruction through couples' group therapy. In R. A. Neimeyer & G. J. Neimeyer (Eds.), *A casebook in personal construct therapy.* New York: Springer.

Neimeyer, G. J. (1993). *Using the repertory grid in vocational counseling and development.* Videotape available from Psychoeducational Rescources, P. O. Box 141231, Gainesville, FL 32611.

Neimeyer, G. (in press). Innovative techniques in personal construct marital and family therapy: A practical precis. In H. Procter & G. Feixas (Eds.), *Personal meanings in systemic therapy: Constructivism in action.*

Neimeyer, G. J., & Hudson, J. E. (1985). Couples constructs: Personal systems in marital satisfaction. In D. Bannister (Ed.), *Issues and approaches in personal construct psychology.* London: Academic Press.

Neimeyer, G. J., Leso, J. F., Marmarosh, C., Prichard, S., & Moore, M. (1992). The role of construct type in vocational differentiation: Use of elicited versus provided constructs. *Journal of Counseling Psychology, 39,* 121-128.

Neimeyer, G. J., & Merluzzi, T. V. (1982). Group structure and group process: Explorations in therapeutic sociality. *Small Group Behavior, 13,* 150-164.

Neimeyer, G., & Neimeyer, R. A. (1981). Personal construct perspectives on cognitive assessment. In T. Merluzzi, C. Glass, & M. Genest (Eds.), *Cognitive assessment.* New York: Guilford.

Neimeyer, R. A. (1985). Personal constructs in clinical practice. In P. C. Kendall (Ed.), *Advances in cognitive-behavioral research and therapy* (Vol. 4). New York: Academic Press.

Neimeyer, R. A. (1987). Personal construct therapy. In W. Dryden & W. Golden (Eds.), *Cognitive-behavioral approaches to psychotherapy.* London: Harper & Row.

Neimeyer, R. A., & Neimeyer, G. (1985). Disturbed relationships: A personal construct view. In E. Button (Ed.), *Personal construct theory and mental health.* Beckenham, Kent: Croom Helm.

O'Hara, M., & Anderson, W. T. (1991). *The Family Therapy Networker, 15*(5), 18-25.

O'Loughlin, S. (1989). Use of repertory grids to assess understanding between partners in marital therapy. *International Journal of Personal Construct Psychology, 2,* 143-147.

Penn, P. (1982). Circular questioning. *Family Process, 21,* 267-280.

Penn, P. (1985). Feed-forward: Future questions, future maps. *Family Process, 24,* 299-310.

Procter, H. G. (1978). *Personal construct theory and the family: A theoretical and methodological study.* Unpublished doctoral dissertation, University of Bristol, UK.

Procter, H. G. (1981). Family construct psychology: An approach to understanding and treating families. In S. Walrond-Skinner (Ed.), *Developments in family therapy.* London: Routledge.

Procter, H. G. (1985a). A personal construct approach to family therapy and systems intervention. In E. Button (Ed.), *Personal construct theory and mental health.* Beckenham: Croom Helm.

Procter, H. G. (1985b). Repertory grid techniques in family therapy and system intervention. In E. Button (Ed.), *Personal construct theory and mental health.* Beckenham: Croom Holm.

Procter, H. G. (1987). Change in the family construct system: The therapy of a mute and withdrawn schizophrenic patient. In R. A. Neimeyer & G. Neimeyer (Eds.), *Personal construct therapy casebook.* New York: Springer.

Procter, H. G., & Parry, G. (1978). Constraint and freedom: The social origin of personal constructs. In F. Fransella (Ed.), *Personal construct psychology 1977.* London: Academic.

Procter, H. G., & Walker, G. (1988). Brief therapy. In E. Street & W. Dryden (Eds.), *Family therapy in Britain.* Milton Keynes: Open University Press.

Reiss, D. (1981). *The family's construction of reality.* Cambridge, MA: Harvard University Press.

Ryle, A. (1985). The dyad grid and psychotherapy research. In N. Beail (Ed.), *Repertory grid technique and personal constructs: Applications in clinical and educational settings.* Cambridge, MA: Brookline.

Ryle, A., & Breen, D. (1972a). A comparison of adjusted and maladjusted couples using the double dyad grid. *British Journal of Medical Psychology, 45,* 375-382.

Ryle, A., & Breen, D. (1972b). The use of the double dyad grid. *British Journal of Medical Psychology, 45,* 383-389.

Ryle, A., & Lipshitz, S. (1975). Recording change in marital therapy with the reconstruction grid. *British Journal of Medical Psychology, 48,* 39-48.

Sanchez, E. F. (1988). *Una vision sistemica de la familia* [The systemic vision of the family]. Unpublished doctoral dissertation, Universidad de Sevilla.

Sanchez, E. F. (1990). Diagnostico sitemico do una familia: El Cuestionario de Interrelacion Familiar (CIF) and la tecnica de rejilla [Systemic diagnosis of the family: The family dialogue questionnaire]. *Psicologica, 11,* 59-82.

Selvini-Palazzoli, M., Boscolo, L., Cecchin, G., & Prata, G. (1980). Hypothesizing-circularity-neutrality. *Family Process, 19,* 3-12.

Sluzki, C. E. (1985). Terapia familiar como construccion do realidades alternativas [Family therapy as a reconstruction of alternative realities]. *Sistemas Familiares, 1,* 53-59.

Thomas, L. F. (1979). Construct, reflect, and converse: The conversation reconstruction of social realities. In P. Stringer & D. Bannister (Eds.), *Constructs of sociality and individuality.* London: Academic.

Tomm, K. (1985). Circular interviewing: A multifaceted clinical tool. In D. Campbell & R. Draper (Eds.), *Applications of systemic family therapy: The Milan model*. New York: Grune & Stratton.

von Foerster, H. (1981). *Observing systems*. Seaside, CA: Intersystems.

von Glasersfeld, E. (1984). On radical constructivism. In P. Watzlawick (Ed.), *The invented reality*. New York: Norton.

Waring, E. M. (1980). Marital intimacy, psychosomatic symptoms, and cognitive therapy. *Psychosomatics, 21*, 595-601.

Watzlawick, P. (Ed.). (1984). *The invented reality*. New York: Norton.

Watzlawick, P., Beavin, J., & Jackson, D. (1967). *Pragmatics of human communication*. New York: Norton.

Watzlawick, P., Weakland, J., & Fisch, R. (1974). *Change: Principles of problem formation and problem resolution*. New York: Norton.

Wijesinghe, O. B. A., & Wood, R. R. (1976). A repertory grid study of interpersonal perception within a married couple's psychotherapy group. *British Journal of Medical Psychology, 49*, 287-293.

Willutzki, U., Grzempowski, B., & Goohs-Kammler, P. (1987, August). *The exchange grid specialized: How do couples conceive each other in problematic situations?* Poster presented at the Seventh International Congress on Personal Construct Psychology, Memphis, TN.

Yorke, D. M. (1985). Administration, analysis, and assumption: Some aspects of validity. In N. Beail (Ed.), *Repertory grid technique and personal constructs: Applications in clinical and educational settings*. Cambridge, MA: Brookline.

6

The Personal Narrative in the Communal Construction of Self and Life Issues

LISA TSOI HOSHMAND

S ARBIN (1986) proposed the narrative as a root metaphor for psychology. Use of the narrative as a means of sense making and knowing is germane to many disciplines (Polkinghorne, 1988). The analysis of narrative discourse has spanned the study of cultures, poetics, philosophy, rhetoric, and linguistics (Mellard, 1987). In psychology, interest in the narrative is reflected in an increasing use by researchers of natural language data obtained with interactive modes of data gathering. Although this is not novel to practitioners in their inquiry, the conceptual and practical implications are worthy of consideration. The social constructionist perspective (Arbib & Hesse, 1986; Gergen, 1985a, 1985b) implies that individual meaning making is always socially embedded and should not be divorced from its embedding context. The contribution of the natural social setting to the construction of personal meanings is a dimension that requires us to look beyond traditional boundaries in individual assessment. The objective of this chapter is to describe a field-tested approach involving the use of personal narratives obtained in a group setting for assessment purposes.

In sociolinguistic terms, *narratives* are organized units of discourse that have as their central internal function the telling of a story. Narrating is a way of recapitulating past experience or of constructing present experience and the future, which often involves a temporal sequence (Labov & Waletzky, 1967). *Personal narrative* in this context is a first-person account that has some degree of apparent organization, temporality, and thematic coherence. The personal narrative is perhaps the most common form of natural language data used by therapists and counselors in understanding their clients. Its use in psychological inquiry has precedent, for instance, in the personological inquiry of Murray (1938). Developmental understanding of life issues can be gleaned from a personal life story (Levinson, 1978; Loevinger, 1976). Recent authors have examined the thematization of personal life history within a structured self-image (Bertaux, 1981), as well as the intertwined relationship between life story and personal identity (McAdams, 1988). Although not all of the conversational data found in a group setting may represent complete narratives in the sense of a complete personal story, the frequent occurrence of narrative-form sharing in groups allows for its use in understanding the self and life issues of the group participants. Practitioners of psychotherapy seem to believe in the healing potentials of self-narratives as they support self-identity clarification and development. Some counselors and therapists would see their role as assisting clients in reconstructing their life stories. Thus there is a further possibility of the communal process of narrative construction serving a therapeutic function (Sarbin, 1986).

As a construction of the self and one's life issues, the personal narrative shares many characteristics with other types of client-constructed data such as discussed in this casebook. The analysis of narratives could in principle be conducted in varied fashion, using different conceptual frameworks (Sarbin, 1986). One approach with which it may be compared is conversation analysis, which is represented by an identifiable body of work (Antaki, 1988; Atkinson & Heritage, 1984; Potter & Wetherell, 1987). Like conversation analysis, which has been associated with ethnomethodology, ethnography, and semiology (Heritage, 1984; Moerman, 1988; Potter & Wetherell, 1987), the analysis of personal narratives can draw on a variety of concepts and methods congruent with its philosophical underpinnings. This possibility allows practitioners and researchers to apply and evaluate those tools that they consider to be particularly useful for understanding personal meanings, life scripts, and experience. As will be explained later, phenomenological concepts (Fischer, 1980; Keen, 1975; Valle & Halling, 1989) and a combination of content-analytic (Viney,

1983) and hermeneutic methods (Kvale, 1983; Van Maanen, 1990) are applied to the narrative analysis in this case.

In recognizing the social dimension of meaning construction, the personal narrative is viewed as a product of a self-directed yet communally mediated constructive process. Gergen (1985a) presented the philosophical and conceptual arguments for the social construction of the person. People personify themselves with socially embedded meanings. In this case, personal narratives obtained from interactions in a group residential setting provide an opportunity to look at self and life issues in their proper communal context. As with any conversation analysis, personal narratives occurring in group conversation need to be interpreted in context and to be viewed as generating contexts to which members of a group could respond. An individual's construction cannot be understood apart from the shared meanings of the group and the apparent group culture that mediates narrative exchanges. This dynamic relationship between inividual expression and group-mediated process means that the unit of analysis can include all of the following: (a) the individual, (b) the individual-within-the-group process, and (c) the group as a collective meaning-making entity. The second unit was found to be the most difficult to explicate procedurally. The group processes mediating meaning making are given only a tentative treatment here in this chapter.

Whereas the use of groups for therapeutic intervention has been described widely in the professional literature, the use of the group setting for client assessment per se has not been systematically documented. For a close parallel, one may refer to the use of group interviews in field research. Morgan (1988) described the use of focus groups as a form of qualitative inquiry. Focus groups that involve an open discussion format have their origin in sociology (Krueger, 1988). They have been used considerably in applied research, such as in the fields of marketing, public relations, and political campaigning. Recognizing the focus group's value as a self-contained research method and as a supplement to both quantitative and qualitative research, Morgan (1988) proposed its increased use by social scientists. The present approach, as will be described subsequently, has certain similarities to the focus group. Group interaction is encouraged as an opportunity for observing naturally occurring discourse. The group facilitator assumes the role of a participant observer. The participants' perspectives are sought and respected. It differs from the focus group, however, in being more phenomenological in orientation and less driven by the agenda of the group facilitator. This is an important distinction in that focus groups tend to be dominated by the purpose and questions of the interviewer, which can keep the process from being more open. The present group is akin to a therapeutic group in terms of the training background of the facilitators and the attention given to the process of meaning making. It differs from a therapeutic group in avoiding intentional interventions or moving the group toward a working stage and final outcome. In other words, its purpose is primarily one of assessment.

The application of discourse or narrative analysis to the developmentally disabled in particular was pioneered by the anthropological work of Edgerton and Langness (1978). Interest in the language and thought of these populations goes beyond the relevance of such functions to their social adjustment. Looking at the lives of these individuals as if they were actors in a play, and listening to their life stories as told by themselves, reflect a constructivist commitment to understanding the interpretations and perspectives of these clients. Perhaps because of the perceived verbal and cognitive limitations of the developmentally disabled, practitioners and researchers have not taken a sufficient interest in their personal narratives and phenomenology. Like the rest of us, these individuals live in language communities and shared experiential worlds. The conversations and personal narratives are part of the essential reality of these groups that professionals can strive to understand.

Background

I began the gathering of personal narratives in a group setting initially in field research with the developmentally disabled, using a "rap group" format (Hoshmand, 1985). Graduate counseling students served as group facilitators. Over a period of 2 years, the group sessions evolved into a tool that could be used for client assessment. These group sessions, conducted in facilities for the developmentally disabled, were welcomed subsequently as opportunities for the clients to discuss their personal issues and daily concerns. Group sessions were held under conditions of confidentiality, with the understanding that the collective concerns of the clients would be communicated to the appropriate agency staff for therapeutic consideration and program planning.

The approach to be described in this chapter had been used with seven different groups, totaling 56 clients (19 males and 37 females, aged 19-57). Each group had seven to nine members. Four groups were constituted in community sheltered workshops for the mildly retarded, with two consisting of clients from high-functioning work areas and two from moderate-functioning areas. The clients had tested IQs ranging from 52-77. The other three groups were offered to clients of a regional center for the disabled. Two of these groups consisted of mildly retarded adults, with tested IQs of 53-79, who were living in board-and-care facilities. The third group consisted of clients with cerebral palsy and an IQ range of 68-113. Thus the approach has been tested with relatively homogeneous groups of clients who apparently shared similar life situations and concerns. Although individual differences were evident within each group, such differences will not be the focus of this presentation.

The number of weekly group sessions conducted in the first year ranged from 15-20. The group sessions were about 50 minutes in length. In the second year, 8-9 sessions were held for the groups, each lasting an hour. It was felt that the amount of time was sufficient to get a fairly good picture of the clients' lived world.

The purpose of the field inquiry described here was to generate hypotheses about the client populations involved and to suggest areas of focus from a service point of view. The general approach and procedures were those of an open-ended explorative study.

Method

It will be appropriate to describe first the present approach in terms of the attitudes and orientation of those conducting the inquiry. We went into the setting with an open, nonjudgmental attitude toward the clients. By adopting a phenomenological orientation, we took special interest in the experiences and meanings of our informants, while making an effort to set aside our preconceptions. The main assumption that we did hold was about self-agency. We chose to see the clients as capable of self-directed discourse about their lives, personal actions, and anticipations. Although our training orientation was "therapeutic," we saw our roles primarily as participant observers engaged in a reciprocal process of exchange with the members of these communities. Besides the interaction within the self-contained groups, the group facilitators were free to observe and study the larger premises of the facilities as naturalistic settings. This immersion was considered to be helpful to developing a sense of the culture and language community to which the group participants belonged. It provided us with the kind of local knowledge that practitioners need to have about their particular client population and program setting.

Our data-gathering method may be described as *ethnographic*. We made audio recordings of all verbal interactions. For our field research, stream of behavior records were kept of related observations in the group sessions. Subsequent assessment groups were taped similarly, with brief observational notes taken by the facilitator to help contextualize the interactions as they occurred. As participant observers, the group facilitators were interested in the "native" perspectives and meanings of the members. An open atmosphere was created for the groups, with the invitation for all participants to talk freely. Confidentiality was emphasized, and privacy from other parts of the facility and nongroup members was provided. Through modeling and gentle instruction, the group participants were given the expectation that everyone should be given ample opportunity for self-expression and should be listened to without excessive interruption. The literature on groups refers to stages in the development of group process and the conditions for optimal levels of participation (Corey & Corey, 1992; Shapiro, 1978; Yalom, 1985). Our initial groups for field research had been analyzed quantitatively for frequency of interactive participation. The results of this analysis indicated that participants from the developmentally disabled population were able to achieve a certain "group-likeness" within a few sessions and to maintain levels of participation sufficient for assessment purposes.

One of the most crucial features of our method was the encouragement of informant-embeddedness, or freedom to be immersed in one's own experience and frame of reference. We wanted the clients to bring in their personal contexts for all discussion. We experimented with using broad areas as suggested topics for initiating group sessions and then observed the degree and nature of participation. We changed to allowing clients to bring up their own topics and monitored the group interaction. After a period of experimentation, client-chosen and client-directed topics were followed predominantly. At all times, the group facilitators werc intent on following the clients' own contexts in the flow of discourse, avoiding the imposition of external agendas or interventions that might result in distorting the clients' meanings. This avoidance required attentive listening and empathic indwelling but not active interpretation or intensive therapeutic reflection. Summarizing statements were used mainly to verify what was being said. The primary objectives were inquiry and developing an understanding of the particular client populations involved.

The group facilitation was aimed at encouraging the sharing of personal meanings and phenomenological descriptions of experience. After a client introduced a topic, we asked such questions as, "What is it like?" or "How does it feel?" but did not routinely react with questions or other comments of a confronting or challenging nature. This did not prevent other group participants from responding freely to a client's remarks in ways that might have shaping effects. We considered this natural dialogue to be inherent to the communal process of meaning making. Not infrequently, when the topic concerned their living experience at the facility, group members would express different points of view. The spontaneous give and take and the confirmation or disconfirmation of experience among group members were accepted as part of the communal process from which the personal narratives took shape. In a sense, our method of data gathering was rather simple, deriving information from the richness of natural conversation.

The group sessions were transcribed verbatim, with the on-the-spot observation notes kept by the facilitators serving as additional guides for contextualizing the narratives. After a period of time, the transcripts of sessions from each facility were reviewed by pairs of independent judges for analysis. The narrative data analysis involved (a) low-inference content analysis that may be regarded as lying on the more quantitative end of the continuum of interpretive methods and (b) a more qualitative, hermeneutic approach (Kvale, 1983). Thus two types of logic or analytic strategy were followed. When recurring topics were identified on the basis of similar descriptive content, a replication logic was followed in the derivation of themes. In addition, the interpretive process also involved any amount of narrative material and observational data deemed relevant as the larger context of the expressed meanings. In other words, the unit of meaning analysis varied as any given part could contribute to a sense of a whole, and the emergent whole could be used to reinterpret any part of the text. This reciprocal interpretive process, based on a part-to-whole logic, definitely depended on the interpreter's tacit reading of culturally shared habits of discourse and meaning-generating narrative

TABLE 6.1 Narrative Data Analysis

Process	Procedures
Literal comprehension of descriptive content[*]	Open coding of meaning categories relevant to general area of interest[*]
Reading and indwelling for metaphoric understanding	Listing of expressive units that symbolize significant meanings
Posing questions to the text, based on conceptual framework, clinical hypothesis, or research interest[*]	Focused coding and interpretation of units relevant to the questions
Inductive derivation of themes from recurrent meaning categories[*]	Identifying themes from coded units based on replication criterion[*]
Hermeneutic cycle of interpretation[*]	Deriving understanding based on part-to-whole relationship of units to emergent pattern as interpretive context[*]
Creative dialogue with interpretive process	Creative rewriting and integration based on fantasy variation, figure-ground reversal, or dramatization
Validation (presumed on reliability checks of prior procedures)[*]	Cross-case replication, verifying with source, and assessing pragmatic value of the obtained understanding[*]

[*] Applied in the present case.

contexts (Mishler, 1986). The comprehension of the text in content analysis and the derivation of themes were presumed on culturally recognizable discourse units by their topical unity, internal organization, and boundedness. The "guidelines" for this cultural aspect of interpretation are thus more implicit than explicit.

Table 6.1 summarizes the process and procedures of conducting narrative data analysis, with those elements applicable to the present case identified with asterisks.

The first level of analysis was in terms of topic areas by descriptive content. Discourse on any given topic was defined operationally by a minimal number of speaking turns on the same topic by different participants. After the topic areas were determined to be sufficiently reliable (over 75% agreement), they were used for coding the interactions of subsequent group sessions, with the option of adding new topics (in a similar way) as they appeared. The number of topics per session varied from one to as many as nine, considering all groups. The coded transcripts were analyzed further in terms of recurring topics, with the appearance of the same topic in more than two sessions regarded as a thematic recurrence. This operational criterion was used in the absence of an inductive basis for predetermining the pattern of recurrence.

The second level of analysis was in terms of themes and patterns. The coded topics were reviewed by independent judges. Overall 22 themes were derived, each noted for unique or multiple group origin. A matching procedure similar to that used by Weenolsen (1985) in the study of life themes was followed, whereby a second independent judge matched topics to the themes deduced by the first judge. Themes receiving moderate to high agreement (75-100%) were retained for interpretation as potential generalizations or hypotheses about the group of clients involved. Strength of themes was ranked on a group basis by the number of related recurring topics and was evaluated for similarities and differences between groups.

The narrative content of each theme was examined from a personological and phenomenological point of view. Temporal continuity and consistency of self-presentation were assumed to represent a sense of personal continuity or identity (Sarbin, 1986). Questions posed to the data included, "How does the information reveal self-identity?" "How is the self portrayed and justified?" "What is the nature of the person's lived world and life purpose?" "What kinds of life issues seem to preoccupy this person's phenomenological world?" and "Does this person's experience resonate with other members of the group, and in which way?" These questions are considered from a hermeneutic point of view to be essential to uncovering the lived meanings of the personal narrations that may not be as apparent from a purely content-analytic approach.

Communal Processes of Construction

In an attempt to understand how social interaction processes enter into the participants' meaning making in the group context, the literature on therapeutic and experiential groups was consulted. The research seems not to be definitive on the exact processes mediating meaning-making activity (Dies & MacKenzie, 1983; Kaul & Bednar, 1978, 1986). The literature only suggests that the search for meaning can occur as early as the beginning stage of a group and that the process may follow various courses, depending on the nature of the group (Yalom, 1985). In the absence of theoretical preconceptions and grounded knowledge about how naturally occurring group processes mediate the construction of personal meanings, an inductive effort was made to discover the social aspects of narrative expression. Our client assessment groups were examined for possible types of relevant communal processes. For a beginning understanding, segments of the transcripts that had been coded as revolving around a given topic were analyzed. Granting that this exploration of communal processes of construction was the most speculative aspect of the analysis, a few types of tentatively inferred interactional mediation of meaning construction are noted.

Echoing. One of the more common forms of group response to a client's narration seemed to be *chiming in* or *echoing*. This could be found in what appeared to be self-centered statements to the same effect as a previous utterance by another person, as obtained from some of the clients with subnormal intelligence. For example, a client was speaking of feeling sad about not being able to see her family often:

Client A	I wish my parents didn't move away. I'm really sad. I don't get to see my family that often.
Client B	My brother is going to get this (waving his fist) if he doesn't show up soon. When my mother was alive, she would come regularly (looking down).
Client C	I'm sad that my sister will be getting married soon. I don't know if I'll be seeing her.

These echoing responses may be taken as a communal validation of a sense of loneliness, even though the narrated content was self-centered. As another example, a client was speaking about his dreams:

Client A	I dreamt that I was in Vietnam. I flew the helicopter and saved a lot of people.
Client B	I dreamt that I was a famous bowler. I won a big tournament.
Client C	Yeah, I was racing cars and I was something.

The communal meaning seemed to be that one could do great things in one's dream.

The echoing response was found in higher functioning groups as well. For example, a client was talking about not feeling safe living at the facility:

Client A	I always leave my bedroom door, my bedroom window locked all the time.
Client B	X (another client) had her TV stolen the day she was moving out.
Client C	They don't care.
Client B	Until something happens.
Facilitator	What do you mean?
Client A	I don't think they do.
Client D	No, I always said they don't care. All they care about is money.

The group members went on to describe various infringements on the residents' personal property and what the agency should have done to better guard the facility. The communal meaning was a lack of protection and caring.

Expanding. In other instances, the echoing type of response seemed to produce an expansion of meanings. For example, a client was talking about what it might be like if life were interrupted by a global disaster:

Client A	We would start all over again. Probably in an underground cave.
Client B	Cutting down trees.
Client A	We'd have to relearn how to do everything all over again.
Facilitator	Um-hum.
Client B	I know what you're saying, but what I'm really thinking . . . if there was some type of a disaster, we'd all have to learn to get to know each other.
Client C	All over again.
Client B	All over again, and get to know different people, because we'd all have to learn from everybody.
Facilitator	Um-hum.
Client B	We'd all have to kind of start back like we didn't know anything or something like that and we'd have to learn. We'd have to learn how to help the people who really need our help. We're kind of . . . we're . . . basically all of us share something in common. We're in chairs and we're disabled, but that isn't so bad. That isn't so bad when you consider that we have a roof over our head, and food in our stomachs.
Client A	And wheelchair buses now.

Client B   I'm not talking about wheelchair buses. I'm talking about the tools
               with which to survive and there are people who are dying 'cause
               they don't have enough food, little kids who don't have clothes and
               don't know how to take a bath. . . . They need us, because if we
               can do something and we don't, we have a crisis. We still have to
               care, about the people that need us.

Client A   I guess that each step forward that we make will help another
               handicapped person a little further.

"Starting all over," as elaborated in the group, not only allows one to
evaluate one's own situation but also to become philosophical about what
it means to be disabled.

   Negotiating. Not all group responses were of an echoing nature. The
negotiation of meanings and one's reality is demonstrated by the following exchange:

Client A   (Referring to another client) She thinks she is married.

Client B   She is—it's just a dream, let her dream it!

Client A   B!

Client B   It's just a thought.

Client A   Yeah, I know that, but . . .

Client B   It's something that's, aah, it's a comforting thought to her. . . . She
               calls her boyfriend her husband. But what A doesn't realize is that
               it's her dream, it's her comfort. And it's just been recently that she's
               been saying he's not my boyfriend, he's my husband. And it's a
               dream. You don't disturb people's dreams.

Client A   I try to put the truth in her mouth. Not that way. I don't believe in
               the make-beliefs.

Facilitator   Uh-huh.

Client B   But A, we don't destroy your dreams.

Client A   I don't like dreams.

Client B   You wanted to live in your own home again, didn't you, eventually
               after . . .

Client A   I know that I'm not going there, I would have . . .

Client B   Okay, but you've been able to go home every once in a while. That
               was your dream, you've been able to do it. You have to let people
               have their dreams. If you don't let people have their dreams, you
               know what's going to happen? They're going to die.

Client A	I do think I'm going to go home sometime.
Client B	Yeah, but see, that dream is going to disappear sometime, but nobody ever said to you, alright, we're going to destroy your dream.
Client A	I know that.

This interchange is particularly significant as some of the disabled clients had been observed to describe their relationship with a boyfriend or girlfriend as "engagement," while the meaning of such engagement and the potential for marriage were being challenged by others.

Attributing. Sometimes a participant assumed an apparently passive role in the interaction, allowing the other group members to construct and attribute meanings to his or her actions. In this example, the group had been talking about different programs and activities and their feeling of purpose:

Client A	We have to go through changes and changes and changes, until we find something that does work.
Client B	And there's always a constant change whether we want it or not. C?
Client C	I ain't got nothing to say.
Facilitator	We're just thinking of being here for a reason, or having something that's unique to you . . . like I've seen you—you have some real pretty artwork in your room, don't you?
Client C	Yeah.
Client B	She's done several things.
Client D	She's sold some of them.
Client B	She's sold several ceramics.
Facilitator	'Cause the first day I was here, I saw some of your artwork. But just inside, in your own feeling, what gives you the most joy in life?
Client C	I don't know.
Client A	Do you really not have anything to say, C?
Client C	Um-hum.
Client A	Oh, I see.
Client D	What I think is her joy of life is painting.
Client C	Yes.
Client B	Whether it's ceramics . . .

Client D   'Cause she paints, she does beautiful clay, she made glasses out of
              clay and stuff like that, and it's all beautiful.
Client C   Oh, D!
Client D   I remember all that.

Following this conversation, Client C became animated in explaining her
artwork, ending in laughter.

The communal process of meaning making deserves further study, both
in practice and in research. The above examples are far from exhaustive.
They are included here to give recognition to the different ways by which
personal meanings expressed in a group conversation are shaped by the
audience and mutually contextualized. The nature of the relationship between each of these communal processes and the specific content of group
conversations has yet to be investigated systematically. Bearing in mind that
such processes were operative, the narratives themselves can be used as
sources of information on the self and life issues of the participants.

Illustrative Findings
on Self and Life Issues

If we take the personal narrative as a construction of the self and life
issues, for individual clients and summatively for the group(s) as the units
of analysis, the data yielded a number of themes. Some of them are
selected for presentation here to illustrate the type of understanding that
we can gain from an analysis of these narratives.

Self-Identity. Sense of identity was conveyed by the cerebral palsy
group as distinctly related to their disability. Illustrative comments were,
"We are the wheelchair people," "Yeah, for all the wheelchair, no walking
people, CP people." As one client said, "The wheelchair should tell my
story." Narrations by the wheelchair were given by some of the clients,
showing humor and a range of intimate emotions.

Normalcy. Closely related to self-identity is the issue of normalcy. This
was found in the groups of mildly retarded clients, as well as in the cerebral
palsy group. For the mentally retarded, it seemed to be associated with frequent remarks about the need to look appropriate and to act with appropriate control:

> Sometimes my clothes don't match and people laugh at me. It hurts. I should look like people outside.
>
> I caught them kissing at the workshop. You shouldn't do that.
>
> Cover your mouth when you cough. They'll think you are dumb.
>
> I was real mad. ___ said, "You are acting like a 2-year-old with a tantrum." I've got to get hold of myself. People would think I'm not normal.

Some of the clients with cerebral palsy found it important to distinguish themselves from other clients who have "mental disabilities":

Client A   I have MD, muscular dystrophy.

Client B   It's not a mental,

Client C   ___ (referring to another client) is lower functioning than the rest of us in this group, so she didn't understand.

When a group member spoke of having had children, the others wanted to find out if the babies were "normal." They considered themselves to be different from people without physical disabilities, yet "just as normal in many ways."

Self-Justification. The narratives reveal that the self and one's personal existence had to be justified:

Client   Because I get help from many, I spread it around and I still can do all the things I need to do with my handicap.

Facilitator   And you don't feel as dependent because you're not depending on just one person for your care?

Client   I'm actually independent by depending upon many.

Facilitator   Um-hum.

Client   And at the other places I went, I felt that I was living and not existing because I was making my own embroidery through Easter Seals. They were helping me draw. My teacher would draw things, then I would embroider them and sell them, or keep them to give away. So I would go on speaking lectures about how even though I was living at a convalescent hospital, I was living and not just existing because of all the different things I was doing.

Life as a Struggle. To understand the ways by which clients justify their being, one can examine their life stories, as well as what they presented as their life purpose. The personal life story was told by many clients in terms of the number of moves they have made and the kinds of encounters they have had with institutions. It was filled typically with episodes about struggles with feelings related to dependence and self-care, as in this narration:

> I'm 50 years old and I started school, if I remember right, when I was 4. I didn't finish high school because handicapped school doesn't prepare you for high school, especially in my time. . . . I left home the first time at 15, and then I came back at 17, and the second time when I was about 21. Took off 'til 24, or 23, something like that. One time was just so that I would learn. I guess my parents wanted me to learn to take care of myself the first time and maybe didn't know what to do with me. They were having marital problems . . . So that's the first time I got to go and I went into a hospital, a county hospital where they tried to fit me into something through rehab . . . . That was before workshops, before I knew about workshops. Then at about 28, I went to the state hospital because I knew my parents couldn't take care of me anymore. They didn't know how to place me anywhere, and I didn't know how to place me anywhere, and I was getting depressed because I didn't want to be with my parents anymore, and then I was scared and depressed because I couldn't leave myself with my parents. I couldn't grow up with my parents, and I also realized they couldn't take care of me anymore, but the only thing I knew of was the state hospital to go to because my mother, when I was little, said things to me like, "People tell me you should be in the state hospital, you should be a ward of the state, I shouldn't keep you." . . .
>
> And I only knew about state hospitals because at the time I didn't know that convalescent hospitals would take you, and I didn't know that even though I had gone to a home when I was, aah, 14 to, I mean 15 to 17. I didn't know that there were more like it or anything, so I said okay and I got really depressed and I said okay, I'll go to the state hospital because I was told that I would be taken care of. And I would get upset with every holiday after, when I was about 28 or so, and so the judge finally said to me, "Well, you keep on coming here at holidays, what do you want?" . . . He sent me to ___. So I went through the front wards of that and in about 3 months I got back to my mother and father because of visits and talking and group therapy . . . The state hospital taught me the bare necessity of just surviving. You were with all kinds of people and you couldn't talk up for yourself. You were just lost, you were just shoved back somewhere and left.
>
> I kept on wanting to go back to the state hospital when I did get into these different homes, I mean different convalescent hospitals, 'cause I still felt

scared because no one was going to take care of me. And then, about, oh when was it, oh about 10 years ago or a few years less than that I learned about the Regional Center, then all my fears settled down.

Life Purpose. The need to have a purpose or some movement in life was another theme:

Client A	Each change I've made I've always pushed forward even if I had to fall back for a while. Always just push forward. It is something you get into something—I need more.
Facilitator	Uh-hum.
Client A	But I have had all my dreams, I asked God. I have had all my dreams. I accomplished all my dreams. I kept on saying to Him, "Give me another dream, I don't know what to dream now. I've done everything I wanted to do. Give me another dream." And you know, He gave me _____ (referring to a program).
Facilitator	What do you mean?
Client B	God.
Client A	God. . . . So He gave me another dream.
Client B	I have no conception of . . . I've done everything, that's what's wrong. My new dream is somebody else's dream, it's not mine. I've done everything that I wanted to do. I just wish that there was still something that I could create and give to somebody, but I've done all . . .
Facilitator	How does that feel?
Client B	Makes me feel bad.

Other life purposes revealed were (a) to show people that they can do what normal people can do, (b) to be helpful to others, (c) to live and experience fully, and (d) to fulfill a higher purpose.

In addition to these themes, issues that were identified thematically include the following:

Control. Having a sense of control over one's life appeared to be a central issue, such as reflected in the following excerpts from two different clients:

I care about you guys, but there are just some things that I have to do and this may sound very confusing, but when I moved here I made some mistakes, to escape and wanting to get rid of it, but I know that was wrong now. I also know that you just can't do that, and now that I'm here I've lost some physical freedom as far as being able to take care of my personal needs, the way that I was taught and the way that I am trained. There are several things that really upset me because I know that the facility cannot be changed over into what I would like it to be. I know that they've got some 80 some odd people that need attention too . . . but I just really miss being able and being in control of my life and being able to do what I need to do for myself. It really irritates me to have to ask somebody to do it because they don't have enough time to set things up the way I need them and let me do it myself. So I'm not saying that the staff here is mean or anything. I'm just saying that I take a look at my feelings . . . feelings and stuff realistically, and now it is coming out all over the place . . . and I just feel really trapped. I feel like I am in a cage, I feel like I have nothing, no control . . . or very little. I think all that I do is just exist here, and that makes me feel real bad and I know it puts a strain on my family because I don't even say anything to them. I know they can see it, and I know the people here see it too.

Sure, it's a board and care, but you don't have 6,000 people going off in 10,000 directions, not knowing right from wrong, or letting them run the whole shot . . . You're going to have nothing. How can you teach people to take care of themselves without teaching them right from wrong? . . . I feel like it's a total zoo. I said on our last . . . I feel like it's a total zoo. Everything's out of control and everything's going off in five different directions.

For some of the clients, control of one's life and destiny meant having better control over their living environment and the care that they receive.

*Transcendence.*To be able to transcend one's disability was important. For one of the clients in the discussion of life purpose, it meant being able to express oneself and to be the self that one wants to be:

Client A   We are more independent. There are people there who can't even hear you. We're also helping them meet their needs . . . and doing something . . . so that if we ever get stuck on our own, or at least partially, we're not stuck wondering what's the world about or anything.

Facilitator   Um-hum.

Client A   We may not, B, we may not agree with what someone does or says, but we can express ourselves, isn't that right?

Client B   Right, uh-huh.

Facilitator	Do I hear you saying that that's connected to your feeling of purpose?
Client A	Yeah, I'm able to be out in the community, and maybe express ourselves. Being out in the world—to be the person that we can be, not the physical strong person. . . . That is helping us, at least me, deal with what I've gotta do.
Facilitator	Um-hum.
Client A	As far as the physical is concerned. But it frustrates me sometimes too, now that I've seen that I can really honestly live with it, not just exist. I can live with my problems, I can solve them, I can get things started, I can actually help somebody else, I can really do something instead of sit there like a stupid bump on a log, watching TV, or just staring into space. I can actually learn something. I can actually be who I want to be. That's exactly what I'm saying.

Collectively the pattern of findings on the respective groups allowed a number of conclusions to be drawn. The self was portrayed by the developmentally disabled clients in terms of their disability, concerns about normalcy, and both positive and negative self-worth. It is justified with life purposes, such as socially approved aspirations of work and learning, and altruistic intentions of helping others. The themes of independence and having control over one's life were major issues. For some of the clients, self-control and self-expression were an integral part of the negotiation of self-esteem among peers. Other prominent life issues expressed by many of the clients were loneliness, interpersonal loss, and survival concerns. Especially for the cerebral palsy group, safety was a prime issue. Their lived world was characterized as a struggle between freedom and constraints. Themes of coping were found across all groups. Some made frequent references to seeking spiritual support or having dreams of self-encouragement and support by deceased loved ones. Others spoke of aspirations as a way of transcending present disabilities. The recurrent strength of the identified themes drives home the quality of existence of these client groups.

Implications for Client Assessment and Therapeutic Practice

The most obvious application of this method is in therapeutic settings where groups are formed readily. A practitioner can learn a great deal about the self and life issues of a client, as well as the collective concerns and meanings of a particular client population, with this method. This approach is especially useful with homogeneous client groups considered to be capable of group participation. It can be used to derive hypotheses on the relevant problems and issues. In this case, the findings have taught us to ask better questions about the psychological adjustment of the developmentally disabled and their service needs. The groups do not necessarily have to be closed. Mixing old with new members probably would change the group process but possibly would add realism. As a means of assessment, this method permits the practitioner to support or modify theoretical formulations with grounded descriptive observations, as well as to discover dimensions of culturally unfamiliar or theoretically uncharted phenomena.

The group format of assessment can be supplemented by individual modes of assessment, such as testing and interviewing. Hypotheses and observations obtained from the personal narratives in the group context can be followed up in counseling and therapy. For instance, in a certain group session, members talked lightheartedly about their fantasies such as traveling around the world and doing things that they were unable to do. One of the mildly retarded clients described a dream house as her fantasy. It was imaged with a lovely garden and the types of flowers that she would like planted in it. When asked to elaborate on what she would be doing in it, however, she stated that she could not let herself be part of the scene. The meaning of her censorship of her own participation in this fantasy can be explored in individual sessions by using cognitive forms of assessment. One may determine the internal dialogue that she has about this and any other forms of fantasizing. It may be fruitful to use guided imagery to discover the lived meanings of being outside as opposed to being inside the garden.

The thematic issues identified in the groups conducted by us led to a number of therapeutic and programmatic recommendations. First and foremost, these clients seem to need an opportunity to express themselves and their concerns and to be listened to without judgment. Internal struggles related to self and feelings of loneliness and other interpersonal concerns could be addressed in individual or group counseling. Specific issues of safety and control over the living environment suggest the need for consulting the clients about facility changes, as well as empowering them in daily arrangements that impact on their autonomy. Learning about the lived world of these clients through their narratives can increase our consciousness of their problems of existence.

The level of interpretation as presented here has tended to be low in inference, which was a choice guided by experience in field research with the populations involved. The transcribed texts contain many more fruitful sources of abstract understanding and clinical speculation. In this sense, the interpretive process is never quite complete. One needs to go back and forth constantly between the original data and the abstracted categories or themes. This brings up the related question of how systematic a practitioner needs to be in analyzing such data for the purpose of clinical inquiry. Although a practitioner may not be able to verify the reliability of observations in an assessment group with the same precision as in research, it is advisable to arrange for some form of peer review or consultation. A cofacilitator or a fellow practitioner can review the taped interaction independently and provide insights against which one can compare one's own interpretations. A very helpful practice is to go back to the source; the informants or clients in the group can be asked to verify the accuracy of one's observations and interpretations. With experience and feedback, the group facilitator's construction of the findings should approximate the communal understanding emergent from the group interaction.

Practitioners who are experienced in conducting therapeutic groups may question the appropriateness of this mode of client assessment. Some may feel that it takes too much time away from active interventions that utilize the group process. Concerns may be raised about the more verbal clients dominating a group, or group interactions getting out of control with minimal leadership and direction. It is important to exercise professional judgment in constituting client groups for primarily assessment purposes. Being more akin to an experiential group than other types of therapeutic groups, they still require qualified facilitators. Although different from the focus group in being less directed by the facilitator, the potential is present for the facilitator and group influence to have restrictive effects on the individual's meaning creation. To the extent that the group members develop trust and feel free to share personal meanings, the group interaction will be more spontaneous and possibly less reactive from an assessment point of view. More needs to be learned, however, about the mediating effects of the group process on the development and communication of personal meanings.

Conceivably this approach can be used by practitioners of diverse theoretical persuasions, provided they find the constructivist perspective to be philosophically congruent with their particular orientation. The areas of conversation analysis, phenomenology, ethnomethodology, and sociolinguistics that are referenced in the earlier sections provide conceptual literature that can supplement the more familiar literature of our own discipline. Group practitioners and trainers and researchers of group practice in particular may find it useful to consider group processes from a social, meaning-making perspective.

Methodological Considerations and Research Implications

Assessment groups of the type described here have advantages and limitations when used in field inquiry. They represent an efficient method of data gathering. Large amounts of information can be obtained from multiple informants within a reasonable period of time. The mode of data gathering is not highly reactive, using participant observation in a relatively natural group setting. The same issues of role management confronted by participant observers in other forms of field inquiry, however, have to be addressed by those who use this method (Jorgensen, 1989; Spradley, 1980). Like focus groups used in research, the present group approach is more contained and controlled than ethnographic research in an open setting. The fact that the group is allowed to be self-managed to a large extent limits the professional's contribution to the data as they are generated.

The degree to which a facilitator actually follows the native contexts of the group members remains a critical issue in the facilitation of the meaning-making process. The balance between active listening and context shaping or context generating is difficult to specify. As pointed out by Mishler (1986), the interpretive analysis of narrative data necessarily involves the introduction of more general knowledge of the culture than is contained in the text itself. We bring into the analysis what else we know about the speakers and their local and general circumstances. If we view the group conversation in this case as a living text, the facilitators' contextual knowledge is limited even as they moderate the group discourse. Not being a native of workshop society or the board-and-care facility for the disabled, our facilitators are likely to have had gaps in their understanding of the flow and contexts of discourse. Only extensive participant observation and immersion in a natural setting would permit us to gain sufficient knowledge of the sociolinguistic rules of a particular speech community (Gumperz, 1964). It may be argued that in some instances of misinterpretation the group members would have negotiated for a modified understanding. Yet unless the reciprocal influence of the group on the facilitator's construing and communication is monitored, this aspect will remain unclear.

The data reduction attempted in this case had been partly dependent on quantitative criteria for establishing topic recurrence and thematic patterns. The method of matching topics to themes does not guarantee the best interpretation of the given meanings or prevent omission. A more systematic approach would have been to follow the constant comparative method described by Glaser and Strauss (1967). Interpretive patterns may be regarded as saturated when additional cases do not add new information and no other theme seems to appear after exhaustive analysis. After establishing a thematic pattern in this fashion, negative cases can be searched for as a test of the interpretation. It is possible to move toward higher levels of data organization in the form of qualitatively construed overarching themes. I was conscious of the intrusion, in this case, of personal perspectives that idealized the existential issues of the client groups in terms of coping and transcendence.

From a communal constructive point of view, more research is needed to give us a better understanding of the group-constructive process in which the personal narratives take shape. Treated as co-constructed data, the narratives from the group should be analyzed with the facilitator's contribution being an embedded part. Drawing on discourse analysis and social-cognitive frameworks, studies of the "languaging" phenomenon in counseling and therapy (Angus & Rennie, 1988, 1989; Martin, 1991; McMullen, 1985, 1989; Pollio, H., Barlow, Fine, & Pollio, M., 1977) may offer ideas for similar studies in groups conducted for client assessment and clinical inquiry. The group use of language represents a new research domain for narrative researchers. Researchers also may examine such forms of social construction from the standpoint of social epistemology (Goldman, 1986). The client groups portrayed here could be viewed as knowledge communities, with personal stories and institutional histories being told, revised, and re-envisioned by its members.

Implications for Training

The group facilitators in this case were graduate counseling students who volunteered to participate in the earlier field research and subsequent assessment groups as a learning experience. From their self-reports, it was clear that serving as a group facilitator was a personally and professionally rewarding experience. They gained a respect and understanding for the client populations concerned that may not have been possible with a less involved role. They learned to listen to what the clients had to say, without feeling the pressure to intervene or to bring about change. This learning experience provided an opportunity to develop the observational base for an accurate reading of the culture of discourse in a group. They also learned about the fruitfulness of group processes of meaning making and how to optimize such group processes. I would recommend this type of experience for the training of scientist-practitioners. In addition to the benefits mentioned above, the narrative data analysis involves thought processes and interpretive strategies highly useful for clinical inquiry and field research.

Concluding Comments

The personal narrative represents a rich source of data that can be tapped with a constructivist approach to client assessment. The constructivist movement advocates the use of natural language data in inquiry. This language of experience and meanings has been illuminating of the groups studied. Due to the social nature of human constructions, data gathering and interpretation are best placed in an interactional context. The group is selected here as one of the natural units of communal construction that constitutes the context of meaning making.

The assessment of clients with a participant observation mode that takes advantage of naturally occurring discourse may have advantages over standardized forms of assessment. The risk of presenting clients with stimuli and tasks alien to their own culture and cognitive organization is lessened. The fact that embeddedness in the client's context is encouraged serves to preserve the meaningfulness of the information obtained. The affinity of the method with other clinical methods for assessing client constructs and with field research methods such as the focus group interview offers possibilities for comparison and linkage.

This particular use of narrative data obtained in group settings is in need of further development as a constructivist method of assessment. Theory and research on group processes as they impact on meaning making will have direct relevance. The fact that the constructivist orientation is beginning to have a multidisciplinary base promises a range of possible conceptual and methodological developments. At the conceptual level, practitioners could take advantage of interpretive frameworks that provide a philosophical match with this format of data generation. From a methodological standpoint, what constitutes a narrative unit of personal significance, how it is to be procedurally distinguished from ordinary discourse, and how group-constructive processes are to be analytically treated as the embedding context of individual narration represent some of the issues yet to be addressed by practitioners and researchers. The evaluation of the use of narrative data in group settings for assessment and research depends on reports of its future use. With more practitioners and field researchers interested in its application, this group-based format of narrative inquiry may be potentiated as a constructivist approach reflective of communal processes of meaning making.

References

Angus, L. E., & Rennie, D. L. (1988). Therapist participation in metaphor generation: Collaborative and noncollaborative styles. *Psychotherapy, 25,* 552-560.

Angus, L. E., & Rennie, D. L. (1989). Envisioning the representational world: The client's experience of metaphoric expression in psychotherapy. *Psychotherapy, 26,* 372-379.

Antaki, C. (1988). (Ed.). *Analyzing everyday explanation: A casebook of methods.* London: Sage.

Arbib, M. A., & Hesse, M. B. (1986). *The construction of reality.* Cambridge, UK: Cambridge University Press.

Atkinson, J. M., & Heritage, J. (Eds.). (1984). *Structure of social action: Studies in conversation analysis.* Cambridge, UK: Cambridge University Press.

Bertaux, D. (Ed.). (1981). *Biography and society: The life history approach in the social sciences.* Beverly Hills, CA: Sage.

Corey, M. S., & Corey, G. (1992). *Groups: Process and practice* (rev. ed.). Pacific Grove, CA: Brooks/Cole.

Dies, R. R., & MacKenzie, R. (Eds.). (1983). *Advances in group psychotherapy: Integrating research and practice.* New York: International Universities Press.

Edgerton, R. B., & Langness, L. L. (1978). Observing mentally retarded persons in community settings: An anthropological approach. In G. P. Sackett (Ed.), *Observing behavior:*

Theory and applications in mental retardation (Vol. 1, pp. 335-348). Baltimore, MD: University Park Press.

Fischer, C. T. (1980). Phenomenology and psychological assessment: Representational description. *Journal of Phenomenological Psychology, 11*, 79-105.

Gergen, K. (1985a). Social constructionist inquiry: Context and implications. In K. Gergen & K. Davis (Eds.), *The social construction of the person* (pp. 3-18). New York: Springer Verlag.

Gergen, K. (1985b). The social constructionist movement in modern psychology. *American Psychologist, 40*, 266-275.

Glaser, B. G., & Strauss, A. L. (1967). *The discovery of grounded theory.* Chicago: Aldine/Atherton.

Goldman, A. I. (1986). *Epistemology and cognition.* Cambridge, MA: Harvard University Press.

Gumperz, J. J. (1964). Linguistic and social interaction in two communities. In J. J. Gumperz & D. Hymes (Eds.), The ethnography of communication. *American Anthropologist, 66*, Part II, 137-154.

Heritage, J. (1984). *Garfinkel and ethnomethodology.* London: Polity.

Hoshmand, L. T. (1985). Phenomenologically based groups for developmentally disabled adults. *Journal of Counseling and Development, 64*, 147-148.

Jorgensen, D. L. (1989). *Participant observation.* Newbury Park, CA: Sage.

Kaul, T. J., & Bednar, R. L. (1978). Conceptualizing group research: A preliminary analysis. *Small Group Behavior, 9*, 173-191.

Kaul, T. J., & Bednar, R. L. (1986). Experiential group research: Results, questions, and suggestions. In S. L. Garfield & A. E. Bergin (Eds.), *Handbook for psychotherapy and behavior change* (3rd ed., pp. 671-714). New York: John Wiley.

Keen, E. (1975). *A primer in phenomenological psychology.* New York: Holt, Rinehart & Winston.

Krueger, R. A. (1988). *Focus groups: A practical guide for applied research.* Newbury Park, CA: Sage.

Kvale, S. (1983). The qualitative research interview: A phenomenological and hermeneutical mode of understanding. *Journal of Phenomenological Psychology, 14*, 171-196.

Labov, W., & Waletzky, J. (1967). Narrative analysis. In J. Helm (Ed.), *Essays on the verbal and visual arts* (pp. 12-44). Seattle: University of Washington Press.

Levinson, D. J. (1978). *The seasons of a man's life.* New York: Knopf.

Loevinger, J. (1976). *Ego development: Conceptions and theories.* San Francisco: Jossey-Bass.

Martin, J. (1991). The social-cognitive construction of therapeutic change: A dual coding analysis. *Journal of Clinical and Social Psychology, 10*, 305-321.

McAdams, D. P. (1988). *Power, intimacy, and the life story: Personological inquiries into identity.* New York: Guilford.

McMullen, L. M. (1985). Methods for studying the use of novel figurative language in psychotherapy. *Psychotherapy, 22*, 610-619.

McMullen, L. M. (1989). Use of figurative language in successful and unsuccessful cases of psychotherapy: Three comparisons. *Metaphor and Symbolic Activity, 4*, 203-225.

Mellard, J. M. (1987). *Doing tropology: Analysis of narrative discourse.* Urbana: University of Illinois Press.

Mishler, E. G. (1986). Analysis of interview-narratives. In T. R. Sarbin (Ed.), *Narrative psychology: The storied nature of human conduct* (pp. 233-255). New York: Praeger.

Moerman, M. (1988). *Talking culture: Ethnography and conversation analysis.* Philadelphia: University of Pennsylvania Press.

Morgan, D. L. (1988). *Focus groups as qualitative research.* Newbury Park, CA: Sage.

Murray, H. A. (1938). *Explorations in personality.* New York: Oxford University Press.

Polkinghorne, D. E. (1988). *Narrative knowing and the human sciences.* New York: State University of New York Press.

Pollio, H. R., Barlow, J. M., Fine, H. J., & Pollio, M. R. (1977). *Psychology and the poetics of growth: Figurative language in psychology, psychotherapy, and education.* Hillsdale, NJ: Lawrence Erlbaum.

Potter, J., & Wetherell, M. (1987). *Discourse and social psychology: Beyond attitudes and behavior.* London: Sage.

Sarbin, T. R. (Ed.). (1986). *Narrative psychology: The storied nature of human conduct.* New York: Praeger.

Shapiro, J. L. (1978). *Methods of group psychotherapy and encounter: A tradition of innovation.* Itasca, IL: Peacock.

Spradley, J. P. (1980). *Participant observation.* New York: Holt, Rinehart & Winston.

Valle, R. S., & Halling, S. (Eds.). (1989). *Existential-phenomenological perspectives in psychology.* New York: Plenum.

Van Maanen, M. (1990). *Researching lived experience.* New York: State University of New York Press.

Viney, L., (1983). The assessment of psychological states through content analysis of verbal communications. *Psychological Bulletin, 9,* 542-563.

Weenolsen, P. (1985, August). *Loss and transcendence life themes.* Paper presented at the 93rd Annual Convention of the American Psychological Association, Los Angeles, CA.

Yalom, I. D. (1985). *The theory and practice of group psychotherapy* (3rd ed.). New York: Basic Books.

7

Constructivist Assessment: What and When

ROBERT A. NEIMEYER

GREG J. NEIMEYER

THE previous chapters have largely addressed the *why* and *how* of constructivist assessment: Why should the practicing counselor consider using this set of methods to complement standard "objective" instruments? and How would such techniques be used? But for these assessment and therapeutic methods to be practical, it is equally important to consider what technique should be used *when.* In this chapter, we will address this question of method selection to convey a better idea of when each technique can be maximally useful.

Simply stated, the selection of a particular technique depends on three factors: (a) the clinical focus, (b) the particular client issue or problem being addressed, and (c) the counselor's preferred role or degree of participation in directing the assessment process. We will consider each of these factors briefly and then discuss each of the techniques presented in the forgoing chapters in light of these factors.

The first factor, *clinical focus,* refers to what you want to assess or achieve in using a particular technique. For example, some methods primarily provide the counselor with *information* about a client's outlook, orientation, or epistemological style, while others enable more self-reflective *exploration* of issues on the part of both client and therapist. Likewise some strategies target subtle *processes* of construing, which may shift from moment to moment (as well as in response to the intervention), while others reveal more enduring *structures* or belief systems. Different assessment methods have quite divergent clinical foci in this sense, as we will describe below.

The second factor, *client issue*, refers to the problem that your client presents with or that evolves over the course of counseling. Of course, these issues may be summarized in many divergent ways, ranging from common sense descriptions of the client's concerns or background (e.g., sexually abused, underachieving, marital problems, low self-esteem) to elaborate diagnostic systems such as the DSM categories (e.g., dysthy mic, bipolar disorder, panic disorder). Most systems of psychotherapy also have their preferred theory-based descriptions of psychological disorders. Thus psychodynamic clinicians may refer to clients with punishing superegos, behavior therapists may attempt to help clients remediate difficulties with low rates of response contingent reinforcement, and systemic family therapists may intervene when family members display weak intergenerational boundaries. Constructivist counselors tend to describe problems at a level about halfway between these more theory-driven descriptions and ordinary language, orienting therapy to a client's developmental issues, sense of fragmentation in personal identity, conceptual rigidity, and so on. Various problems conceptualized at this level invite different strategies of assessment and intervention, as we will outline selectively below.

In addition to the clinical focus and the client issue, a third consideration guides the selection of constructivist assessment: *the degree of preferred counselor involvement*. Involvement can range from minimal intrusion into a client's spontaneous storytelling, reflections, or associations to relatively directive forms of assessment and intervention. Constructivist methods of inquiry span this entire range, although they tend to share the same respect for the client's meaning-making activity. Both more and less directive assessments have their role in constructivist practice, with minimal counselor participation in the assessment giving maximum latitude to the expression of the client's personal reality, and higher degrees of counselor involvement promoting a "conversational construction of meaning" in the therapy dialogue (Loos & Epstein, 1989). Methods characterized by a higher degree of counselor directedness also are more likely to facilitate change by prompting shifts in a client's self-awareness.

Figure 7.1 presents various assessment techniques described in the forgoing chapters, organized along two dimensions. The first corresponds to your clinical focus: Is your goal to tap into your client's moment-to-moment construing process, or is it to help articulate the relatively enduring structure of his or her belief system or assumptive world? The second dimension represents your level of involvement in the assessment strategy: Do you want unobtrusively to monitor the content, sequence, and organization of your client's constructions or to assist or challenge him or her through more directed inquiry? Of course, your position on these dimensions will shift over the course of counseling, perhaps even within a single session. But thinking in these terms will help you select when a given technique fits with your intent or intervention plan.

Although every client is ultimately unique, some broad recommendations can be made about the appropriateness of each of the assessment methods contained in this volume for various presenting problems. For example, stream of consciousness work may be a preferred method for a client attempting to gain greater self-awareness about her or his "internal dialogue" but may be inappropriate in the early phases of counseling for clients struggling with issues of trust. We will use the scheme represented in Figure 7.1, in combination with our thoughts about the appropriateness of each technique to various client issues or circumstances, as a way of summarizing factors to consider in selecting an assessment method for use in a particular case.

Stream of Consciousness

Of all the techniques covered in the preceding chapters, streaming (see Mahoney, 1991; Neimeyer, R., Chapter 3, this volume) is perhaps the least directed and the most sensitive to a client's ongoing shifts in awareness. Thus the technique is an excellent choice when your goal is to develop a more intimate appreciation for the complexities, conflicts, and concerns of your clients—or to help them do so. Encouraging the client to "let go" of conventional norms of communication (speaking in full sentences, following a "logical" line) gives both partners in the counseling relationship a chance to appreciate more fully what it "feels like" to live out the

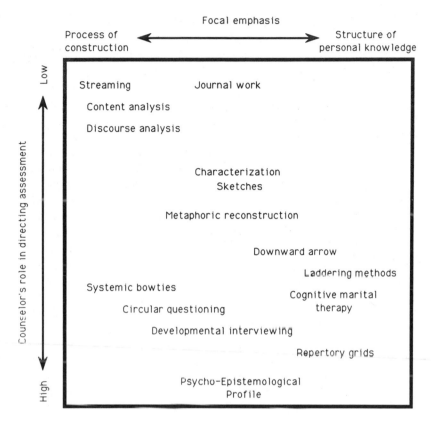

Figure 7.1. Representative Constructivist Assessment Techniques Organized by Focal Emphasis and Counselor Directiveness.

client's frame of reference. By observing the flow, blockages, and redirections in the client's stream, the clinician can flag central concerns and recurrent themes that can be explored later during a more dialogic phase of the therapy. If the streaming technique is to have maximum impact and disinhibit the client to share experiences honestly and deeply, however, then the counselor must avoid the temptation to interpret, challenge, or even directively inquire into the material that the client chooses to share. Instead the counselor should use this technique only when he or she can maintain an attitude of quiet, almost reverential support for the client's constructions, providing only occasional nondirective encouragement for the client to enter his or her stream more deeply.

Because it tends to "loosen" conceptually rigid clients, streaming provides a useful method of self-exploration for highly "cognitive" individuals, encouraging greater attunement to fleeting emotional nuances and imagery that may otherwise escape notice. It is also well suited to the depth exploration of childhood abuse in adult survivors, the original context in which Freud employed the related technique of free association. It is critical to emphasize, however, that streaming requires a very high degree of trust on the part of the client and for this reason is a poor choice when working with guarded, extremely vulnerable, or recently victimized individuals. It is also poorly suited to a crisis intervention or brief therapy context, both because the requisite degree of trust in the working alliance is not yet established and because the lessons learned through streaming often require careful "winnowing" over a considerable period of time. Finally the intimacy and "loosening" associated with streaming may be too threatening or disorganizing for severely dissociative or fragmented clients, for whom it can sometimes amplify destructive "voices" over which the client may experience little sense of control.

Content Analysis

Of all the methods presented above, the content analysis of a client's spoken (or written) narrative comes closest to being neutral and nonreactive. Content analysis does not even require therapist prompts beyond the simple invitation to "say how things are going, the good and the bad" (see Viney, Chapter 4, this volume). But while this is true of the method as an assessment technique, it is worth remembering that content analysis is typically applied to therapy transcripts in which the therapist has played a significant part. Thus it may or may not be used in conjunction with a more directive style of interviewing or interacting with clients, unlike streaming, which requires minimal intrusion into the client's shared reflections.

Content analysis shares with streaming a focus on the thematic content of the client's construing, but the two methods differ in their timing. Whereas streaming is an "online" technique that is informative during the exercise itself, content analysis is inherently a post hoc procedure that must be applied at some point after the session has ended. For this reason, content analysis is better suited to research or case study applications in which the counselor wishes to monitor changes in a client's sense of agency, depression, and so on across time.

The relative neutrality of content analysis makes it amenable to almost any case, although it requires extensive verbalization on the part of the client to yield reliable categorization of session content. This implies that it would be inappropriate for clients who have great difficulty expressing themselves verbally, as well as for those whose (sub)cultural or personal communication styles involve the extensive qualification or amplification of verbal messages through nonverbal or coverbal channels (e.g., gesture, vocal tone). Its inherently classificatory nature also renders content analysis a relatively crude way of discerning idiosyncratic meanings within individuals or families. For this very reason, however, it may promote useful comparisons of two or more clients (e.g., family members) in terms of their predominant content (e.g., degree of acknowledged emotion).

Discourse Analysis

As used by Hoshmand (Chapter 6, this volume), the analysis of group discourse shares many of the strengths and limitations of the content analysis of an individual client's speech. Because the therapist uses primarily nondirective prompts, the method allows for the ethnographic analysis of themes deriving from spontaneous conversation within a group and in this respect is flexible enough to apply to a wide range of client issues. It is perhaps best suited to consulting contexts requiring the assessment of intact groups, whether these are work groups, task groups, residential groups, or the like. Although the method might be extended also to mutual support groups that assume an attitude of exploration of members' perspectives and the expression of common feelings (e.g., Mallory, 1984), it may be limited in its application to therapy groups per se that require the group leader to play a more active interpretive or directive role. Thus, like streaming and content analysis, discourse analysis requires a fairly low degree of counselor activity, permitting the observation of naturalistic communal construction processes and self and life issues.

Contraindications for the use of this method in group settings include significant problems in group dynamics (e.g., the inclusion of a particularly needy, reserved, or dominant group member, the emergence of high levels of conflict), that would require more assertive therapist management. The method works well, however, in groups that share a common climate of self-disclosure, particularly when the assessors can ground their understandings of the group in serious participant observation of the mutual lives of group members outside the group session. Perhaps the most serious constraint from the standpoint of the practicing counselor would be the limited ability of group-based discourse analysis to reveal the private concerns of individual group members, insofar as the resulting material inevitably is shaped by unpredictable processes of group interaction that are more influential and directive than the anthropological reserve of the group leader.

Journal Work

The personal journal or diary has particular affinity for constructivist counselors. By encouraging the client to maintain an honest, deep, and therapeutically relevant "conversation with self" in the form of a personal journal, the counselor can promote a process of reflection and reconstruction that ultimately may obviate formal therapy. The diary typically is minimally structured by the therapist, although the client may experiment with a great range of formats and write in a variety of "voices," to different real or imaginary audiences, and so on (see Rainer, 1978, for useful guidelines). As a narrative technique par excellence, the journal invites attention to a client's shifting moods, significant life events, and attempts at sense making in confusing or conflictual situations. Because it evolves over time, it also portrays the flow and change in his or her awareness and promotes a consolidation of the client's outlook that suggests new courses of action or decision making. The diary becomes an assessment technique for the counselor, as well as client, when you invite the client to bring in the journal periodically and to share entries selectively from the previous week. This sharing can itself be powerful if the passages are read aloud by the client (or therapist) as a prelude to further therapeutic discussion.

In terms of Figure 7.1, the journal is oriented predominantly toward the monitoring of the client's construction and reconstruction processes but, to a greater extent than streaming or content or discourse analysis, contributes to the articulation of the client's belief system as well. In journaling, writers often begin to identify more and less fundamental values, to list priorities, or sometimes even to depict interrelationships graphically among their ideas or to trace their origins. Frequently it also has a strongly interpersonal tone, providing a safe forum in which the author can reflect on his or her relationships (past, present, and future) and can share the results of these reflections with the counselor on a discretionary basis.

Because of its adaptability, the diary can be a useful adjunct to therapy for nearly any client issue or problem. It can be inappropriate, though, for some clients who feel constrained by the written word or who use it only to report on daily events in a merely factual, journalistic fashion. The use of personal journals should be discouraged also in marital or family therapies whose goal is to promote greater commonality and sharing among family members rather than greater differentiation. Finally it can prove frightening for severely disorganized clients for the same reason as stream of consciousness work, providing a setting in which extremely destructive "voices" may eclipse the client's fragile sense of self control. If these limitations and threats can be managed, the diary can be a powerful means of coming to know the client's fundamental concerns and of fostering greater self-knowledge, mastery, and coherence even in severely distressed individuals. Mahoney (1991) offered several poignant illustrations of the use of journal work with adult survivors of physical and sexual abuse.

Characterization Sketches

Originating in the work of George Kelly (1955), the self-characterization offers an efficient narrative approach to assessment that is amenable to both brief and long-term therapies. It is especially helpful in the early sessions of therapy, when the counselor is attempting to understand the client on his or her own terms, or at later points of therapeutic impasse, when a larger and more inclusive view of the client's outlook is needed. In terms of our organizing scheme, the self-characterization or its family variant (Alexander & Neimeyer, G., 1989; Feixas, Procter, & Neimeyer, G., Chapter 5, this volume) is somewhat more directive than the techniques reviewed above, mandating that the author(s) write from a particular hypothetical external perspective about the self or family unit. The degree of counselor "lead," however, is limited intentionally to give the writer(s) considerable latitude in deciding what content to address and in what fashion.

Like other narrative methods, characterization sketches can be applied to a broad range of client problems and are somewhat more attentive to the thematic flow of the author's story than to the structure of personal knowledge. They also can be used, though, to conduct a "dimensional analysis" of the client's identity constructs. This reason makes the characterization sketch a good choice for the client who is struggling with issues of self-definition or who experiences conflicts with others as a function of her or his "personality." In a family setting, the characterization sketch can provide a window on the operative family construct system, revealing dimensions of meaning that reflect important similarities and differences among family members. It can be a risky procedure to employ, however, when the family apparently has joined to "scapegoat" one of its members, in which case the shared sketches may read more like verdicts than family portraits. Characterization sketches are perhaps most useful when both clients and therapists would benefit from grasping a more comprehensive and sympathetic view of the individuals experiencing the problem. They are also helpful as a first entry in a personal journal or as a way of consolidating previous journal entries on a periodic basis.

Metaphoric Reconstruction

Like the various forms of characterization sketches, methods of metaphoric reconstruction require relatively little counselor directiveness. Some initial setup facilitates the metaphorical expression, but the extent and directiveness of this guidance can vary widely. As discussed in Chapter 5, providing short sentence stems for metaphorical projections (e.g., "Families are like ___") often will give enough initial structure, and simple prompts (e.g., "You see your family like a ___ in what ways? Can you say more?") frequently encourage the client to enrich and embellish the metaphor.

Less directive methods of eliciting metaphors are discussed by Woolum and her colleagues (Woolum, Dow, Senese, Berg, & McDonald, 1987), who gradually draw metaphorical expressions from their clients in the course of therapeutic conversation. Paying attention to emotionally charged, frequently used, or idiosyncratic words all enhance the likelihood of eliciting metaphorical construction. As the client struggles to bring clarity to an area of personal uncertainty, he or she spontaneously will import metaphors to bring familiarity to unfamiliar territory. Reflecting these wisps of metaphorical expression back to clients encourages them to build on them by stretching and molding the metaphor to help map the emotional terrain. Here the counselor's role is largely nondirective, somewhat more directive than in the use of streaming or journal work, perhaps, but less so than in instances of directed questioning (see next section, below).

Just as metaphorical reconstruction occupies a midpoint in terms of counselor directiveness, it likewise occupies a midpoint in relation to the process versus structure dimension, depending on the intended purpose of its use. The use of the family metaphors described in Chapter 5 were directed largely toward making relatively inaccessible family beliefs more readily available for discussion. As windows onto the family construct systems of various family members, this use of metaphorical construction is aimed mostly at understanding existing structures (beliefs). Other uses of metaphorical reconstruction tip the balance in favor of a process application, though, as in Woolum et al.'s (1987) description of the creation of personal metaphors.

For Woolum, an important aspect of the metaphorical construction is that it permits movement and fluidity. Constructing something in metaphorical terms breathes life into it so that it can grow and change and evolve or diminish across time. According to this perspective, the precise content of the metaphor is in some ways less important than the process of metaphorical construction itself. This is because Woolum is less interested in what the particular metaphor may say about enduring structure than she is in using the metaphor as a way to dislodge people from their struggles, and the metaphor provides a route for this transportation.

Metaphorical construction can be useful at several points in counseling. It can be useful, for example, in helping articulate difficult emotional struggles or in helping facilitate expression in emotionally "blocked" or otherwise reticent clients. Because it requires some degree of trust and therapeutic rapport, however, metaphorical methods are more commonly used after a good working alliance has developed.

The power of metaphors to capture meaning that may otherwise escape representation or expression means that their use may carry some warnings as well. Premature use of metaphors may not give the person adequate time to adjust to the expression of emotional material, for instance, resulting in the introduction of sudden or alarming realizations. Because metaphors are so malleable, it is easy inadvertently to furnish or elaborate a metaphor in a way that does not adequately represent the client's own concerns. A good therapeutic relationship is a reasonable safeguard against the intrusion of such material, though, because clients who feel sufficiently comfortable will frequently reject unwanted or misplaced metaphors or metaphorical extensions.

Systemic "Bowties"

The use of systemic "bowties" involves a higher degree of counselor direction than do the above techniques and requires that the counselor systematically inquire about the constructions and associated actions of each member of a problem system. This form of "zigzag interviewing" unfolds the process of mutual escalation or impasse experienced by family members and offers the counselor a means of joining with the positions of each individual, whose actions are fully coherent with his or her (plausible) interpretation of the others' outlooks and behaviors. A skillful therapist even can generalize this approach to family assessment to the individual therapy context, where one partner can be encouraged to make "educated guesses" about how the partner views the client's own behavior, in a way that makes the spouse's reciprocal actions comprehensible.

In spite of its flexibility, in some clinical situations the use of the "bowtie" assessment is not recommended. For example, some client actions are so dangerous or destructive (e.g., child or spouse abuse, severe suicide threat) that more directive management of the problem behavior needs to precede any attempt at interpreting the underlying pattern. It also becomes pragmatically difficult to apply to each member of a multiperson system (beyond two or three), at least if the counselor remains true to the intent of the method to look at reciprocal interpretations and reactions on the part of all family members. The technique is extremely useful, however, in marital therapy or family therapy involving adolescent children, when it can highlight recurring dysfunctional reactions marked by anger, escalation, or withdrawal with remarkable clarity. A graphic portrayal of a family's vicious circles often proves both eye-opening and reassuring to clients, who may glimpse for the first time an explanation for their difficulties that does not require the attribution of malevolence to any family member. Finally it can provide a road map for intervention with the family, with each "node" in the diagram suggesting means of intervening in the meaning or actions of family members in a way that promotes transformation of the system.

Laddering

Both the laddering technique and its dialectical variant (see Chapter 3) move strongly in the direction of a structural assessment of relatively enduring personal belief systems, while remaining only moderately directive on the part of the counselor. By establishing an initial bipolar construct (e.g., through comparison and contrast of a set of people, things, or events) and by teasing out the respondent's preferences and higher order rationale, laddering elicits hierarchical aspects of a client's construct system, ranging from the more concrete to the more abstract. This aspect makes it especially useful in values clarification or in career counseling situations when the client needs to explore the broader implications of a particular occupational choice. Indeed it is a valuable adjunct to any form of decision making, especially when the client complains of conflictual or ambivalent feelings about a choice (e.g., moving to another city, staying in a relationship) that are difficult to articulate. It may be less appropriate, though, for highly abstract clients who need to concretize their intellectualized discussion in order to examine the behavioral implications of their stated values. It also may be difficult for extremely concrete clients, who may be virtually unable to express a higher level reason for their choice of a stated alternative. But for the majority of adolescent and adult clients, laddering and dialectical laddering can represent a beneficial and nonthreatening aid to self-exploration, as well as an informative probing strategy for the counselor.

Downward Arrow

Exploring a client's problematic reactions through the use of the downward arrow requires about the same degree of moderate counselor involvement as laddering methods. Both are essentially series of recursive questions whose goal is to tease out more fundamental or core issues arising for a client in a more concrete context or situation. But the downward arrow is somewhat more process-oriented than laddering because it involves the pursuit of a series of inferences or implications apparently already drawn at an emotional level by the client. This orientation makes it a good strategy for exploring emotional "overreactions" to events, whether these eventuate in depression, anger, anxiety, or other compound emotional states. As illustrated in Chapter 3, the downward arrow can be adapted to group as well as individual therapy settings, although it assumes at least a moderate level of trust and support among group members.

Application of the downward arrow can be premature if it is used before the client has had a chance to experience the distressing emotion fully. If used sensitively and slowly, though, it can deepen the client's awareness of otherwise suppressed feelings. Tears are not unusual as one approaches the core issues signaled by the lower rungs on the ladder. But for this very reason, the counselor should exercise caution in using it with very vulnerable clients or in using it toward the end of a session or series of therapy sessions and leaving too little time for processing of the material that results.

Interviewing Methods

Many of the interviewing methods discussed in this volume occupy the lower right section of Figure 7.1. In general, they involve fairly high levels of counselor directiveness and are more concerned with assessing enduring features of structure rather than the processes of construction per se.

Circular questioning is among the most process-oriented and least counselor-directed of these methods (see Chapter 5). In circular questioning, for example, the counselor is not seeking to determine the clients' placement in relation to any preestablished scheme. Nor is the counselor interested primarily in the content of the family members' responses; equally important is understanding the nature of the interrelationships among family members and the processes that reveal these relationships. Nonetheless circular questions are clearly counselor-derived questions that direct the discussion into specified areas of the counselor's choosing. As such, they involve fairly high levels of counselor direction but seek to assess aspects of family process, as well as structure.

Cognitive marital therapy is somewhat less directive but more clearly oriented toward uncovering the content of enduring beliefs or underlying relationship theories. This procedure largely preempts the assessment of process issues, at least at an interpersonal level, in that it encourages interaction primarily with the counselor.

Developmental interviewing involves more directed counselor intervention but also seeks more process-oriented insights into the nature of construing. In developmental interviewing, the counselor assumes an active role in asking questions and in using his or her interaction style to elicit client responses (see Chapter 2). These responses are taken as indicators of the individual's stage, level, or orientation toward interpersonal relationships. These indicators, however, tell more about an individual's process of construing than about any enduring content or belief structure. As is implied by the name itself, developmental interviewing is concerned chiefly with the expected movement, change, and processes of interpersonal construing.

This focus contrasts, for example, with the use of standardized instruments, such as the Psycho-Epistemological Profile (PEP). As an instrument given to the client by the counselor, the PEP is clearly counselor-directed, and it aims to provide information about some durable, structural features, as well as process features of construing. Endorsing a strong belief in empiricism, for example, carries implications for what a person believes about the world, as well as his or her process of knowing. It means, for example, that the individual probably prefers a careful, systematic, and controlled approach to information gathering and may value change more than is behaviorally evident. Because it provides information about what an individual believes, as well as how he or she comes to believe it, the PEP occupies a midpoint in relation to the process-structure dimension.

Each of these methods can be useful in different ways at different times, of course, and may be complementary when used jointly. Circular questioning is a provocative, dislodging means of assessment that clearly encourages insight and reconstruction as well. Cognitive marital therapy is intended for more limited use, either as an experimental "time-out" in conflict-habituated couples or as a means of encouraging deeper disclosure when core relationship issues need to be brought to the surface in a nonthreatening context.

Developmental interviewing is an appropriate approach at any point in the therapeutic process as a means of contextualizing the nature of the presenting problem. It may be useful from the outset of counseling as a way of better understanding the limitations and directions of anticipated client change. Or it may become important at points of impasse when you experience a "glass ceiling" in your work with a client; in other words, you find that the client is stuck in a way or place that does not quite make sense or is difficult to understand. Developmental interviewing might provide a context for understanding otherwise invisible boundaries that limit or curtail expected levels of client change.

Repertory Grid Techniques

Both the content and form of repertory grid techniques can vary according to the counselor's interests (see Chapters 3 and 5). Grids may be directed toward assessing constructions in a wide variety of intrapersonal and interpersonal domains, and their format is adaptable to the context of their administration. In clinical contexts, they have been used to understand how eating-disordered clients feel about themselves (Button, 1992), the ways in which conflictual and abusive couples construe their relationships (G. Neimeyer & Gold-Hall, 1988; Neimeyer & Hudson, 1985), and people's threat in relation to death and dying (Epting & Neimeyer, R., 1984). As discussed in Chapter 5, the focus may be on clients' self-constructions, on their constructions of other people, or on their constructions of the relationships between themselves and other people, among many other possibilities.

In each of these applications, though, the emphasis of grid techniques is to uncover structural features of the individual's idiosyncratic world view. This structure can take many different forms, but all aim to articulate relatively enduring aspects of the person's unique worldview.

At the simplest structural level, the grid involves the elicitation of a set of personal constructs. These constructs take the form of bipolar dimensions of meaning (e.g., trustworthy vs. untrustworthy). Each dimension forms a basis for ordering perceived events within its domain. The construct "conservative vs. liberal," for example, provides a dimension that is useful for ordering politicians and related political beliefs. The set of personal constructs that is elicited from any repertory grid technique is assumed to reflect a representative and fairly stable sample of the overall set of constructs used by an individual in making sense of his or her experience. As such, it provides a window on the unique worldview that each client brings to bear in construing events.

The relationship among these constructs can be assessed in a wide variety of ways, yielding assorted measures of construct system structure. Measures of structural differentiation, integration, and hierarchical organization can be assessed with simple computer programs, for example, as can a host of other structural properties. One issue of the *International Journal of Personal Construct Psychology* (Vol. 5, Issue 1) has been devoted exclusively to repertory grid methods, and it provides a wealth of information on the use of structural scores and their psychometric properties.

Concerned primarily with providing insight into structural features of a person's worldview, repertory grid techniques are nonetheless quite adaptable in their form of administration. Although they tend to involve fairly high levels of counselor directiveness, this can vary somewhat.

On the low end of directiveness would be a more conversational and interactive administration of the grid. Dolliver (1967), for example, described a form of repertory grid administered interactively in a card sort format. Most forms of repertory grid administration, however, involve the counselor in providing a set of instructions and guiding the client through the completion of the instrument. Some forms of the grid are completely self-instructional and just can be handed to the client for completion (e.g., Bodden, 1970).

Repertory grid methods tend to be concerned primarily with the structure of personal knowledge and involve fairly high levels of counselor directiveness. They can be quite useful in a variety of ways, though, regardless of the particular form or method of administration. Foremost among their uses is in determining the unique language and structure of experience that a client brings to counseling. Woolum et al. (1987) made the excellent point that we often assume the meaning of socially shared words and that this assumption sometimes can be in error. One of the major advantages of the repertory grid techniques is that they highlight the meaning of personal constructs in their relational context. A client who describes him- or herself as "anxious," for example, may be reluctant to give that up if he or she views anxiousness as preferable to the personal contrast of "vulnerable." Repertory grid techniques provide immediate access to such idiosyncratic views and for that reason can be useful forms of assessment for exploratory purposes.

An indirect advantage of the grid method is that it is an organized and structured technique. For clients who experience difficulty with ambiguity, a repertory grid method may prove quite useful. In contrast to a free-form method, such as streaming, the grid method structures and channelizes a process of personal exploration and for that reason may help reduce anxiety.

Many of the grid's advantages can be viewed as disadvantages. Some clients will experience the grid as too structured, for example, and may benefit more from less counselor-directed forms of self-exploration. Likewise, because the grid is aimed largely at uncovering structural features, it reveals little of the actual process of construing, where methods of streaming, content analysis, and discourse analysis may prove more useful. Finally, like the Psycho-Epistemological Profile, or any other counseling instrument, the administration of the grid interrupts the ongoing, conversational flow of therapeutic dialogue. Other qualifications regarding the use of repertory grid techniques are discussed by Yorke (1989).

Conclusion

In this chapter we have tried to convey the idea that sensitive use of constructivist assessment and change methods, like any other counseling technique, requires timing and sufficient "goodness of fit" to the client's issues, as well as to the counselor's objectives. These objectives may include two complementary avenues of exploration: *process* (the examination of the flow of the client's moment-to-moment experience) and *structure* (the identification of enduring values, core beliefs, and central dilemmas that constitute part of the structure of the client's personal knowledge). Both aims are essential to successful counseling or psychotherapy, the first to promote a keener sense of "being with" the client in her or his experiential world, and the second to move therapy to the deeper levels necessary to promote "second-order change" in the problem system (Lyddon, 1990).

The intelligent use of constructivist assessment can help achieve both objectives. Moreover, although some of the measures presented in this volume can precede or follow actual therapy and thereby provide a useful index of therapy outcome, most can be integrated fully into the process of therapy without disrupting the counseling relationship. Indeed the seamless blending of compatible constructivist assessment methods with an existing repertory of therapy skills can augment, deepen, and direct your practice, as it has for the therapists of many theoretical persuasions who have been drawn toward constructivist forms of practice (Neimeyer, R. & Neimeyer, G., 1987). We hope that your own exploration of these techniques extends your set of options for understanding human distress and increases your range of strategies for fostering the process of human change and reconstruction.

References

Alexander, P. C., & Neimeyer, G. J. (1989). Constructivism and family therapy. *International Journal of Personal Construct Psychology, 2,* 111-121.

Bodden, J. (1970). Cognitive complexity as a factor in appropriate vocational choice. *Journal of Counseling Psychology, 17*, 364-368.

Button, E. (1992). Eating disorders and personal constructs. In R. A. Neimeyer & G. J. Neimeyer (Eds.), *Advances in personal construct psychology* (Vol. 2, pp. 187-215). Greenwich, CT: JAI.

Dolliver, R. (1967). An adaptation of the Tyler Vocational Card Sort. *Personnel and Guidance Journal, 45*, 916-920.

Epting, F. R., & Neimeyer, R. A. (Eds.). (1984). *Personal meanings of death: Applications of personal construct theory to clinical practice.* New York: Hemisphere.

Kelly, G. A. (1955). *The psychology of personal constructs.* New York: Norton.

Loos, V. E., & Epstein, E. S. (1989). Conversational construction of meaning in family therapy: Some evolving thoughts on Kelly's sociality corollary. *International Journal of Personal Construct Psychology, 2*, 149-167.

Lyddon, W. J. (1990). First- and second-order change: Implications for rationalist and constructivist cognitive therapies. *Journal of Counseling and Development, 69*, 122-127.

Mahoney, M. J. (1991). *Human change processes: The scientific foundations of psychotherapy.* New York: Basic Books.

Mallory, L. (1984). *Leading self-help groups.* New York: Family Service America.

Neimeyer, G. J., & Gold-Hall, A. (1988). Personal identity in disturbed marital relationships. In F. Fransella & L. Thomas (Eds.), *Experimenting with personal construct psychology* (pp. 297-307). London: Routledge.

Neimeyer, G. J., & Hudson, J. E. (1985). Couples' constructs: Personal systems in marital satisfaction. In D. Bannister (Ed.), *Issues and approaches in personal construct theory* (pp. 127-141). London: Academic.

Neimeyer, R. A., & Neimeyer, G. J. (Eds.). (1987). *Personal construct therapy casebook.* New York: Springer.

Rainer, T. (1978). *The new diary.* Los Angeles: Tarcher.

Woolum, S., Dow, E., Senese, R., Berg, J., & McDonald, T. (1987). *Therapeutic use of metaphor in counseling.* Unpublished manuscript.

Yorke, M. (1989). The intolerable wrestle: Words, numbers, and meanings. *International Journal of Personal Construct Psychology, 2*, 65-76.

Author Index

Subject Index

About the Authors

Darlys J. Alford is currently a faculty member in the Psychology Department at the University of Southern Mississippi, Hattiesburg. She worked as a marriage and family therapist before completing her doctorate in social psychology at the University of California, Santa Barbara. Along with teaching courses in group dynamics and multicultural counseling, she conducts research on cognitive changes in self-identity that accompany the process of reference group exit.

Guillem Feixas is currently a faculty member in the Division of Sciences, Department of Personality, at the University of Barcelona, Spain. The author of more than 30 professional publications in the area of constructivist psychotherapy, he is recognized internationally for his contributions to the interface between constructivist and systemic therapies. He is co-editor of a forthcoming volume titled *Personal Meanings in Systemic Therapy: Constructivism in Action.*

Lisa Tsoi Hoshmand is Professor in the Counseling Department at the California State University, Fullerton. She has published on the teaching of inquiry and alternative research methodologies. She is completing a book on reflective orientation to inquiry in professional psychology, and co-editing a volume on method choice and the inquiry process in programmatic research on therapeutic practice.

William J. Lyddon is Assistant Professor and Director of the Counseling Psychology Clinic in the Department of Psychology at the University of Southern Mississippi, Hattiesburg. Coauthor (with Michael Mahoney) of the 1988 major contribution to *The Counseling Psychologist,* on constructivist versus rationalist therapies, he has focused his professional attention on epistemological issues in counseling theory and practice. In addition to these empirical and professional contributions, he also serves as Assessing Editor for the *Journal of Mind and Behavior* and Assistant Editor for the *Journal of Cognitive Psychotherapy.*

Greg J. Neimeyer is Professor of Psychology and Director of Training in the Department of Psychology at the University of Florida, Gainesville. Coeditor of the *International Journal of Personal Construct Psychology* and two volumes on constructivist assessment and interventions, he also has published more than 100 articles on aspects of counseling and personality and has served on the editorial boards of *Journal of Counseling and Development* and *Counseling Psychologist.*

Robert A. Neimeyer is Associate Professor and Director of Clinical Training in the Department of Psychology at Memphis State University, Memphis, TN. Author of more than 100 publications within clinical psychology, he is also coeditor of the *International Journal of Personal Construct Psychology* and four books devoted to issues of constructivism and clinical practice. In addition he is author of *The Development of Personal Construct Psychology* and is an editorial board member of the *Journal of Consulting and Clinical Psychology.*

Harry G. Procter is Professor of Psychology in the Department of Psychology at Tone Vale Hospital in Somerset, England. He has written extensively in the area of family construct systems and is coeditor of the forthcoming volume *Personal Meanings in Systemic Therapy: Constructivism in Action.* An active practitioner in a hospital setting, he brings considerable clinical expertise to his professional scholarship.

Linda L. Viney is Associate Professor in the Department of Psychology at the University of Wollongong, Australia. She is a widely published international figure in constructivism and is the author of several books and more than 40 professional publications in the area. In addition, she is currently editor of the *Australian Psychologist* and an editorial board member on several other journals within her field.